THE WORKS OF SRI CHINMOY

ANECDOTES & RECOLLECTIONS

VOLUME II

THE WORKS OF SRI CHINMOY

ANECDOTES & RECOLLECTIONS

VOLUME II

★

SALUTATIONS

I LOVE SHOPPING

THE WORLD-EXPERIENCE-TREE-CLIMBER

SRI CHINMOY VISITS INDIA

MY EXPRESS VISIT TO INDIA

LYON · OXFORD

GANAPATI PRESS

LXXXIX

© 2019 THE SRI CHINMOY CENTRE

ISBN 978-1-911319-05-4

See appendix for notice regarding this edition.

FIRST EDITION WENT TO PRESS ON 27 MAY 2019

ANECDOTES & RECOLLECTIONS

VOLUME II

PART I

SALUTATIONS

BOOK 1

I – SALUTATIONS TO SWITZERLAND

1. Meditation in Zurich

In Zurich over five hundred people came to the meditation. The seekers in Zurich were so good. They took prasad with real devotion – "devotion" is the right word. I am always deeply moved that when seekers in the audience in San Francisco take prasad after a public meditation, they show tremendous respect. Here in Zurich it was truly like our San Francisco experience. With such devotedness, hundreds of people took prasad.

2. Zatopek arrives

As you know, the immortal runner and Olympic gold medalist Emil Zatopek spent two days with us in Zurich on 14 and 15 June. Right from my childhood I have been a great admirer of his, so I am deeply grateful that Zatopek came from Czechoslovakia to visit us. So many unforgettable experiences we all had with him and his wife, Dana!

Our plane reached Zurich at eleven-thirty and at twelve o'clock Zatopek's plane was supposed to arrive. Kailash, Abarita and I went with two photographers to another platform to wait for him. His plane came on time, but there was a problem with his bag. He had a small bag – you can call it a briefcase even – for his wife and himself. But they wouldn't allow him to carry the bag on the plane. It had to go in the baggage compartment. He said later that in America we can take big, huge boxes and all that, so he felt it was ridiculous that they wouldn't allow him to carry such a small bag.

We were watching him through the glass door as he was waiting by the carousel for his bag. Everybody's luggage came, but his was missing. He is my best friend in that way. So many times everybody's luggage comes except mine. Even returning to New York this time, I arrived yesterday and only today my luggage arrived. You can call my stories hilarious or painful.

We were all excited because we could see him, but he couldn't come outside to meet us because he was looking for his bag. At one point while we were waiting, ten or more middle-aged and elderly ladies asked me, "Is Zatopek here?" We pointed him out, "Yes, he is there." They had gotten their bags and everything, and, O God, now they wanted to see him. For about half an hour or more they were waiting outside – only to see Zatopek. They were so eager and anxious to meet him. Perhaps, for the first time, they were getting the opportunity to see him in person. When he was young, when he was a champion, they had heard his name. Now they wanted to see him.

At long last he came out and I approached him. He recognised me. I wanted to shake hands with him, but he immediately folded his hands in the Indian way and said, "Namaskar." Then he started talking to me in Hindi, using a few Hindi words. He was asking me if I wanted to drink hot tea. Then he asked, "How is it that Hindi is easy, but Urdu I could not learn?" He and his wife were in India for four months. We were talking and talking about various things.

A French disciple was using my movie camera, but there was nothing inside it – wonderful! But fortunately thirty or forty very nice pictures were taken by Marco. Then Zatopek and his wife went to their hotel to take rest.

3. The athletic meet

In two hours' time we met again at an athletic meet. A few world champions were there, and people had come from different countries. We were sitting together in the gallery with Zatopek and his wife. In the beginning he was so shy that his wife did most of the talking. It was not that Zatopek was snubbing me, but he would look to this side and that side and sometimes even close his eyes. His wife was absolutely at ease while we were chatting. Zatopek speaks many languages, but his wife seems to speak better English than he does.

During the five thousand-metre run, Zatopek picked a runner that he wanted to be first. He was telling me, "This runner is going to be first." It so happens that that particular runner had written me a letter about a year ago. He had heard about me and congratulated me on something that I had done. I forgot to tell Zatopek that it was the same person. Zatopek was clapping and screaming the runner's name, but that runner didn't come in first. Afterwards, the runner wanted to see me. I went and congratulated and consoled him.

When Zatopek went to give the prizes for the five thousand-metre race, the whole audience cheered him. Everybody in the stadium honoured him like anything.

4. The uncooperative camera

Kailash was using my camera to take pictures at the athletic meet. It seemed that the camera was on exposure number eight, so Kailash took nine, ten and all the way up to thirty-six pictures. Then for some reason suspicion arose. He opened the camera and there was no film in it.

But there were three other photographers, so there was no problem. Marco and others were taking pictures; so it was not necessary for Kailash to take pictures also.

5. *The great man*

The funniest thing happened when it was time for the awards ceremony for the women's discus. For each event the organisers of the games had arranged for a "great man" to give out the prizes. They were looking for the great man who was supposed to give the prizes for the discus, but he was missing. Then it was discovered that this great man was none other than Abarita himself.

They called Abarita over the loud-speaker and begged him to give the prizes. Abarita dropped from Heaven! How could he go to the centre of the stadium and give the prizes? He knows nothing about the discus and he does not consider himself a great man. But those people were saying, "You are great."

In the ceremony there was a line of three or four girls, and the official had to put a medal around each girl's neck. The winners were all three and four times as large as Abarita; they were like Tejiyan and Bhima. They were absolutely from another world. Abarita became nervous, but since he had become the great man, he had to go and give out the prizes.

6. *The relay race*

The girls in the four hundred-metre race ran so fast! You could barely see them even. It was very good and it reminded me of my races in India. They were all thin, like skeletons.

After the relay race, I was supposed to give out the prizes in the stadium and speak about Zatopek to honour him. I spoke for four or five minutes appreciating him, and I mentioned his wife's name also. Then Zatopek also spoke, thanking the organisers and encouraging us.

The German disciples sang *Run and Become* and the Marathon song very nicely.

7. The big prize

Another calamity! Zatopek was supposed to get a very nice prize from the club and from us. But, God knows, there was some confusion and the prize we wanted to give him did not arrive in time.

All the disciples had was a very tiny – tinier than the tiniest – medallion. I said, "What am I going to do?" Abarita said, "What can you do? If you don't give a big prize, what will everyone think?" The disciples thought it would look odd for people to see such a tiny thing, so they wrapped a very big chocolate bar and put the medal on top.

But that night we compensated for this and gave Zatopek some very nice things that he liked – a very big cuckoo clock and other things. We told him afterwards that the other prize was all deception. But what could we do? Thousands of people were watching.

8. Zatopek and water

We were at the stadium for hours. There I usually drink tea and all that. I don't know how, but this time I became a good man and was drinking only water. Perhaps I didn't have the heart to ask the disciples to bring me tea. Three or four times I drank water. I was very thirsty and hot. Zatopek watched me – although at the time I didn't know that he was watching.

Zatopek likes drinking beer. When we went back to his hotel, there was a tiny refrigerator in each room. So he asked his wife to give him a beer. Then he changed his mind and said, "Oh, no, no! I saw Sri Chinmoy drinking water. After seeing him drink water, I can't drink beer." These were his words. So he asked his wife to give him water.

His wife was so happy to give him water, because she had been telling him for years that he should drink less beer. Then, to make her happier, he said, "Now, I am not going to drink beer anymore. Only on very rare occasions will I drink it. Otherwise, I will drink only water. I saw Sri Chinmoy drinking water; I can't drink beer anymore."

That night he didn't take beer and the following day also he didn't drink beer. He was drinking only water. So for two days he didn't drink beer. His wife was happy that he was fulfilling her wish.

9. *Zatopek and the Russians*

In the running world, the Russians were Zatopek's worst enemies. Sometimes he used to break a world record and hold it only for a few days before the Russians would break it. The Russians tried in so many ways to defeat him. They used to give him bad advice. Outwardly they pretended to be very good friends, but often they told him everything wrong so that he would practise wrong and then lose. That kind of trick he didn't play on the Russians.

10. *Stories from Zatopek*

Zatopek told me so many stories, and I asked him many questions. He said that his father was so sad and mad when he took up running. His brother was also sad. He said, "You have cast a slur on our family. The neighbours have seen you running in another village. They are saying such bad things about us." He said that in his own village he didn't practise, because the people criticised him and hated him. So his father was very, very sad.

Then, when he became a champion, his father used to go to all the paper stands and collect the newspapers that had his picture. He kept album after album, only with Zatopek's pictures. When friends and relatives came, he would show them the albums, even before they asked anything about his son. Before that, his father was dead against his running. But when the neighbours started appreciating him, his father used to get much more joy from Zatopek's running than he himself got. This happened in my case also. When I used to stand first, my brother Mantu would get much more joy than I got.

When I asked Zatopek about his timing for one hundred, two hundred and four hundred metres, to verify what I had read in the book, he told me the timing. Believe it or not, my timing was better than his timing. But I didn't tell him that. Of course, I was a sprinter and Zatopek was a middle-distance and long-distance runner.

11. The television trick

One television station was supposed to interview both Zatopek and me. Then they changed their mind and said that they would interview only Zatopek. But Abarita said, "No. Zatopek came to Zurich at our request. If our Master cannot be there, then we will not allow Zatopek to be there." So Abarita cancelled it.

Then these rogues said, "We have changed our mind. Both of them should come." Around ten o'clock we went there and were taken to the main studio. In fifteen minutes' time we were supposed to be on television. A young girl came and put powder on Dana's face and on Zatopek's face. Then she went away. Immediately I got the point. I said, "They are playing a trick." So I stood up and asked Abarita, "Now, go and ask them if I will be in the interview." Abarita asked them and they said, "No, we have changed our mind again. Only Zatopek and his wife will be there."

It was so hot there with all the studio lights. I started going into another room – but not actually outside the building – so I could watch the interview more comfortably on a television set. But then Abarita came up to me and said, "It will look very odd if you go away. No, please stay here."

I said, "I know, but it is so hot."

Then the interviewer came up to me and said, "We have a special place for you. Please come."

The special place was a seat with the jokers in the studio who only clap. There were about sixty or seventy who had come to watch the show. They put me in the front row. As soon as I joined them, they began cutting jokes and screaming and doing all kinds of things. Fortunately, I didn't understand their language. They were behaving as if they had come directly from a zoo; they were mocking and all that – the way you see them behave on television.

While Zatopek and his wife were being interviewed, they showed pictures of his Helsinki performance. At one point, Zatopek broke in and started talking about me. The interviewer immediately changed the subject. But when Zatopek mentioned my name, for two seconds the camera turned towards me and I was on television. So people saw me for two seconds. The rest of the time it was all about Zatopek. They did not allow him even to talk about me.

When it was all over, immediately Zatopek grabbed me. He felt very sad. With a very sorrowful face he said, "You are a very, very great, creative personality." I said, "What can you do? It is not your fault. Everything is for the best."

12. Zatopek's Guru

Later we went to our dining place and I played for ten or fifteen minutes on the esraj. Both Zatopek and his wife were listening very attentively. In a book about him, I had read that he used to play on the guitar, so we asked him to play for us. He took the guitar and for two or three seconds he played. Then he gave it to his wife, saying, "She is the one who plays."

She took the guitar and played. Then we asked them to sing one or two songs; but to our delight, they sang one, two, three, four, five, six, seven, eight. They went on and on. I must say, they and I have some similarities. When you ask me to sing, I don't stop. They said, "We don't sing spiritual songs. We sing folk songs." So they sang many songs in different languages. I have a tape of them. It is very nice.

Both of them have excellent singing voices. He sang while she was playing on the guitar. Then, at one point, we again asked him to play. He didn't want to. He said, "No, as you are their Guru, she is my Guru." He used the term "Guru" quite a few times.

13. Glued to the screen

When we showed the movie we had made for them of the singers in New York performing the songs I had dedicated to Zatopek, he and his wife were sitting literally on the edge of their seats. Pictures are there to prove it. They wouldn't look to this side or that side. During the serious songs I could understand it. But even during the joking sections they were sitting like that. In the movie at times our people joke and perform short skits to illustrate the songs; everything is going on. But even then Zatopek and his wife didn't laugh. Usually they are not so serious. They smile and joke and do all kinds of things. But during the movie they were so moved. They watched in pin-drop silence, as if they were glued to the screen.

14. Zatopek the reader

After the movie I presented Zatopek with the book I had written about him. It seems that Zatopek does not like to read anything. Perhaps he thinks it is a waste of time. I do not blame him. His wife reads on his behalf. He turns the pages, but he doesn't read. But his wife reads everything carefully. She will read my book and tell him about it. He liked very much the songs and also the movie we made for him.

15. Sri Chinmoy Lauf

The following day was our main race, the Sri Chinmoy Run. The disciples had found a very beautiful course around a lake with two or three small loops and one big loop. Zatopek was supposed to start the race. He was so enthusiastic, as if he were running himself. He called out, "Where is the gun?" He was screaming, "No gun? No gun?" We said, "We don't use a gun." Then his wife said, "You don't need a gun." When his wife said that, Zatopek said, "All right, I will clap."

The race was to start on a small bridge. There were a little over two hundred people on the bridge. They were standing under a big banner saying "Sri Chinmoy Lauf". "Lauf" means race. Zatopek was standing on one side. He started the race by saying something in German, ending with a final clap. When he clapped, everybody clapped, and the race started.

All the London disciples – even elderly women – were running. Our very good runners were also there. Among the disciples, Sundar came in first and then Janaka. But they were defeated by local Swiss boys. I was not feeling well and was running last, behind everybody. When I ran along the small loops, Zatopek was so excited. He was clapping like anything. His wife stood up also and was clapping and clapping, although I was running behind everybody.

Some of the girls who are useless runners kept taking short cuts at the places where the monitors were directing them around the loops. I told them later that they were all rogues. If they were supposed to run around someone who was standing in one place, instead they cut across. They saved fifty or seventy metres on four occasions. I was so disgusted. On one loop, at least two hundred metres they didn't run. They took a short cut. What were they doing? Just because they were third-class runners, they felt nobody would pay any attention.

When it was over, Zatopek gave the prizes. I was so embarrassed. The first, second and third prize trophies were of the same size, with the same figure. Only it was mentioned on the trophy, "first" or "second" or "third". I said, "How can it be?"

Phillip announced the winner's name and handed the trophy to Zatopek, who handed it to the person. To each person who came up for a trophy, Zatopek had something encouraging to say. He was very, very nice. There were also health food prizes – honey and other things – for the winners. Zatopek was so happy to see that we had health food for the winners. After he gave each person his trophy, he pointed to the health food so happily and said, "Take this. You select."

I thanked both Zatopek and his wife, and Zatopek spoke, appreciating us. Then he came up to me and grabbed my hand and said, "Our Guru, this is the best." That was his comment. The race and the atmosphere – everything – pleased him, so he said, "Our Guru, this is the best."

The Mayor of Zurich, who comes from Canada, sent his assistant to honour me. He came with a proclamation and he spoke so highly of me for about seven or eight minutes. All of a sudden, his wife, who was very tall – much taller than her husband – came and gave me a huge bouquet. She was smiling at me. The husband said, "She wants to offer you this bouquet." So I took it and I thanked her.

16. Signing autographs

After the race, people were all standing in a queue for Zatopek's autograph. Some people came up to me and asked me to autograph a small scrapbook. Some also came and asked me to sign their running numbers.

Everybody liked Abarita's book on Zatopek. It was in German and included conversations with Zatopek during Abarita's stay at Zatopek's home. Before they ran, and afterwards as well, many runners came up to Zatopek and asked him to sign the book. Carla was selling the book, and Zatopek and his wife were sitting together side by side, signing it. When there were people he considered important, he asked his wife also to sign. Otherwise, his signature was enough. Hundreds of people came and stood in line.

When the line began fading, I also came. Before me there were seven or eight people. But Abarita had to ask those people to let me go ahead of them.

When I stood in front of Zatopek with one of Abarita's books, he wrote, "With great admiration for the greatest Guru." Then he signed his name and he drew a picture of a javelin aiming at someone. Like me, he became an artist and illustrated his signature. When I sign, I draw birds. In his case, he drew a javelin.

SALUTATIONS

17. The ball collector

Many times Zatopek had talks with Abarita about me and the Centre. When we went to play tennis, he came to watch us play. His wife went to see one of her students, who has now become a coach.

For over an hour, Zatopek was watching our games. There were no good players there, so I looked like a great player, defeating all the European disciples.

While he was watching, four or five times he ran after the ball to collect it and give it to the person throwing balls to the server. He was enjoying the game like anything, but he never played.

Zatopek and his wife were very nice. Everything went perfectly well. They were so happy that they had come, and we were so happy to have them. They liked the disciples and they were very, very deeply moved.

18. The Director-General of the United Nations in Geneva

The Director-General of the United Nations in Geneva, Mr. Luigi Cottafavi, is an Italian. For about forty-five minutes we met with him and talked all about different religions. We also spoke all about Hinduism and about India.

He was very nice and kind, and full of life and enthusiasm. Physically he was very tall and strong. There is a great difference between the Director-General in Geneva and the Secretary-General here in New York. The Secretary-General has luminosity; the Director-General has dynamic vigour.

19. Other meetings

In Geneva I met with the Vice President of the International Red Cross. He was very humble and modest. Our people sang the *Red Cross* song. It was a very soulful atmosphere that our singers created. Everything went well.

In Switzerland I also met with the Indian ambassador, who was extremely nice and very kind. Daily we went to three or four different places.

20. *A visit to Einstein's house*

Visiting Einstein's house in Bern was an unforgettable experience. Before Einstein came to the United States, he had lived in these three or four small rooms. There are four floors and one has to walk up. It is a very old building. Einstein's pictures were there and different examples of his research work. Einstein became very soulful and spiritual in the evening of his life.

The greatest living authority on Einstein was there. He has written a book on Einstein. I don't know what the professor saw in me, but he went on talking and talking, literally not allowing me to come down the stairs. He talked all about Einstein's spirituality and this and that.

Finally he said, "Please, you have to write down something," so I had to write something in the guest book. They don't ask for an autograph; they ask for a few lines. It was a big page and while I was writing he was standing beside me and watching. I was so moved.

II – SALUTATIONS TO ITALY

21. *The excited Cardinal*

As you know, on the 18th of June, at seven o'clock, I was supposed to meet with the Pope. At five-thirty they wanted me to be present. I came at five-thirty on the dot and stood not at the Vatican Gate, but about twenty or thirty metres away. A Cardinal was waiting for me but he could not see me, and he was very excited because he thought I was late. When he finally saw me, he took my papers and led me inside.

22. *My Italian photographer*

I had invited our Italian disciple Giorgio to come with me when I went to see the Pope. He does not speak English; he does not even speak French. And I don't speak Italian. So we talked through our smile – no other language, only smiling language we understood.

Giorgio went with me to take pictures, because with the previous Pope we had had problems. The first time I saw Pope Paul VI, we got good pictures. The second time, nothing that was taken by the Vatican photographers ever came out. The third time I was there, the Vatican photographer came to me and asked how many pictures we wanted taken. But when I actually met with the Pope, that was the moment that the photographer left the room. We were looking for him, but he had gone.

This time, with Pope John Paul II, we did't take any chances. I was allowed to bring one person, so as a friend and a student Giorgio came with me. Another reason I took him was because he speaks Italian.

23. The Pope arrives

Inside the Vatican, there were ninety thousand people. They had all come to hear the Pope speak. Since it was summer, the audience was held outside, in a corridor. But the Vatican is so big that the corridor easily housed over ninety thousand people. The people were all excited that they were going to see the Pope.

Around a quarter to seven, the Pope arrived in his small van or car. His car was moving down a passageway, and he was blessing people from the car. Then, when he came out of the car and was making his way to his throne, he would go and bless one person, shake hands with someone else, pat somebody's shoulder and do all kinds of things. He was like an affectionate grandfather greeting his family.

There was a group of African singers wearing special uniforms. Sometimes they would sing and sometimes they would slap their face or head. It was a part of the performance. The Pope was so satisfied with them. He clapped and clapped and clapped.

24. The Pope's speech

The Pope read out his speech in, I think, seven languages. First one of the Cardinals said something in Italian, and then the Pope read out his message in English, French, German, Spanish and a few more languages. But before he read out his serious message in all the languages, he cut jokes and made everybody laugh. You can't imagine, for two hours or more, he only smiled and smiled and smiled. He would look to one side and smile and then to the other side and smile. He would all the time smile, bless people, talk and cut jokes.

Like the last time I was there to see Pope Paul, this time also I was put in the front row. Beside me were a Cardinal and two or three priests from Africa. They were also supposed to see the Pope. It was a private audience in the sense that the Pope would speak to each person personally. Behind me was another row; so there were two rows altogether.

The Pope's throne was very, very simple and his shoes were also very simple. He was in a white robe. Six or seven times during his talk he looked at me and smiled. I was sitting only ten or twelve metres away from him. He looked at me and greeted me six or seven times during his speech.

25. Meeting with the Pope

After the speech, it was time for the private interviews. Three or four black priests were ahead of me. The Pope came up to them and they all knelt down and kissed his ring.

As soon as the Pope came near me, I stood up and one of the Cardinals said, "He is Sri Chinmoy from the United Nations."

I gave the Pope Sanatan's plaque, which was so beautiful, and the pamphlet with the song about him. As I was giving him the plaque and the pamphlet, the Pope said, "You are from the United Nations."

I said, "Yes, Father, I am."

Then he asked me, "Are you an Indian?"

Again I said, "Yes, I am."

Then he said, "India, India, India!" with such joy and enthusiasm in his face. He was absolutely beaming with joy.

He very powerfully grabbed my elbow with such affection, and looked at me as if I were an old forgotten friend or grandson. He was holding me firmly and talking to me, and he patted my shoulder seven or eight times.

Then he said to me, "Special greetings to your members. Special blessings to you. We shall continue together."

The words we exchanged were few, but he spent time looking at the plaque and appreciating it. I also showed him the picture of me with the previous Pope that was in the U.N. booklet, *Our First Ten Years.* He looked at the picture and also at the pamphlet with the song about him.

26. The Pope's affection

Pope John Paul has tremendous warmth and he is very sincere in expressing affection. He is very sociable, very affectionate, very compassionate. He has sincere compassion and affection. He was beaming with joy and showed me tremendous affection, love and concern when he offered me his benediction.

The Pope has compassion on the human level, the physical level, which others can immediately see and feel. Pope Paul VI had compassion in a luminous, ethereal way. The previous day, I saw the soul of Pope Paul four or five times, filled with real aspiration. His psychic presence I saw and I felt most powerfully.

27. Giorgio versus UPI

There is a funny story about our photographer-disciple, Giorgio. When the UPI photographer saw Giorgio there, he asked him to leave, saying he had no right to take pictures. Previously, Giorgio had asked me if I wanted pictures taken during the Pope's speech, and I had said yes. God knows where the UPI man was then, but Giorgio took three or four pictures of the Pope from over my shoulder.

When it was time for the private interviews, the UPI photographer came and told him to leave. Giorgio looked at me and I just smiled at him. So he gave a similar smile to the UPI photographer. The UPI man got mad and made complaints to one of the Cardinals. The Cardinal asked Giorgio to leave immediately, but he was not listening. He kept looking at me and I kept smiling at him.

At least four times they insulted him, all in Italian. Still he didn't listen. He took four black and white pictures and four colour slides. Eight or nine pictures he took, and UPI took, I think, three.

28. The Pope's hair

The Pope has much more hair than I have. Once, the wind blew away his cap and four or five Cardinals ran after it, almost colliding. That was the time I was able to see. I said, "O God, so much hair!"

29. The meditation in Italy

In Italy I was supposed to give a talk. It was in a small hall in a very big building. For the first time, perhaps, I went to give a talk in a track suit, but the audience didn't mind. There were about seventy or eighty people.

Indians, as usual, dominated the question and answer period. Three Indians did not allow anyone else to ask any questions. One question was about pressure in the third eye. Another question was about reincarnation. They went on and on.

Before that, a tall young man came up to me and introduced himself as one of the secretaries of the Italian Ambassador to the United Nations. He said he had come to our meditations at the U.N. five or six times and had enjoyed them very much. He couldn't believe that I came to such a small gathering to hold meditation and give a talk. He was very, very nice. Also he came to the meeting later.

The lady who organised the meeting had wanted to come to New York to see me and become my disciple. But instead of coming to New York, she went to Miami and met another Master and became his disciple. She was asking me, "Did I do the right thing? Did I find the real Guru?" So I said, "You did absolutely the right thing. You found the real Guru." She was so happy that she had found the real Guru and the real path.

III – SALUTATIONS TO GERMANY

30. Marathon champion

While in Germany, I met with the previous women's world marathon champion, a German girl, Christa Vahlensieck. Projjwal had invited Christa to get a trophy from me. You can't imagine how spiritually developed that girl is. She doesn't speak English, but she gave the sweetest smile each time we talked to her. She had come by bus from forty or fifty miles away. The disciples sang for her and we gave her gifts. Many pictures were taken. She enjoyed everything.

Christa is a very good runner. She is very short and her strides are also short. In 1978 she came to New York, but she could not finish the marathon. She said that the New York heat was unbearable and she was miserable. That was when she lost her world record; Grete Waitz broke it by seven minutes. Then, for one year she could not run because she was sick. Now she will be running a marathon in Britain. She was very, very nice and everybody liked her.

31. Jharna-Kala exhibit

My paintings were exhibited in a very beautiful museum in Bonn. Many dignitaries were there, including a Harvard professor. She was a very nice elderly lady who liked the paintings very much.

The curator came up to me with a guest book and said, "Please, you have to write something; you have to sign this."

"Write something" means what? I wrote a full page, and he was very happy. He is a professor also. It was a very good experience.

32. The mayor of Cologne

We also saw the Mayor of Cologne, who gave us a proclamation and very nice gifts. He was so nice. Three or four times he talked about me, all from his heart – what he was feeling about me. Then there was an immediate translation by a lady who had been in New York for only three years. But her English was excellent. When I spoke, she translated for me.

Of all the twenty or thirty mayors that I have seen, this German mayor was the one who touched most deeply the very depth of my gratitude-heart.

33. Composing songs

On Father's Day I asked all of my disciples to meditate once for each year that they had been with me. I am sure they listened to my request. On Father's Day I composed a song. It was translated into twelve languages. The best was an African language. Devadip translated it into Spanish and Haridas arranged it.

I also composed a song on France – *Vive la France.* The European disciples enjoyed it very much and now they are learning it.

I gave a name to Projjwal's printing press: Perfection-Glory. There I composed a song dedicated to his press.

34. My coach Saumitra

Last but not least, I visited my former coach, Saumitra, a German runner who coached me in India. Now he is head of a school which has three or four thousand students. He is the father of three sons and he does not run anymore. He has lost a lot of his hair, but nobody can defeat me in losing hair. He looked at me and I looked at him. In silence we talked about our hair.

I spent an hour and a half with him. What a moving experience! We talked and talked and talked about many, many things. He gave me the greatest surprise. In 1958 I had given him a small album with some pictures. Also, I had composed two songs about him. One was sung in front of the head of the ashram by two hundred athletes. He has kept that song plus the other song I had composed, one of my pictures and the album. Projjwal had sent him a photograph of me running a marathon. He has kept everything like a treasure. I had totally forgotten about the album and the pictures, but he has preserved them under lock and key in a cupboard with his most valuable things. He brought them to me with such concern and care.

We discussed many, many things and gave each other tremendous joy. His wife is extremely spiritual. When he was in India, he was not yet married.

Our old friendship we revived. At one point I said, "You were an excellent coach but I was a hopeless case."

He said, "I never told you that you were a hopeless case. It is all your mental creation!"

I said, "I could not learn your way."

He said, "But that does not mean you were hopeless. In your own way you did so well."

That was Saumitra.

IV – SALUTATIONS TO PUERTO RICO

35. Pan American Games adventure

I am telling you about my adventure at the Pan American Masters Games. As you know, I was invited to go there to offer a short meditation. Also, I was requested to dedicate one of my songs to the Pan American Masters Games. So, the good singers sang the *Run and Become* song extremely well for a tape and I dedicated that song to the Games.

There were quite a few thousand spectators. Some young men used coloured flags to say "welcome", "thank you" and all kinds of things – as in the previous Pan American Games. It was quite beautiful and charming.

The speaker read out ten or twelve lines about me in Spanish and then I was escorted by a lady to the platform. Uttama followed me. I was not supposed to inaugurate the Games; I was supposed to hold the opening meditation after the inauguration. The Governor himself was supposed to inaugurate the Games, but God knows what happened. The Governor was delayed for some reason. So the official said, "Sri Chinmoy will offer us the inaugural benediction."

I went to the platform and Uttama said a few things. He thanked all the celebrities and then introduced me. I meditated for about two or three minutes, facing the audience. Then I turned around and meditated on the people who were showing the coloured flags. Afterwards I spoke for a few minutes, thanking them and bringing down the Supreme's Blessings for the athletes.

Thousands of people were there, but they remained in pin-drop silence. I told them I was dedicating one of my songs to the soul of the Pan American Masters Games and they played the tape over the loudspeaker. It sounded extremely good. It was simply marvellous.

36. The march past

After the inauguration, we were in the march past. You laugh, at times, at our marching on Sports Day. But if you laugh at our marching, then you would have perhaps jumped and danced if you had seen them marching. The musicians in the band were really good, but nobody paid attention to the drum. Everybody had his or her own inner drum.

37. The grace descends for the mayor

After the march past, the Mayor of San Juan was supposed to speak. We were standing in the field and the Mayor was taking a little time to start speaking. O God, from Heaven real Grace descended. There was a real downpour, and I was not brave enough to stay. I ran inside the stadium, but others were brave. They stood there in the rain and listened while the Mayor spoke for a few minutes.

God knows what Uttama told him about me. Afterwards the Mayor came up to me, walking at least 200 metres out of his way. He thanked me profusely for the trouble I had taken to come to the Pan American Masters Games. I thanked him and said quite a few nice things about the athletes. He was very happy.

After the Mayor came, the president of the organisation, a tall young man, introduced himself to me. I thanked him and he thanked me. He was very nice.

Then a man, sixty-seven years old, came up to me. Last year he was decathlon champion in his age group. He started telling me about himself. He said he had seven children and eighteen grandchildren and that whenever he won it was all God's Grace. The next day, the newspaper had his timing. My timing and throwing distances in the ashram were far, far better. But I can't brag, since I was twenty-six or twenty-seven at that time and he is sixty-seven.

38. The rainy race

I was supposed to join in the 100-metre dash. Just before the race, it started raining. Many others didn't run because of the rain, but I wanted to show off. During my twenty years of competing in India, I never used starting blocks. I lost my balance at the start and I was last. God wanted me to have this experience.

Once upon a time I was first – for sixteen years. But here, there was at least a fifty metre gap between the first runner and me. The audience was enjoying the fact that there was such a gap between us.

On the board it was mentioned, "Sri Chinmoy, Puerto Rico". The Puerto Rican disciples were so delighted. I had said that I was not going to run the 400-metre dash, but they didn't listen. My name still appeared on the board: "Sri Chinmoy, Puerto Rico".

39. Old friends

A thin, tall black man came up to me and said, "Guru, don't you remember me? The other day I ran 800 metres with you." Then I recognised him. He was in the Randall's Island race in New York City. I had told Danny to videotape him. I said, "Yes, you ran extremely well. I was far, far behind." He is national champion in his age category. He was so happy to see me. He couldn't believe that I was in Puerto Rico. At Randall's Island he ran a 2:10 and my timing was 3 minutes. But in India in the 800 metres I had stood first.

In half an hour, again he came up to me just to chat. In the Pan American Games he defeated everyone in the 800, but in the 100 he didn't get a place. So, he said nice things and I said nice things.

Then some elderly athletes were showing that they could do the high jump and pole vault. One of them pushed the bar with his shoulder, so everybody laughed. One or two athletes were good when they jumped. I was watching and enjoying. Sometimes when people were throwing the javelin, it did not point. Even world champions have that problem.

One seventy-five-year-old ran very fast. Then, when the race was over, the first, second and third place finishers embraced one another and took pictures. It was most thrilling. Many times the experiences were very, very good.

40. A man of peace

Today something very significant took place. When I arrived at the airport, there were only twelve minutes before the plane was scheduled to take off. I went hurriedly to the last check point. As soon as I came near the door and saw the man who was in charge of checking, he came running towards me and grabbed my right arm powerfully. Then he embraced me and said, "Sri Chinmoy, you are a man of peace. The other day I got so much peace from your meditation at the Pan Am Games."

He asked me how old I was, and I said, "Forty-nine."

He said, "You look younger every year. I need peace. The world needs peace badly."

Then he asked me for my ticket. I had my ticket and boarding pass. But I was looking for my passport, because they always ask you for a passport when you are leaving Puerto Rico. He said, "What are you doing?"

I said, "I am looking for my passport."

He said, "You are a saint. You don't need a passport. You are universal. A man of peace is universal."

41. First class

I gave the man at the check point my boarding pass. God knows what he did with it. He said to me, "You will get a refund of sixty-nine dollars." Then he said, "I just put you a few seats ahead."

I had bought a ticket for the coach section. But when I entered the plane and showed the stewardess my pass, she took me to the first seat of the first class section. So I got a sixty-nine dollars refund plus first class accommodations.

In ten or fifteen minutes' time, the same man entered into the plane. There was some bad news: all the breakfasts were rotten, so they had to take them out of the plane. I thanked him for what he had done. He said to me, "It is my honour, my pleasure. At least I can do this much for you. I am so honoured."

So, if you can really bring down peace, at least one person may get peace. And because he got peace, he put me in the first class section and gave me a cheque for sixty-nine dollars.

42. Before take-off

I was sitting in the first seat of the front row. One of the stewardesses said, "Please let me take the bag that is in front of you until the plane is in the air. Then I will bring it back."

So I gave it to her. Then there was an announcement that the plane would be delayed for twenty minutes. When I went to the stewardess to get some books out of the bag, a tall man came and stood in front of me and said, "Master, Master, why didn't you run yesterday in the half-marathon?"

I said, "I couldn't do the 400-metre dash. How could I have done the half-marathon?"

He said, "Your races are so good because they are held early in the morning. I always enter your races. Early in the morning I run."

Here the half-marathon was held at three-thirty in the afternoon, so he didn't run. And he is Puerto Rican! Puerto Ricans are accustomed to that kind of heat.

So you see, if you start races early in the morning, there will be at least one person who will be happy and grateful.

He said, "Your students, your disciples, are so good."

Another stewardess happened to be there and she said, "Because the Master is good, the disciples are good." Then she said, "Master, I have been to your meetings quite a few times, but now it is different. At the meditations you are very distant. It is good, but you are somewhere else. Now you are talking."

I said, "At that time I meditate."

She said, "Yes, that is why you are so distant."

43. *The stewardess' job*

That particular stewardess was supposed to serve the first-class passengers. She asked me what I wanted to drink. I said, "Seven-up." She felt that I had given her a special job. During the flight I didn't ask her again for Seven-up, but she was watching my glass. I was writing poems, in my own world. Whenever my glass became empty, she came and filled it. I didn't have the heart to tell her I didn't want any more.

NOTES TO SALUTATIONS, BOOK I

1–20. *(p. 5)* Sri Chinmoy visited Switzerland in June 1980 as part of a European lecture and concert tour.

21–29. *(p. 19)* Sri Chinmoy visited Italy and the Vatican in June 1980, lecturing in Rome and meeting with the Pope.

30–34. *(p. 25)* In June 1980 Sri Chinmoy visited Germany as part of a European lecture and concert tour.

35–43. *(p. 28)* In September 1980 Sri Chinmoy was invited to Puerto Rico to deliver the opening benediction at the Pan American Masters Games.

SALUTATIONS

BOOK 2

V – SALUTATIONS TO FLORIDA

44. The plane ride

When I arrived at the airport for the flight to Florida, I entered into the plane and sat down quite comfortably. O God, right behind me two young men and their girlfriend were talking so loudly about the dates they had been on and all that. The girl's name was Jill and one of the boys' names was Michael. The girl kept speaking to Michael only to annoy the other boy.

It was ruining my concentration, but what could I do? After twenty minutes I got disgusted, saying to myself, "I won't be able to write anything." So I moved to another seat.

Then I saw that one row in front of me a baby was sleeping. I said, "At least let him sleep. I will be able to finish my writing." The baby remained fast asleep, so I was happy. Suddenly his mother started shaking him. I said, "O God, only in Indian villages do they do this kind of thing – showing their affection this way." Then, finally, she pulled away a pacifier that was in his mouth. As soon as the pacifier was taken away, the child started screaming. The hostile forces were acting through the mother.

She gave the child a toy and the child kicked it. Of all places, it fell at my feet. The mother said to me, "Can you hand it over?"

I gave back the toy, but I said in silence: "You want to show your possession to the world at the cost of others' suffering. You have got a child, but why do you have to ruin our peace?"

Her husband was sitting beside her. He got mad at her and said, "Had I known that you were so ugly I would not have married you. You are inwardly so ugly."

Then she said, "Had I known that you were outwardly so ugly, I would not have married you."

The husband left his seat and sat some other place, four or five seats ahead. I said, "Here is God speaking on earth. The wife is a hostile force, and the husband is God." I took his side.

After an hour the two boys and their girlfriend came and sat right behind me again. But this time they did not talk at all. All three were absolutely peaceful. But why did they have to come and sit behind me? There were only forty or fifty people on the plane; it was totally empty. I thought they would again start their business, but they were quiet.

45. *The first night*

The first day I was in Fort Lauderdale alone and I went out to run at night – around ten o'clock. After I had run about two and a half miles, I became quite hungry. I had some money, so I went into a restaurant. But they said to me, "No, you can't eat here. You are not properly dressed." I was wearing tennis shorts which came right to my knees. They were quite modest – not the thin, Bill Rodgers running shorts.

So I left and went to another place. There was a guard sitting at the door. He said to me, "Do you want to eat?"

I said, "Yes, I am very hungry."

He said, "You can go inside and eat."

I went in, but here also, one of the waiters saw how I was dressed and said to me, "This is not the place for you. Here you can't eat." They also asked me to leave.

There was a place beside the main restaurant, like an adjacent dining hall. Nobody was there. I asked, "Can I not eat there?"

They said, "No, you are not properly dressed. You have no tie, no suit, nothing."

Two places had thrown me out. Now it was like a challenge to find a restaurant. Otherwise, I wouldn't care. But since I live in America, American blood has entered into me, and Americans love challenges. So I was running and running. Finally, around eleven o'clock, I came to an Italian restaurant. I saw a menu on the window, and I was reading it with the hope that I would be able to go inside. Somebody came out and looked at me. I said to that person, "I want to speak to the manager."

The man said, "I am the manager."

I asked, "Can I go inside and eat?"

The manager asked, "What is wrong with you? You have no money?"

I said, "I have money, but I am not properly dressed."

So I went inside. Except for one table, all the tables were occupied. I ordered eggplant, as usual. Beside me there was a group of people at a big table: an airline pilot and his wife, the co-pilot and his wife and their parents. The wives were sitting on the right side of the husbands and next to them were the parents. It was one of the fathers' birthday and they were all very happy. They had ordered a cake, which one of the waiters brought, and they were about to sing *Happy Birthday*.

Quite unexpectedly, a middle-aged couple came over to them. The couple had been sitting at another table. The co-pilot stood up and shook hands with the man and kissed the woman. O God, the co-pilot's wife became furious. She stood up and walked out of the restaurant. Her husband's father and some others went to bring her back. At the table, some were laughing, some were serious, some were shocked. Even people from other tables came over to see what the commotion was. But the co-pilot just said, "Let us sing *Happy Birthday*."

My bill was for seven dollars and something. So I put a ten-dollar bill on the table and left. I was not enjoying my eggplant. "Next," I thought, "will come a fight. Before bottles fly in the air – bottle-bullets – let me leave this place."

46. The police chase

It was around midnight and I was going back home. There were some grocery stores that were open twenty-four hours, so I went into one and bought a Tab, some fruit and juice – no candy at that hour. Two or three other people were also inside the store.

A middle-aged lady was behind the counter. Each time a person wanted to come in, she would open the door from the inside and then bolt it again. She was very nice. O God, suddenly three young men tried to open the door forcefully, but the lady would not let them in.

The three young men were being chased by the police. While the other two were still banging on the door, trying to escape, one fellow hid under a car. There were three or four cars in front of the grocery store. The police were having such trouble getting this man, because they were too fat to get under the car. They were screaming at the fellow, but he continued to stay under the car. The other two had already been arrested, and they were laughing at the police. I said, "O God, O God, I don't want to know the remainder of this story." So I bought four or five dollars' worth of things and I left.

47. Looking for Sally

I was coming back home around twelve-thirty. About three hundred metres from my apartment was a small hospital, with windows facing the street. One fellow was standing on the street drinking and calling for his girlfriend, "Sally! Open the window. I want to see you. I have not seen you for a long time." He was screaming up to the second or third floor for the patient, Sally, to open the window and talk to him.

But she was not opening the window. Another man from upstairs started screaming at the drunk fellow, "What are you doing at this hour?" He used all American slang, screaming at him from the third floor.

48. The hat

The next day I went to the airport to meet Alo. I am on a diet, but only my soul knows it. I bought candies and cookies. It was very hot and I was suffering so much. All I had was a headband, so I wanted to buy a hat. I picked one out and put it on my head. I picked up a newspaper and a few other things also. The cashier was an old lady. For the newspaper, this and that, she charged me two dollars and some change. I gave her a ten-dollar bill and she returned the change. Everything was perfect.

After I left the store, inadvertently I put my hand on my head. I said, "O my God, I didn't pay for my hat."

I went back to the cashier and explained, "I didn't pay for the hat. It was on my head."

The lady said, "There should be another person like you on earth."

The hat was five or six dollars, so the lady was very happy that I had come back.

49. The taxi driver

Alo and I were looking for a taxi for about ten minutes. We wanted to get Savyasachi from the airport. Finally a taxi stopped, but there was a man in the back seat, so we didn't want to take the taxi. The driver explained that the man in the back seat was blind, and that he was supposed to help the blind man out of the car. The blind man had a machine for Braille, and Alo was asking about it. The man said that his mother came from New York.

The taxi driver was so nice. After he let the blind man out, he took us to the airport. He said he came from Flushing five years ago. He does not run at all, but he swims. His girlfriend compels him to swim, so he swims.

We arrived at the airport. The fare was eight dollars, but I gave the driver two dollars more. He looked at me. I said, "You are such a kind-hearted man. You helped that blind man."

I had been sitting in the front beside him. He said, "Now I see that your vibration was too high for me."

50. The muggers

Alo, Savyasachi and I were out shopping for furniture, this and that. At one point, when I came out of a big department store, three black teenagers came up to me and said, "Mister, what time do you have?"

I said, "Four forty-five."

Then they came closer to me and said, "What we really want from you is the wristwatch, and not the time."

I got so furious! I pushed my elbows out, but I didn't touch anybody, and I screamed, "What!" When I screamed, all three disappeared. There were hundreds of people around at the time.

51. You need daily church

As you know, I am always fond of entering into bookstores, especially if they are Christian bookstores. I am just the right person. So I went into a bookstore run by an old couple and asked the lady if she had a daily prayer book. She could not understand my pronunciation. She said, "What, what?"

Then I said, "Everyday prayers."

"Oh," she said, "You are saying 'daily prayers'. My son, you don't need a daily prayer. What you need is daily church. You must go to church every morning. Daily you must go to pray. You don't need a prayer book."

She looked like she was in her seventies. She wanted me to go to church and pray.

52. *A young running companion*

One day I was out running. A beautiful six- or seven-year-old child, wearing a necklace, came up to me and asked, "Mister, can I run with you?"

I said, "Why not?"

I had been running at an eight or eight and a half minute pace. Now, very slowly I ran with her. We covered three blocks, and then she stopped near her house. She came from a respectable family. She was so happy and proud that I ran with her. She thanked me and gave me a broad smile.

53. *Mister, will you help me?*

Two days later, a little child, even younger than the other little girl, was on her way to school when I ran by quite fast. All of a sudden she said, "Mister!" There were no cars, but she wanted me to help her cross the street. So very slowly I walked across the street with her. I didn't even need to hold her hand, because there was no traffic. As soon as we had crossed the street, she thanked me and entered into a little school.

54. Lost and found

The other day, I went out to run for two hours. After I ran for about an hour and forty minutes, I got totally lost. It was raining. I said, "O God, where do I go? I don't have any money." Luckily, I remembered the apartment number and, with greatest difficulty, I even remembered the name of the street – Las Olas. I said, "This is the time for me to look for a taxi."

I asked a lady where Las Olas Street was. I had to listen for at least five minutes while she explained which road to take and where I should turn. I didn't understand her in spite of her five-minute explanation. I said, "All right, let me take this street."

Then whom did I see running down the street? Savyasachi! I said, "How can it be?" I had run six or seven miles. He was staying only one mile away from where I had stopped running. He had just gone out for a short run, and he got great joy when he saw me. Then we ran together.

When I play tennis with Savyasachi, his standard always makes me laugh – not only inwardly but also outwardly. But when he runs with me, I feel that inwardly he is laughing at my standard.

55. The braggart

As I was running the next day, a young man went ahead of me. Four men saw him run past. They said to me, "He is bragging. Don't pay any attention." The runner went four or five hundred metres ahead, while I continued slowly running. Then he stopped and began to walk. His bragging was over. I passed him. When I was returning from my run, he was still walking.

56. Competition-blood will never leave me

Another day I saw an old man running. I said, "If my speed has really increased, I will be able to pass him." I came nearer, only to discover that the runner was a lady. I said, "Let me run according to my speed." After two hundred metres, I turned around. O God, she was so far behind!

I tell the disciples to have no competitive feeling, to compete only with themselves. Here I was competing with an old lady! Competition-blood will never leave me.

57. Dog problems

While running in Fort Lauderdale, as usual, I had dog problems. A dog started barking at me and didn't allow me to go by. When I returned home, I told Alo about the dog.

The following day she went to look for it, so that she could insult the owner. Luckily she found a different dog, so everything went peacefully.

58. The lost running companion

Another day I was running about seven miles. At one point I was about to make a right turn, but something within told me to make a left turn. Alo was there looking for me!

Another day I was running and she was following me. I would go ahead two hundred metres and then come back, go ahead and come back. Once, after running two hundred metres and coming back, she was not there. I said, "Where can she be?" But she was not to be found.

What happened was that she had gone across the street to look at a clothing store. I didn't see her standing across the street, so I kept going up and down the block – three or four times.

When I came back home, she was there, worrying about what had happened to me. She had gone out two times to look for me. But she did not find me because she just went in front of the building, and I was somewhere else.

59. The best shopping in the world

A few years ago I told you I went to an Indian bookstore in Calcutta called "The World's Best Bookshop". In Fort Lauderdale there are also shops with that kind of name. One shop is called "The World's Best Sport Shop". Another place is called "The World's Best Tea Shop". Hardly four persons can sit there, but it is called "The World's Best"! Other places are called "The World's Largest". Our small meditation hall is three times as large as those places! In other places, if they have four or five pairs of skates, they will put them on a table with a sign: "World's Best". If you ask the price, it is twenty-nine or thirty dollars – very expensive.

And these stores have very, very few things. You can go to ten athletic stores, and you will be finished in each place in five minutes. Very few shops have a second story; there is no upstairs. Sandhani's sports store is bigger.

The shopkeepers are rogues. I was looking for the kind of belt that weightlifters use. One shopkeeper told me, "We don't have what you are looking for, but our branch in Coral Gables definitely has it." He said that their branch store in Coral Gables was more established, whereas this store was about to close down. I believed him, and Savyasachi drove us to the store. It took us twenty-five minutes. But when we reached Coral Gables, they didn't have one single belt. What can you do? The shop was smaller than the smallest and everything was so expensive!

60. The ignorant shopkeeper

I went to a particular store and bought something. Then I sent Savyasachi to get something else from that store. It was mentioned that the item was twenty-five per cent off. Savyasachi said, "Twenty-five per cent off, your sign says."

The owner of the store said, "Oh, I didn't know that." He asked his assistant, "Is it twenty-five per cent off?"

His assistant also said, "I don't know."

The owner did not know and his assistant did not know. Did I go there and write "Twenty-five per cent off"?

Then I went to another store, just to browse. I got the same item, but it was of far better quality and the price was also far better. I asked Savyasachi to return the item to the first store. He is an American, so he was a little embarrassed because first we had asked for the twenty-five per cent discount, and then we wanted to return the thing. But they gave all our money back, and then we bought one dollar's worth from their store.

61. The Paradise Whydah finch

On my way back home to New York, I came to the airport with a bird called a Paradise Whydah, a kind of finch. It has a very long tail and is very beautiful. Alo was holding the bird in a box. An official at the check-in counter said, "Oh, you have to make a reservation for the bird. There will be an extra charge."

I said, "I have carried birds from so many places. There is never any problem."

The man said, "No, the bird is an animal. You have to pay."

We didn't pay any attention to him. We just went to another check-in counter. Alo felt really sad that she had been holding the bird near the people who check baggage. She said that she always brings good luck, but that this time she had brought bad luck.

This time Savyasachi held the bird. The people at the other check-in counter said, "You have to pay twenty-one dollars for the bird, because it is an animal."

We were disgusted with their behaviour, so we didn't pay right away. Alo and I went to have some dinner, and Savyasachi stayed to watch our bags. While we were gone, one of the clerks came over to Savyasachi and asked, "Are you with the people who had the bird? Where are they?"

Savyasachi said that he didn't know anything; he was only watching the bags.

The clerk said, "They have to pay for the bird."

The people were very bad. When we returned, we argued with them again, but our arguments were in vain. So Alo paid twenty-one dollars, and I entered into the plane. One of the stewardesses saw the box and asked, "Is there a bird inside?"

I said, "Yes."

She asked, "What kind of bird?"

I replied, "A finch, a Paradise Whydah."

She said, "Oh, I adore finches."

I looked a little sad and said, "I had to pay twenty-one dollars to bring it on the plane."

She said, "Twenty-one dollars! Those men are crooks! I would have given them a mouthful. If my superiors were not here, I would go on your behalf and speak to the people who charged you."

The plane was about to leave. Half an hour after take-off, the stewardess came and sat beside me and started talking to the bird. She said to the bird, "Hello, darling, talk to me."

I said to myself, "Oi! As if finches will talk!"

Then she said, "Finches are adorable. You had bad luck. Those men were crooks. Next time, you tell them that it is a bird and not an animal. Or take a small box and put the bird in your briefcase. They do that just to make money. The money will not even go to the airline. It will go into their own pockets."

She was talking to the bird and it was making noise.

VI – SALUTATIONS TO CANADA

62. *Looking for the Ottawa Holiday Inn*

Yesterday in Ottawa I went out to run early in the morning. I had been running for about an hour and fifteen minutes when I realised that I was lost. I asked a very nice and kind-hearted black lady where the Holiday Inn was. She said, "Oh dear, where are you? It is so far. Go straight down for at least twenty blocks and then ask people to show you where it is. You won't be able to understand how to get there from here, so after twenty blocks you ask someone where it is."

I ran about twenty blocks to a place that I later found out was only two or three blocks away from the hotel. Unfortunately, when I asked a young boy where the Holiday Inn was, he told me exactly the opposite way. Instead of telling me it was two blocks in one direction, he turned the other way and said, "Run that way. Go only a couple of blocks – two or three more – and then you will find it." He even pointed the way with his finger.

I ran two or three, then six or seven blocks, and still I didn't see the hotel. Finally, I approached someone else, "Somebody told me that the Holiday Inn was only two blocks in this direction."

The man said, "Not this direction. It is in the other direction. Turn around and go the other way."

I said to myself, "Whom to believe?" The first time, when I was following the young boy's instructions, I was having no doubts. But by this time real doubt had started. O God, what could I do? When one is a stranger, one has to believe in these people. Finally I said, "All right." So I covered six or seven blocks in the other direction, and finally I found the Holiday Inn there.

63. Pizza for breakfast

Before I left on the Canadian trip, I had taken a solemn oath not to take solid food during the whole tour, depending only on water, ERG, juice and, of course, my best friend and enemy – nuts. I really did keep my promise.

In Montreal, early in the morning, Savyasachi, Alo and I went to the Montreal Mall for breakfast. As usual, I asked for a cup of tea and Savyasachi ordered his breakfast. Alo said she didn't want anything. Then I pointed out a pizza parlour about five or six metres away, asking, "Do you want to have pizza?" She said, "Yes, yes," and went to get some.

The pie in the tray had meat on it – sausage or whatever. So she asked one of the men if they could give her vegetarian pizza. They said, "Yes, we can give it to you, but come back in five minutes." After five minutes when she went back, to her surprise she saw that one of the workers had just removed two slices from that same pie and then taken off the meat. When they gave the pieces to her, Alo said, "You people are not honest. Definitely you have taken these pieces from the sausage pie and have just removed the meat."

One of the workers answered, "There is no meat inside it. I told you there would be no meat."

Then Alo said, "You people are dishonest."

They said, "You are also not honest."

Alo said, "Can you not look into my eyes and my soul?"

One of them answered, "Can you not look into my soul and into my eyes? I am honest. You are dishonest. You talk too much."

Then Alo said, "You people do not have the Canadian good nature. Of the three of you, only one has a little sincerity," and she pointed to one of the workers.

Then the other two started cutting jokes with the one who, according to Alo, was a little sincere. Savyasachi and I could overhear the whole conversation, and we were deeply amused.

64. *"Your smile is our meditation"*

When we were coming back from Halifax to Quebec, we had a short stopover at one of the towns. Just as we were about to get out of our seats, a young man, very nicely dressed in a suit and tie, came over to me and said, "So, were you successful last night?"

I said, "What do you mean?"

He said, "Last night you gave a concert. I was there. It was so moving."

I said, "If people are receptive, then I am successful; and if they are not receptive, then I am not successful. But I place my success and failure at the Feet of my Lord Supreme with equal joy."

Then he said, "I wish to tell you one thing. You didn't have to play, you didn't have to sing, you didn't have to do anything. If you had only given us a smile occasionally we could have stayed in our highest, our best consciousness. From time to time you did smile at the audience. That was the best meditation and the best music for us. I am a disciple of Maharaji. I initiate people here in Canada. Would you be able to listen to a short tape of a Hindi song?"

I said, "I know very little Hindi. Also, I won't be able to understand the words from the tape. Even when they tape my own songs in Bengali, which are sung by my students who are excellent singers, I can't understand the words. So I know I won't be able to understand this."

He said, "Please try."

So I said, "I can try."

The tape was very short. It was a short bhajan, a Hindi religious song. I said, "All right, this much I can say. It is dedicated to Lord Krishna and it is about the gopis in Brindaban, but the actual translation I won't be able to give."

He was very happy that I had listened to the tape. He opened up his briefcase to show me a picture of his Guru wearing a suit. Now the Maharaji has grown a moustache, a long beard and long hair.

It was time to get off the plane and I said, "How can we keep our seats?" There were no reserved seats but we wanted to save our places. Immediately the young man took from his pocket a piece of plastic that said "Occupied" and put it on our seats to save them.

65. *The Japanese robin*

I went to a pet shop that had three Japanese robins. I wanted to buy two, but the lady said, "Don't buy two, buy one."

I asked, "Why?"

She answered, "If you buy two, they won't sing. Only buy one; then it will sing. When they are alone, they sing a lot. But if you have two or three, as we have here, they don't sing."

The price was thirty dollars. I asked her, "Can you reduce the price?"

She was so nice. She said, "I have to ask my boss."

Her boss came over to me and I asked her, "Can you make the price a little less?"

The boss said, "Oh, twenty-five dollars." I agreed, "All right. I will buy it for twenty-five dollars."

The bird started flying all over the store, and with greatest difficulty the saleslady caught it. When she brought it to the register, her boss said, "I am going out now. I will be back in a few minutes."

As soon as her boss left, the saleslady rang up twenty dollars on the register.

I said, "Why, it is twenty-five, not twenty." She just gave me a smile. I continued, "But your boss didn't agree to twenty. She said for twenty-five I can have it."

The saleslady gave it to me for twenty. She was so nice to me. And she was right; the bird sang for three days in the car. For fifteen minutes it would sing one song, then another song. Japanese robins sing different songs with different notes. At least twenty times we heard it sing.

Before this incident, I had gone to another store where the owner was so rude. They had a beautiful parrot. I made him an offer, but he said, "No! It is about a hundred dollars."

I said, "But I will give you American dollars."

He exclaimed, "What?"

I said, "Perhaps you know that American dollars are worth more."

He said, "What does it mean? So what!"

I said, "Come to America. Then you will see."

These people are all rogues. In so many places they don't give the right exchange rate for the American dollar.

66. *Practising what you preach*

In Toronto there was a two-mile race. I had already run a lot early in the morning before the race, so I was very tired and exhausted. Also, I didn't have any energy because I had not been eating solid food. But I started running anyway.

There were about twenty-five runners in the race. Four girls who were running started to pass me. I said, "I have no more strength to run. I preach all the time 'surrender, surrender, surrender' to my disciples. Now God wants me to practise it."

O God, one, two, three, four – the girls all went ahead of me. Then, after one mile, one by one I caught three of them. But one girl was still ahead of me. After a mile and a half, O God, I had absolutely no energy left. I started walking very nicely and the girls whom I had passed went ahead. I said, "Oh, now I am practising and practising. Not only do I preach surrender but I practise it also."

A young man, a new disciple who still has long hair and a moustache, came up to me near the end of the race and said, "Guru, I want to run with you because I want peace. I am getting so much peace from you."

I thought, "Oh, he is getting peace and I am dying."

So, near the finish line, when I started walking, he also started walking. Then about a hundred metres from the end I told him, "Now, please, you go and run. Finish it running." So he completed the two mile race running.

67. The well-established seeker

Right after the concert in Halifax, when I was coming out of the hall, I had no guards except Utpal, who went ahead to the car just as Alo and I were about to get in it. All of a sudden, a young Indian man fell down at my feet and prostrated himself, just as if he were going to do pushups. Then he did do four pushups, touching my feet with his forehead each time. I said, "Oi, oi, oi, please, please get up."

He wouldn't get up, so I placed my hand on his head and he finally stood up with folded hands. Alo said, "You are so nice, you have such a fine soul. If you want to come tonight, Sri Chinmoy will see people who are interested in his path."

Then the Indian man said, "Oh no, I am well-established here. I come from New Delhi and I am well-established here. But I was so moved when Swamiji was playing."

Later Alo said, "Look at that fellow! He prostrates himself, doing pushups at your feet, banging on your foot. Then he says he is well-established, so he can't come!"

68. Devotees from the Indian Consulate

There was an Indian girl, Vijaya, who worked in the same section with me at the Indian Consulate. She came from south India, from Kerala, our divine Shivaram's place. She was very nice and kind to me, very fond of me. Some time after I left the Indian Consulate she also left to get married. When she had a child, she wanted me to bless it because, according to her, I was a real swami, a real saint and all that. A few years ago she brought her child to our Centre in New York for blessings. She said, "Look, we were in the same section and you became a saint, a swami." She was very proud that I was an Indian. She was very nice and I blessed the child.

In Toronto, this same Indian lady wanted to come to see me, but she could not come because of family problems. Her husband also likes me very much. In India, whenever you see a swami, a spiritual man, you give him something. So she put fifty dollars in an envelope and wrote, "For the Swami". She gave the money to Shivaram so that she could get inner blessings for her family and for herself. Shivaram gave the envelope to Alo and Alo opened it in the plane, saying, "Shivaram told me that this Indian lady had given some money so that she could have your inner blessings, even though she could not come to see you."

What I am saying is, even in those days, when I worked at the Consulate, people saw something in me. Now I have become a Guru, a Master, but even now some people don't recognise anything in me. Such a difference between their spirituality and the spirituality of some of my former colleagues, such as Vijaya. In those days, when I was a junior clerk and she was a junior clerk, she recognised me. Of course, when I was a clerk, Shivaram was also a clerk. Shivaram and I used to talk about Ramakrishna and different spiritual Masters. He saw something in me and he became my disciple. Look at his divinity! My best friend at the Indian Consulate has since become my disciple. Whoever thought, when we were working at the Indian Consulate, that Shivaram would someday become my disciple?

Yesterday an Indian man became a disciple. His brother used to work with us at the Consulate. I don't recollect who he was, but Shivaram says definitely I knew him. He used to work in another section. He used to take photographs. Now his brother, who is also a photographer, has become a disciple in the Toronto Centre!

69. *The musician's plight*

In Canada when I was flying from Halifax to Quebec, I was carrying my smallest esraj. When I went to sit in my seat, a stewardess asked, "How is it you have brought that in here? Did you pay for it?"

I said, "No, they didn't ask me to pay."

She said, "It is illegal. You have to pay and you can't bring it here."

I said, "They allowed me to come in here and they saw that I was carrying this."

I was sitting on the extreme right. A musician happened to be on the extreme left. He took my side. He got furious, and started abusing the stewardess, "You make your rules every second. All over the world we go and here you won't allow us to carry an instrument."

I said, "When I went to Halifax, Air Canada allowed me to bring this with me."

Then the stewardess got frightened or perhaps she was amused. She said, "Please give me the instrument. I will keep it very safe and give it back when we land." She kept her promise. As soon as the plane touched the ground, she brought the instrument back.

VII – SALUTATIONS TO ENGLAND

70. *The good and bad shopkeepers*

One day I went to buy an alarm clock for Alo because she needed one badly. First I went to one store and bought a pair of shoes. Then I went to another store to look for the clock. The man was extremely kind and polite and showed me five or six alarm clocks. I selected one that I liked and bought it.

When I walked out of the store, I left the bag with my shoes there. I had covered about four blocks when all of a sudden behind me I heard some footsteps and panting. The gentleman from the store had come running after me, saying, "Sir, Sir!" Then he gave me my shoes.

I was so moved, and I wanted to give him a tip. He said, "Oh no, I can't take that." The gentleman had run four blocks to catch me. I was so grateful.

I entered into a meditative consciousness and continued walking back to the Palace Gardens Hotel. After I had covered another three or four blocks, I saw a small shop selling bags. It was like a boutique. When I entered the store, the owner, an Arab lady, said to me, "You not good man. Go away."

I looked at her. Then I saw a beautiful scarf and asked, "How much is this?"

Again she said, "You go away my shop. Go away."

This is what happens when you are in a meditative consciousness. Finally I went away. The following day, I told Alo about the incident and she was so mad and furious. She wanted to go there.

So these are two experiences with shopkeepers, one good and one bad.

71. The Palace Gardens maid

When I was staying at the Palace Gardens Hotel, one day around six-thirty or a quarter to seven in the morning somebody opened my door. Usually they don't clean so early so I asked, "What is it?"

A maid answered, "Sorry, sorry," and went away.

Then I came out and put the "Don't Disturb" sign on the door and went back into my room. In twenty minutes, the same lady again opened the door. This time I insulted her: "You don't read English? Here is the 'Don't Disturb' sign. You speak English, but you don't read English."

After that, I left my key at the desk and went out for about three hours. When I came back to my room, I realised I had left the key downstairs. I saw the same lady in front of my room, so I said, "I am very sorry, but I left the key downstairs. Would you kindly open my door?"

She said, "How do I know you are staying in that room?"

She would not open the door for me, so I had to go downstairs to get the key. When I came back, she was watching me open the door and laughing at me. For twenty minutes she had bothered me. Then, three hours later, she said she did not recognise me. By not opening the door, she was punishing me for insulting her.

72. The Indian exchange rate

I went into an Indian store to buy a few things for the children of the London Centre. The lady quoted prices in American dollars. I was buying scarves, saris and all kinds of things.

O God, when I gave her the money, the lady reduced the exchange rate because she was so eager to get American dollars.

When she saw American money, she gave everything to me much cheaper.

73. *Two Indians*

When Haridas' choir sang at the Bharatiya Vidya Bhavan School last year, the head of it wrote me a nice letter. This year I had not the slightest idea that we would have that place for our evening functions, which are all plays, songs, jokes and all that. When we got to the school, I thought, "Perhaps the head of the school will be here." But, as usual, I was wearing a running suit. I only wear *dhotis* on special occasions.

Right away the registrar came up to me with folded hands and said, "I have to honour you." When he returned half an hour later, he was wearing his Indian kurta and dhoti and had put a tilak on his forehead. Also, he had brought a garland to garland me.

We were both on the stage. He spoke very highly of me for a long time. An Indian was honouring me, saying nice things about me! I was embarrassed. Although I was unprepared, I spoke very highly of the founder of his organisation and of my personal experiences with him.

Another Indian, a Bengali, happened to be there. When I returned to my seat, he came up behind me and started showing off. He touched my feet and then gave me a pound as a gift. Since I am a Bengali, he started talking all about Bengal. Finally Alo stopped him, saying that we had many important things to do.

74. A song for Malcolm

I composed a song for Malcolm while I was in Europe this time. As soon as people think of Malcolm, they laugh. But he has a very good soul and I am really pleased with his exemplary dedication. I wanted to make him happy, so I composed a song.

The children in our London Centre are better singers than the children in America. They learned so many songs and performed them extremely well. They also performed excellent plays.

One boy, in a play, recited the Sanskrit for "The Soul cannot be won by the weakling", *Nayam atma balahinena labhyo*. Then, instead of singing that song, he sang instead *Tomai dite*. I said, "Wonderful!" I called him down from the stage after the play and set tune to the Sanskrit words. I taught the song to him, and then all the children learned it.

75. Buying a newspaper

When I bought an English newspaper, I couldn't understand the shopkeeper's pronunciation. It was thirty pence, but I thought he was saying twenty pence. I gave him twenty pence and he was saying, "Wan mo', wan mo'," but I couldn't understand him.

VIII – SALUTATIONS TO BRAZIL

76. The cup of coffee

In Rio, we went to a shop where it said a cup of coffee was fifteen cruzeiros. We gave the man twenty. But, instead of giving us change, the man asked for another twenty. Alo got mad at him. When our bus driver came, he said to the man, "How can you ask for more than what it says?" Finally, he returned five cruzeiros as our change.

77. The beer drinker

In one hotel in Rio, the Riviera, as usual we went to pay the bill at check-out time. My bill and Alo's bill were not the same. Alo hadn't made any phone calls, but her bill exceeded mine. When we checked it, we saw that they said she had taken two bottles of beer from the refrigerator.

Alo got furious and insulted them very nicely. Finally they said it had been a mistake. The chambermaid had said that Alo had drunk two beers, but when Alo got furious, they said it had been a mistake. The two beers should have been billed to another room.

78. The hotel rogues

At another hotel in Rio, the Luxor Regente, Alo stayed in room 509 and I was in 408. After two days, Alo left for Puerto Rico. I had given them a deposit of sixty dollars for our rooms, although they didn't want it at the time. Alo left at 9:30 at night and they called me, asking me to come down to settle the account. I said, "I have given a deposit and I am still here. I will settle it tomorrow."

An hour later, somebody else called, asking me to come down to settle the account. I got mad and insulted them. I said, "I am here. My things are here. I have given a deposit."

In two or three days, when I went to check out, again I had problems with them. At some hotels if you stay for half a day, they charge you only half. But these people were such rogues. Checkout time for half a day was six o'clock. If it is a little past six, even five minutes, you pay the full amount for a whole day. At a quarter to six, I came down to check out. Then they took twenty-one minutes to check my room. They sent a bell boy or someone to see what I had taken from the soda and juice stocked in the refrigerator. They were delaying and delaying, just so they could charge me for a full day.

79. *The holster*

We went to see Brazil's world-famous statue of the Christ. On the way back, I wanted to buy a belt, but they only had a holster. I said I couldn't buy it because it was for a gun. They removed the holster piece, but still kept the price very high, so I didn't buy it.

I walked out of the store and entered into a bus, leaving behind something I had bought in another shop. O God, the owner of the shop came running to the bus to give me the things that I had bought at another store – even though I hadn't bought anything from his shop.

80. Breakfast for two

We were in Sao Paulo, which has the world's largest population – eighteen million. It is twice the size of New York City. We were staying in the El Dorados Hotel.

Early in the morning, around eight o'clock, I went to Alo's room, which was 610. She was having breakfast. She said that since I had come, we could order my food too. Alo told them that I was from room 503 and she asked them to bring the same food for me – milk, bread and, God knows, maybe an egg. Breakfast is always included with the room.

When I went downstairs to check out, they charged us for the food, saying that Alo had to pay extra because she had had a guest. I had given my room number and I had had my keys with me. There were two separate registration forms for us, and I had registered properly. Still, it took them fifteen minutes to look into the problem. Finally, the manager came. Not only did he cancel the extra breakfast charge, but he also deducted six or seven dollars from the total bill for the rooms.

81. Blouse bargaining

In one shop I wanted to buy a blouse for Alo. The lady said it was twelve hundred cruzeiros, and she wouldn't lower the price. I said to All, "Since you like it, let us buy it," and I gave her the money. Then I went next door. When Alo gave the shopkeeper the twelve hundred cruzeiros, the lady returned four hundred.

81. The grandfather

I went to a shop to buy Joanna a present. I said to the owner, "I am looking for something for a little girl."

The man asked, "Is it your daughter?"

I answered, "No, my granddaughter. The only problem is, I don't know her size."

The man said, "What kind of grandfather are you? You don't know your own granddaughter's size?"

I said, "Whenever she wears a sari, she looks very stout and fat. But whenever she wears Western clothes, she looks thin and skinny."

Then I just picked out something, without knowing whether it was too small or too big.

82. The stranger from Texas

In Brazil there was a seven or ten mile race. I was tired, exhausted, since I had run eight or nine miles that morning, so I didn't join.

I saw a man with a dog near the start of the race and I said to him, "Excuse me, can you tell me how many miles they are going to run? I see there is going to be a race."

The man said, "I don't understand your English!" in a very abrupt way.

Immediately I saw that he was an American. I asked, "Where do you come from?"

He answered, "I come from Texas. Where do you come from?"

I said, "I come from New York."

He said, "Now I understand your English. Ask me again."

When I asked him, he said, "I am also a stranger, like you."

83. Getting through customs

When I was coming through American customs, the immigration officer was an Indian. He noticed that I was also an Indian and, when he saw my green card, he said, "What have you been doing here for such a long time?"

I said, "What have you been doing here for such a long time?"

He said, "I am here for the money."

I said, "I am also here for money."

If I had said, "I teach philosophy and yoga," then he would have given me his philosophy about how we are ruining the prestige of India. So I just said, "I am also here for money." This is how one can get through customs.

NOTES TO SALUTATIONS, BOOK 2

44–61. *(p. 37)* Sri Chinmoy visited Florida from 11 March to 20 March 1981.

62–69. *(p. 50)* From 4 May to 10 May 1981, Sri Chinmoy gave a series of lectures and concerts in Canada.

70–75. *(p. 59)* From 14 to 20 May 1981, Sri Chinmoy was in England for a lecture series at Oxford and Cambridge.

76–83. *(p. 63)* From 21 May to 1 June 1981, Sri Chinmoy was in Brazil.

SALUTATIONS

BOOK 3

IX — SALUTATIONS TO FLORIDA

84. *Do you want a cigar?*

The first day in Florida while I was running, I saw a young man smoking a cigar. He said to me, "Do you want to have a cigar?"

I waved my hand and said, "No, thank you."

The man ran after me and said, "You thank me and you are not taking one?"

This time I got mad at him, and he stopped bothering me.

85. *Strengthening the chest*

After fifteen minutes I saw a very nice old man running with his hands behind his head. He said to me, "Good morning."

I asked him, "Is there any reason why you are doing that?"

He answered, "To strengthen my chest."

In silence I said, "You don't need to, but I want to strengthen my chest."

86. *A cold day*

Another time I was running on a very cold day. Florida also can be quite cold in the winter. A newspaper boy saw me around five o'clock in the morning. He said to me, "Don't keep running. Go home. You will get frozen."

He advised me not to run, but on that day I ran thirteen miles.

On that cold day I ran by a girl waiting for the bus. Half an hour later, when I was returning, she was still waiting in that cold weather.

87. A cold day

One day I went to Sears because somebody told me that there was a section with a variety of birds. But there were no birds there; they had only bird food. It was quite cold, so I bought a long-sleeved T-shirt for nineteen dollars. Then, since it was cold, I put the shirt on in the store, and I was wearing it.

O God, one of the guards came up to me. He suspected that I had just taken the shirt, and he was about to ask me to show him the receipt. Usually, I never keep any receipts; that is not in my line. Luckily, this time I had put the receipt in my pocket, so I showed it to him. After I showed it to him, he said, "Oh no, I was not suspecting you." But he did take the receipt from me and look at it.

88. The toy elephants

The people at Sears told me about another shop very nearby which sold flowers, plants and so forth. When I went there, I saw two toy elephants for six dollars. Sometimes I tell you people what you were in your previous animal incarnations. In Sharon's case, in her last animal incarnation she was an elephant, so I wanted to buy her these elephants. By this time she has a very large collection of elephants.

I said, "Let me buy these two toy elephants." I went to give the lady behind the counter six dollars. She said, "Why six dollars?"

I said, "It is mentioned there, six dollars."

She said. "The price is three dollars."

I said "Three dollars?"

She said, "Yes."

Here this lady was telling me that I was giving too much money, and just two minutes before that I was about to be arrested.

89. *The combs and the beach towel*

The same night Alo and I went to a store and saw a very nice comb. You pressed a button, and immediately the comb came out of the case. I said, "This is something cute. I will buy it for Pahar, our Centre barber."

I wanted to buy one dozen. The man said, "If you come back tomorrow, the price will be reduced."

Since I went to that store quite often, I said, "I will come back."

Then Alo saw a beach towel with a sea horse on it. She thought it was very nice and wanted to buy it. But the man didn't want to sell the one on display, and they said that they didn't have any more in stock.

The following day I went to the store to buy the combs. Two old ladies were working there. One was very fat; one was very thin. The fat one was very, very good, and the thin one was very, very bad.

I said, "Can you ask your boss if there is a reduction on these combs?"

The thin lady said, "How can we ask that?"

But the fat one said, "Why not? Let me ask."

Immediately the thin one became insecure and jealous and said, "I will go and ask him." She went away but she didn't ask him. When she came back she said, "The boss told me that I can give you ten per cent off."

If I hadn't begged her, she would never have told me about the ten per cent discount. Then I asked her about the towel again. She said, "They are 12.99 dollars. But you can't get it. We don't have any more in the store."

I asked, "Can I have this one?" I pointed to the towel hanging on display.

She said, "No, you can't have it. I don't have a young man working here today, and I can't climb up and get it myself."

The towel was hanging near the ceiling, and one would have to climb up a ladder to get it. I said, "I can climb up and get it. I will be responsible."

She said, "No, you can't climb up. You are an old man."

Then the fat one said, "Let me go upstairs and see if we have any there."

The thin one insisted, "No, we don't have any." But the fat lady went upstairs anyway to look for the towel. I followed her. She looked in one place, but there was nothing there. Then she went to another place, where there were not supposed to be any towels, and she found them. She saw that the price was 8.99 dollars. She said, "That rogue! She told you thirteen dollars."

I gave the fat lady thirteen dollars and said, "Since you were kind enough to tell me the correct price, you keep the difference."

She said, "No, I can't. Why do I need money? My children are grown up. Now they have children. Why do I need money? I only want my family – my children and my grandchildren – to be kind to me."

When both of us reached the register the fat lady was still mad at the thin one for quoting a higher price. She pointed to the price of the towel and said to the thin lady, "Not 12.99 dollars!" The thin lady was a real rogue.

90. *Buying a moustache bird*

I went into a pet shop to buy a moustache bird. I was wearing shorts at the time. A young couple happened to be in the store, and the wife was a real joker. She came up to me and said, "What muscles you have! How I wish I had your thigh muscles!"

Her husband was so embarrassed. She asked, "Are you a good runner?"

I said, "No, I am a very bad runner."

She said, "But you have good, strong muscles."

The husband was embarrassed and he started laughing because she was laughing. Since he was there, I was polite to her.

There was also a taxi driver in the store who was from Stamford. He started telling me that his brother had a cockatiel. The young girl interrupted him to say, "My husband has given me three cages but no birds. Can you tell me what I am going to do with empty cages?"

The owner said to the wife, "Why don't you buy a bird?"

She said to the owner, "I want a bird for twenty dollars. More than that I can't afford." The husband didn't say a thing.

Finally I bought my moustache bird. It was from India or Pakistan. The young girl said, "Don't forget to take care of the bird." Then she asked me how many birds I had.

I wasn't sure exactly how many birds I had. Recently Ranjana had told me about eighty-nine, so I bragged and said, "About a hundred."

She said, "You liar!"

I had to hear the word "liar" from her! I didn't argue with her. The taxi driver asked me, "Is it true?"

I said, "I have over eighty at least. I think I have eighty-nine."

I couldn't solve the mystery of why the young girl's husband didn't buy her any birds, just cages. Perhaps he wanted her to buy the birds herself, so afterwards she wouldn't say that she didn't like them.

91. The magic of the train

While I was running, I saw a train going by, and I stopped to watch it. After it passed by, even then I didn't have the inclination to start running again. I was only enjoying the magic sound of the train.

I really like train journeys. In my childhood my only desire was to work for a railroad. I never lost my fascination for trains. Even after realising God, I still have that fascination. So every time I see a train I get a very special thrill.

92. Airport rogues

I brought three birds to the airport with me to take back to New York. The last time I came back from Florida, some rogue airport workers charged me twenty-seven dollars for carrying a bird, but this time I didn't have to pay anything. Savyasachi put the birds in a box, and I kept the box with my hand luggage.

I was originally supposed to leave from Fort Lauderdale, but I was returning from Miami instead. The lady at the ticket counter asked her supervisor if there was any difference in the price of my ticket. The supervisor looked at my ticket and said, "Six dollars," very quickly. If I were supposed to pay extra, they would have told me. Since they did not ask me to stand in line and pay, that meant that they were supposed to give me back six dollars as a refund. But instead of giving me my refund, the lady said, "You don't have to stand here," and she told me to stand in another line at the boarding gate, beyond the place where they check your bags. I didn't have the heart to fight with them. They would have kept me for twenty minutes just for six dollars!

These two were not losing or gaining anything by not giving me the money. But who wanted to stand there and argue with them? The last time I flew back from Florida, the airline workers charged me twenty-seven dollars for the bird I was carrying, and then they put the money in their own pockets. The man from whom I bought the birds told me that he takes birds quite often on airplanes and never pays anything. He said that the men who charged me twenty-seven dollars last time at the airport had cheated me. But this time these people were not even gaining anything.

X — SALUTATIONS TO MEXICO

93. *The blue birds*

In Mexico City we went to a store where there were unbelievable birds. Had I been a millionaire, I would have bought them all, but instead I bought five. One bird I got was so beautiful. I couldn't have imagined that such a beautiful bird existed! It is called a golden pheasant. I have been to so many places and seen many, many beautiful birds. But all the birds we got that day were exceptionally beautiful, and I had never seen any of them before.

When I was about to pay for the birds, there were six persons standing near the cash register. One of the two blue birds flew out of the cage, but nobody noticed, including me. Then a young boy standing nearby grabbed the bird. It was only after he brought the bird back to us that we looked into the cage and saw that one bird was missing. After that we saw that the boy's thumb was bleeding. We thanked him, but the boy didn't speak English.

If he had not been kind enough to catch the bird, we would have had only one of the blue birds and not two.

94. *Good and bad runners*

One morning I saw Snigdha running. She was on one side of the street, and I was on the other side. She stops her watch when she stops running, even when she pauses for a minute at a side street.

Later that day we went to watch a three mile race. There were many good runners and many bad runners. But the bad runners were many, many more in number.

95. *A soul's message*

The next morning while I was running seven and a half miles, Garima's soul sent me a message. Then two seconds later I saw Garima running. I was running on one side of the street, and she was running on the other side.

96. *The show-off*

Another morning Anupadi was showing off. For a while she was running near me, and then she went ahead. Her strides have become longer now. Previously her strides were so short!

97. *The untouched wallet*

One day in Mexico City I left my hotel room early in the morning, leaving one of my wallets on the dresser there. It had a large amount of money, both in American dollars and Mexican bills. I knew perfectly well that the wallet was in the hotel room. You can call it lethargy, or you can call it confidence and faith in the chambermaid, but I didn't take the trouble of going back during the day to get it.

I came back at night only to discover that my wallet was intact; not even a dollar was removed. I know how I keep my dollar bills, and the wallet had not even been opened. To have this kind of experience anywhere in the world is very, very, very rare.

So some people are very nice. I am Pranavananda's disciple. After he lost his wallet, he said, "Some people are space cadets." I still can't believe that I left my wallet on my dresser, and at night it was in perfect order.

Later I asked who the lady was who cleaned my room. Then I gave her some money because nothing had been stolen.

98. Lost pocket money

From my previous experiences I have learned always to carry money with me when I go running. While we were in Mexico, Alo sent one of my track suits to the laundry, and I am sure she didn't take out the money from my pocket. That money I never saw again. That time I had the opposite experience from the one with the chambermaid.

99. The hotel manager

The day before we left Mexico City, we went to pay the balance of our hotel bill. The people at the desk said it wasn't necessary for us to pay early. They asked us to come back in the evening.

It is very rare for hotel managers to be so nice. Usually they are very suspicious.

100. The shrunken shoes

Whenever I take off my shoes in the plane, afterwards I can't put them back on. This always happens to me! The same shoes, same legs, same feet – but I can't get them on. This has happened to me when I have gone to Mexico, Australia, Japan and many other places.

101. Indian-style shopping

At one place in Mexico City I spent forty-five minutes or more trying to buy some things for the San Francisco girls' singing group. But I had bad luck. Finally I got something in the Mazatlan market.

SALUTATIONS

The Mazatlan market reminded me of India, where I was born and brought up. There they had little shops where you could bargain with the people as much as you wanted to.

The first time I went to the market, Hashi was the interpreter. The rule was never to accept what they said, because they knew you were not going to buy it at that price. No matter what they said first, you had to ask them to come down.

102. The opportunist

This is a story about your Guru, about what kind of opportunist he is. In Mazatlan every day my mantra was that nobody should follow me when I went to the market. Everybody listened, but sometimes unconsciously people made mistakes.

One day, after I said that nobody should follow me, whom did I see in the market? Nayana! So I gave her an undivine look and she disappeared.

Then I bought something for Kanan's singing group. Just then I saw Hashi, and I gave her a very divine look. Do you know why? So that I could give her the things that I had bought. After I handed her the packages, I said, "Now, go away!" Then again I didn't let anybody come near me.

103. The extra member

Before I went to buy gifts for Kanan's group, again and again I had asked him how many were in his group. Each time he had told me that there were ten members.

O God, right after I had bought ten gifts, I saw Kanan in the market. He said, "O Guru, our group has eleven members. But I won't mind if I don't get a gift."

Then I told him that he was hopeless.

104. Dog attacks

The morning of our seven-mile race in Mazatlan, I ran seven miles by myself just before the race started. At least four times I was attacked by dogs. Perhaps the reason they attacked me was because I was wearing a red shirt. When they came at me, I stood there very bravely until they stopped barking at me. In one case a dog crossed the street to where I was running, but it didn't bite me.

Especially when you are running fast, you get alarmed when you suddenly see a dog. If you are running slowly, it is not such a shock. In my case I was going so slowly – at bullock-cart speed.

None of the disciples were attacked by dogs during the race. That was because they were running in a group.

105. Birthday driver

Later that day I went out to go shopping, but it was cold. I thought perhaps Gayatri would have a car, so I came back to the Social Security Building, which we were using for our meals and functions. By that time Gayatri, Garima and Sarah had all disappeared. But who was there? Pragati. It was her birthday, so I asked her to take me in her car. So Pragati had good luck on her birthday. She drove me here, there, everywhere. Then Tanima joined us. After that we saw Garima walking, so we also stopped for her. Then again we went to the market.

106. Buying a sari

Since it was Pragati's birthday and she was driving me, I said, "Let me buy her a gift." I entered into a fabric store, but they didn't have a proper sari. I asked, what is the price for a yard of this particular fabric?"

The lady said, "Fifty pesos."

I said to myself, "Let me not bargain, since I like the fabric. Today let me be a different person."

So I said to her, "All right. I would like six yards."

The lady started measuring it, and I began browsing in the store. By the time I came back, the fabric was all cut and properly folded. She had put it on the counter and had written down on a piece of paper, "Seventy-five pesos times six yards."

I said, "You told me it was fifty pesos."

She said, "No, while you were looking around the store, I saw that the actual price was ninety pesos. I told you fifty, but I was wrong."

I said, "Then you should have asked me if I wanted to pay more than fifty."

She said, "From ninety I have made it seventy-five."

She was showing me the price. It said ninety. But God knows if she had written it after she told me the price.

I said to myself, "Since she has told me one lie, how can I believe that this is six yards?"

I asked her to measure the fabric in front of me. She pretended it was beneath her dignity to do this, so I started measuring it myself. It was just a little over four yards – not even four and a half. Instead of fifty pesos, it had become seventy-five, and instead of six yards, it had become four.

Then she came up to me and said, "I told you fifty, so you can have it for fifty pesos a yard." She spoke good English. There was no problem with the language. Perhaps if it had been six yards, the length of a proper sari, I would have paid seventy-five pesos. But it was not even four and a half yards, so I just left the store.

That was my first bad experience with a Mexican shopkeeper. All frustration! If I had believed the lady that it was six yards, I would have given it to Pragati. Perhaps she would never have told me that it was only four yards. She would have kept it on her shrine instead of wearing it.

107. The pair of sandals

Then I saw a pair of white, plastic sandals in another store. I said, "These are very nice." But when I went to look, I saw that they were not actually a pair. They were two different sizes. One was size eight and one was size six.

I took the sandals to the shopkeeper and asked her to give me either a six or an eight, since she didn't have seven or seven and a half. She said that she only had this one pair of sandals. She said, "No, you take these."

Was I going to buy one size six and one size eight? Naturally, I didn't buy them. That was my second experience.

108. Success at last!

Then I went into another store. There I saw a very simple but very beautiful deer made of styrofoam. I said, "Here I will have no problems regarding the size." A deer stands for Pragati's speed, so I bought the deer.

I said, "If the deer wins the race, she will have victory. A peacock means victory." So I bought her a peacock as well.

SALUTATIONS

109. *Wasting time*

Another day in Mazatlan I went to a sporting goods store. The two ladies there were so callous. They were just wasting my time. After I had stood there for ten minutes, I gave up and left.

110. *Employees only*

That same day I went to the store on the ground floor of the Social Security Building and bought Alo a track suit. There was a sign that said the store was for employees only, but I didn't understand the sign because it was in Spanish. Perhaps they thought that I was an employee.

The next day I went there again, but this time they said I couldn't go in. They must have realised that I was not working there.

111. *Thanks a lot*

The day before we left Mazatlan, I was running early in the morning. At one point a small car that was going quite fast came near me and stopped. A little boy five or six years old got out and asked me for directions in Spanish. He said three lines of Spanish, and I could not understand anything. I had been running fast, doing speed work, and I was exhausted. I don't know Spanish, and I was so tired that I couldn't talk. I was helpless.

When the boy saw that I didn't understand him and also that I was too tired to talk, he said very soulfully, "Thanks a lot." There was no sarcasm involved. Then he ran back and entered into his father's car.

Another day while I was running in Mazatlan very early in the morning, I saw an American running. This man I had previously seen playing tennis. He was bearded and not very nice-looking. He asked me the time. So I said, "Five fifty-six."

Then he said, "Damn you! Why can't you say 'four minutes of six'!"

I never use the expression "thanks a lot", but I told him, "Thanks a lot," and continued running.

112. An Acapulco welcome

Sometimes when I first arrive in a country or city, the soul of that place will greet me at the airport. Sometimes after a few hours or a day or two it comes to greet me. Other times I am greeted even before I arrive – either on the plane or at the previous place I am visiting. Sometimes the soul of one country or city comes to the previous place to escort me to its own place.

In Acapulco the soul of the city greeted me one morning when I was coming by taxi from my hotel to the hotel where the disciples were staying. At first the taxi driver did not understand my pronunciation when I said, "Hotel Versailles," so I showed him my key where the name of the disciples' hotel was written. I didn't see any meter inside the taxi, so I asked him how much it would cost.

He said, "Forty pesos." Then he said to me, "Hindu?"

I said, "Yes, Hindu."

Then he put his hand on my shoulder very hard and said, "Amigo!"

As soon as he touched me on the shoulder, right on the windshield of his taxi I saw the soul of Acapulco welcoming me. The taxi driver was the instrument. This time the soul greeted me through an outer gesture.

Unfortunately, the taxi driver was a rogue. He saw the key, but he wanted to leave me off seven or eight minutes' drive from the hotel. When I showed him the key again, from forty pesos the fare rose to eighty pesos.

113. Three countries in one

Acapulco is a combination of India, America and Switzerland. At one place it looks like Switzerland, at another place it looks like India and at another place it looks like America. It has everything.

114. The moustache combs

In Acapulco I went to the market with Garima and Niriha. I got a few things and also some nice brooches for people who had not come to Mexico. The man selling the brooches wanted to fool us. They were butterflies and he was saying they could fly.

At one point I saw some tiny combs. I thought they were real combs to comb your hair. Niriha gave me proper wisdom. She said they were not hair combs; they were moustache combs.

I asked, "Who has a moustache?"

Niriha said, "Rabindra."

The man was asking four dollars for the combs. I definitely wanted to buy them, but, as usual, I wanted to bargain. Sometimes the shopkeepers pay no attention to the customers. I was standing there arguing to see if he would lower the price, but the man wasn't paying any attention to me. Finally I went away without buying the combs.

115. *The bottle thief*

Another time in Acapulco, Pulak bought a soda for me and Rabindra was holding it. O God, the store owner started screaming at us to give the bottle back. Rabindra was pretending he didn't understand.

116. *Shopping with the disciples*

I was out shopping in Acapulco when I saw Shephali buying a very expensive gift. I said to her, "You are the richest person!" I didn't know she was buying the gift for me. Lucy was standing nearby, but she didn't see me.

Then Subala and Chandika were fighting at the counter over who was going to pay for something. I wanted to go and pay, but I was engrossed in buying something else at the time. Later I was told that Chandika was having difficulty finding her money.

117. *The circus*

In Acapulco we went to see a circus which I liked very much. If we had not had anything else to do that night, I would have stayed to see it again. That kind of circus gives me innocent joy. Some of the acts were daring; others were absolutely easy.

118. *The run in the dark*

One morning I ran seven miles while it was still very dark. When it is dark, you forget about speed. You feel that as long as you continue running, it is enough. The first mile I did in nine minutes and the last was at an eight-thirty pace. Altogether I averaged only a nine-minute pace, so God knows how slowly I ran the other five miles. A nine-minute pace is very bad. Of course, I was not racing. But if it had not been dark, I would have taken off at least fifteen seconds per mile.

119. Counting the change

Later that day I wanted to buy a dress for Shubhra for her birthday. The price was a hundred and seventy pesos, so I gave the lady two hundred. As she was giving me my change, I was listening to her count. After twenty-four, she said, "Thirty." I hadn't watched her, but it sounded wrong to my ear, so in front of her I started counting the change. She had only given me twenty-five pesos.

XI – SALUTATIONS TO PUERTO RICO

120. Send a prayer

I was standing on line to get my seat assignment on the plane to Puerto Rico. The ticket agent was taking care of the man in front of me. All of a sudden the ticket agent said to me in a very contemptuous way, "Are you going first class?"

I answered, "Yes. I am."

Then she said to me, "Smoking or non-smoking?" in the same nasty tone of voice.

I said, "Non-smoking." Then I said, "What is the matter with you so early in the morning?"

She said, "Man, my husband is in the hospital. I am worried!" She was white, not black, but she spoke like a black lady.

I said, "Just because you are worried, do you have to be so nasty?"

She said, "Send a prayer to him."

I said, "I have already sent one."

Then she put a sticker with my seat number on my ticket and gave it back to me.

121. The box of ERG

Ashrita had put a big box of ERG with my luggage for Bansidhar to use in our marathon. When my luggage passed through the machine, the inspector said something to me half in English and half in Spanish.

I said, "Please tell me in English."
She said, "What is in this box?"
I said, "ERG."
She said, "ERG? What's that?"
I said, "You don't know what ERG is?"

She said, "No!"

I said, "Runners use ERG."

Then she said, "Wait." Four or five minutes I waited. Then I asked the inspector, "Have you sent for someone?"

She said, "No, I am waiting for someone to come."

A very fat old lady was passing through the line. She had overheard our conversation, and she got the point. She turned around and said to the inspector either "Honey!" or "Dummy!" Then she said, "My grandson lives on ERG. In the New York Marathon he did so well."

Then the inspector allowed me to go through the line. She told me to go in Spanish.

122. *The grandmother and mother*

There were two ladies sitting near me on the plane. One was an old lady, a grandmother, and the other was her daughter, whose son had just died. The mother had her arm around the grandmother, and she was consoling her. They were both crying.

At one point the mother said, "I am his mother. Do you think I didn't love him?"

The grandmother said, "Yes, you loved him, but I loved him much, much more than you did. Now keep quiet!"

So the mother kept quiet. In this way the mother was insulted by the grandmother.

123. *The Indian*

The man who was sitting next to me on the plane had three newspapers: the *New York Times*, the *Daily News* and the *Post*. He was reading the *Daily News* and the other two papers were lying next to him. After an hour a lady came up to him and said,

"Sir, hello. Can I borrow your *New York Times*? I see you are not reading it."

The man answered, "No, you can't!"

The lady said, "But you have three newspapers."

Again he said, "No, no!"

From his accent I could tell that he was an Indian. Previously I had noticed that he had dark skin, but I had been in my own world.

I turned to him and said, "Where do you come from?"

He said, "India." Then he asked me, "Where are you from?"

I answered, "India."

I said I was from Bengal, and he told me he was from Bombay. I said, "You have three newspapers. You can't give her one?"

He said, "A few days ago I took an oath that I will never do anything for an American. I will not do any favours for any Americans. I hate them, I hate them!"

"Where are you living?" I asked.

"America," he said, "but that is between the government and me."

We were speaking in English since I didn't know Gujarati and he didn't know Bengali. Strangely enough, we also came back on the same flight. We saw each other before we entered into the plane. He was carrying a box that contained a wine bottle. This time he was in first class and I was in economy class.

124. *Govinda's restaurant*

While I was in Puerto Rico I took Shubhra to do a little shopping. After that we went to an Indian restaurant called Govinda's. A few years ago when I went there, I told the workers there that I had known their Guru, that he used to come to the Indian Consulate and talk to us. One disciple said, "You are so fortunate that such a great soul blessed you."

SALUTATIONS

This time, as soon as I entered the restaurant, a young black man came up to me and said, "Namaste, Guruji, Namaste! I went to New York in 1974 for your initiation. I used to go to your St. Louis Centre. I came five or six times, and then I had a dream that you would initiate me. So I went to Jamaica. You gave a concert there and your meditation was so powerful. Even now it is still so vivid in my consciousness. I went to be initiated by you and I saw Alo Devi. She greeted me with kindness and said that you would take me to the destined Goal.

"Once I even came to meditate at a meeting held in your backyard. As soon as you came out, everybody stood up and meditated so powerfully, with such love and devotion. Again I asked for initiation, but Alo Devi said that you rarely initiate people outwardly. So right from New York I went to India and got initiated by Swami Bhaktivedanta."

Again and again this young man came to me with folded hands to tell me how powerful my meditation was.

I bought food for Shubhra and myself. Then I gave the lady at the counter a ten-dollar bill. It was the same old lady who had been there the last time I had come. She gave me five dollars and five cents change. Right in front of the counter was a box marked "Donations". So I put the five dollars in the box.

The restaurant was self-service. I thought that Shubhra had got dal for me, and she thought that I had got it. She hadn't taken any and I hadn't taken any either. So we went back and got some dal. They charged us one dollar for that, even though I had just put in a five-dollar donation. Business is business!

As we were leaving, the young man came up to me with his Master's biography. He said, "I will be so grateful if you take this book." As a sign of respect he gave the book to Shubhra to give to me instead of handing it to me directly. He said, "Please give this book to Guruji."

Then I said, "I can tell you an amusing incident about your Guru. One time when he came to the Indian Consulate, he was very mad at four or five of his disciples. They had taken his typewriter and thrown it out of the window. It had fallen on the street and broken into pieces. They had also stolen his Bengali manuscripts, because they thought that they contained occult knowledge. That is why he called them beasts."

The boy said, "That very incident is described in this book."

This disciple was given a long Indian name by his Master. It started with Mani, which means "ruby". He was very sweet.

125. Running the marathon

I ran ten miles in our Sri Chinmoy Marathon in San Juan. Many of the runners recognised me. About a hundred people joined, but only two were women. There were national guardsmen in uniform helping out in the race, since we had only nine disciples there. We got a lot of help from the guards and other organisations. Everywhere people gave out water, ERG and time splits. The time splits were in Spanish. I would say, "Please tell me in English." Then they would tell me after I had already gone ten metres past them.

We had to do five and a half laps on the track before leaving the stadium. For the good runners they kept track of the laps. But for the runners like me, who cared? If we deceived anyone, it did not matter since we were not going to get any place. So they did not count our laps.

Even after one mile it was so hot! You just died! I ran five miles at an 8:43 pace. Then I started walking and running. I would run three hundred metres and walk thirty or forty because I had a lot of pain in my foot. In this way I completed ten miles with an average pace of 9:24. Then it started raining heavily.

The winner got cramps at twenty-four miles. Only with greatest difficulty he kept going and stood first. The second runner was only a hundred metres behind him. Both of them entered into the stadium at practically the same time. Last year's best time was 2:27, but this year the winner finished in 2:37 because of his cramps.

At the awards ceremony afterwards there was a large banquet. I would say one line thanking everyone, and Uttama would translate it into ten lines. Usually he translates exactly what I say, but on that day he was elaborating and elaborating.

The Director of the Montreal Marathon happened to be in Puerto Rico on that day, and he had signed up to run in the race. The Montreal Marathon is a very big race, with eight to ten thousand people. He had registered, but then on the day of the marathon, he got sick. He did come to the awards ceremony after the race, but I was in a terrible hurry to catch my plane. Otherwise, I would have spoken to him.

126. The sympathetic inspector

I got two birds in Puerto Rico and I wanted to bring them back to New York. The pet shop told me they were Quaker parrots.

Usually you need a certificate to bring birds into the United States. When I went to get the certificate, they told me it would take four or five days. So I couldn't get it.

When I arrived at the airport, the inspector opened my bag and saw the box with the birds in it. He told me, "I have to see the birds. If they are very small, I will allow you to take them. Otherwise, I will have to charge you. And if they are very rare, you will need special permission to take them."

I said, "Just yesterday I came here and today I am leaving. How could I get a certificate, since it takes four or five days?"

He asked, "Why did you come here?"

I said, "I came here to run the marathon."

He said, "What marathon?"

I said, "The Sri Chinmoy Marathon."

He said, "The marathon of Master Sri Chinmoy?" He did not know who I was. He just knew about the Sri Chinmoy Marathon from the radio and newspapers.

I said, "Yes."

He said, "How did you do?"

I said, "I ran only ten miles."

He said, "Poor man," and he didn't even open the box with the birds. He just let me go through.

127. *The stewardess*

On the plane I was sitting in the front row of seats near the wall where they show the movie. I had a bag with me which I put at my feet. The stewardess, a black lady, said, "You can't put it there. You have to put it in the cabinet."

Inside my bag was the box with the birds in it. If I didn't keep my bag open, I was afraid the birds might die. So as the stewardess was putting the bag into the closet I said, "I would like to open up the zipper on the bag. There is something in there."

She laughed and laughed at me. After fifteen minutes, when the plane was about to take off, she closed the cabinet and locked it. I was worried that perhaps there was not enough oxygen for the birds, but the seatbelt sign was on, so I stayed in my seat. Finally, after fifteen or twenty minutes the sign went off.

I went to the stewardess and said, "Please, I have some birds in the cabinet. Can I get them out?"

There was a sign on the cabinet that said while the plane is leaving the ground and while it is landing, the cabinet cannot be opened. But even though the plane was in the air, the stewardess said, "We are not authorised to open it."

Then I went to a steward, a black man, and I said, "Really, I don't want my birds to die."

He said, "We are not authorised to open the cabinet, but I will do it for you."

When he opened it, I immediately took out the box and put it in front of me. Then the stewardess came near me and called out to the steward, "Robert, how are your birds doing?"

She was bothering that fellow because he had helped me. So I looked at the stewardess and showed her a very disturbed face. Then she smiled at me and said, "What would you like to drink, sir?"

I said very abruptly, "Seven-up."

Then she brought it for me.

Beside me was a couple from Syracuse. The lady was so nice. She had heard my conversation with the stewardess and was cursing her. She said, "Some of these stewardesses have no feeling."

The husband asked me, "Do you think the birds are alive?"

I shook the box and said, "I think they are alive." The husband was so happy to hear that. The wife continued to curse the stewardess.

128. *The tooth problem*

Before I left for Puerto Rico, my dentist said that my teeth were in "top shape". But while I was in Puerto Rico, I had such tooth pain! My gums were badly swollen and I had an abscess. So I had to take penicillin, this drug and that drug. What an experience!

I went to one dentist, a young man, who said to me, "I have seen you many times, not in this capacity, but in another capacity." He had seen me many times on television in Puerto Rico.

The following day when I went back, he said, "It is a great pleasure to serve you. You are a man of insight." Then he said, "But I am sorry, I can't help you."

He refused to take money for the x-rays he had taken.

129. *The excellent magician*

In Puerto Rico we went to see the performance of a man from Cuba who had been a magician for many years. It was excellent, but from the beginning to the end, Alo didn't like it because the magician was telling all lies.

In the beginning of the performance he did a mind-reading act. He looked into a crystal ball and said he clearly saw that somebody in the audience had a particular problem. He said that this person had sat for an examination and was worrying like anything whether he would pass or fail. Then he said, "Now, if the person I am speaking about is here, please raise your hand." Someone raised her hand and everyone was so moved. Then two other ladies stood up and said, "Shame, shame! She works for you. She was at the gate collecting tickets. She only changed her dress." So the trick was ruined.

Then the magician said that somebody else in the audience was working very hard to discover something, and he asked whoever it was to stand up. This person was also one of the magician's workers. Stupid fellow, he started to get up but then he hesitated because he was afraid of being challenged like the other lady. Then another fellow who was sitting in the audience pulled him up. Alo said, "Look at this!"

Then the magician hypnotised a young girl. She was his daughter. He told her to stand up and then he took out a stick and put it right under her and raised her sideways off the ground so that she was floating in the air. Bansidhar had gone to the stage to be a helper. Later he told us that he had clearly seen that the girl had a very thin but very strong iron plate inside her trousers. So when the magician was doing all this, one of his assistants was holding the girl up with wires attached to the iron plate.

At one point during the performance, the magician entered into a big cauldron filled with boiling water, and then they put on the lid. Bansidhar and three other observers were watching. Bansidhar said that he had seen another compartment underneath the cauldron where the magician could move.

At another time the magician asked a little boy from the audience, "Will you allow me to chop your head off?" The little boy ran away. Then another one came up on the stage. He was about ten years old, and he was laughing while the magician was chopping off his head.

At another point, a lady was lying on a bed, and the magician said that with his occult power he would make her levitate. Then he passed his stick near her, and the lady went up.

Then the magician asked a young girl, "Tell me correctly, who discovered America?"

The girl said, "Hernandez Colon," their former Governor, my friend. She was a little girl, so everybody laughed.

The *San Juan Star* had said that his performance was excellent – the best in San Juan. That is why we went to see him. But Ashrita is a far better magician. When Ashrita performs, quite a few things fool me. But here, four or five things I could see how he did, and some of them I could even do myself. But we knew it was all in fun. I enjoyed it from beginning to end.

130. The Canadian magician

The day after we saw his performance, some other magicians who didn't claim to have occult power spoke against this man in an article in the newspaper. One of those who spoke against this Cuban magician was a magician from Toronto who happened to be in Puerto Rico at the same time. He could not bear the way the man we had seen was getting name and fame. So he invited the reporter from the *San Juan Star* to see his own performance. He told the reporter that he was a great magician and that he had even defeated Houdini by forty-five minutes in escaping from jail. He said that on one occasion Houdini had not even been able to escape from jail. Houdini had had all kinds of keys hidden away, but he could not open the lock. So he told the jail guard that something was wrong. The guard laughed and said, "The gate was not locked!"

This Canadian magician wanted to show his capacity. So first he took a spoon and broke it. Then another spoon appeared out of the blue. Next he took the spoon and started banging it on the table. Suddenly it became twelve spoons. Then the magician asked the reporter to give him a dollar bill and said he could turn it into a ten-dollar bill. So the reporter gave him a dollar bill, and immediately he turned it into a ten-dollar bill. Afterwards, a friend of the reporter came running to the Canadian magician with three dollar bills, hoping to get thirty dollars. He knocked and knocked on the magician's door, but the magician would not let him in.

131. More magic

In India we have a magician like Houdini. People hide a certain kind of mineral. Then they blindfold the magician, and he finds it – even if he has to walk three miles to the place where it is hidden. This is our occultism. He is considered to be as great as Houdini. His son has written a book about him.

Once a magician came to the ashram. He gave a ring to the Mother, and she was holding it. Then, in two seconds that same ring disappeared from her hand and appeared in his hand inside a handkerchief.

Next he showed us some ink. Then he threw the ink at the Mother and it turned into flowers. He said, "I don't want to ruin your clothes."

Then the magician threw a rope up into the air. It stayed in the air and he started climbing it. But that was not enough. In front of everybody he suddenly disappeared. Many people have written books about the Indian rope trick.

Another Indian trick is when they cover the magician's eyes and then place a coloured handkerchief in front of his face. They ask, "What colour is it?" and immediately the magician identifies the colour. These magicians are so tricky. When they do this trick, they stand on a small platform which has a hole in it. There is a tiny string which goes through the platform and is attached to one of the magicians feet. If the colour is red, the person with the string pulls two times; if it is green, three times. The magician says that he has occult power, but actually someone is telling him what to say.

When I was six or seven years old, I tried some magic tricks. Even now I can still do a few tricks. One of the tricks that the Cuban magician did in Puerto Rico I showed to Bansidhar at the Centre the following day. He said, "How did you do it?" He couldn't believe the trick!

XII – SALUTATIONS TO BERMUDA

132. The lost ticket

The day I left for Bermuda, Savyasachi drove me to Kennedy airport. Ranjana, Lucy and Sharon also came in the car. At the airport everything was fine. I passed through the check-in area and then, at the last point where they give the boarding passes, I showed my ticket. They said, "This is the return ticket. Where is the front part?" O God, I didn't have any idea where it was. By this time the girls had left the area, so I was absolutely panicking. Luckily, they had not yet left the airport, and I ran and caught up with them. They told me that the first part of the ticket was inside my pocket. Ranjana had put it there, but I had forgotten.

On the plane I was inspired to write fifty-eight poems. That saved me! Before the flight I had said that I would not eat anything; I would take only tea. So I just wrote and wrote, and I didn't eat at all.

When I arrived in Bermuda, a man from immigration asked me how many times I had come to Bermuda.

I said, "Four times."

He said, "That means you like it."

I said, "Definitely I like it!"

The man said, "That means you have friends here."

I said, "I don't have any friends, but I have seen some good people here and I like the place."

He checked all my things very nicely but didn't find anything for my friends.

133. The hundred-dollar room

I stayed at the Princess Hotel. It was supposed to be quite elegant, but inside I saw only dirt and filth. Everything was broken and everything smelled. My room number was 226, but I had to press "3" in the elevator to go to the second floor.

In that place everything went wrong. When I went to take a shower, in a few minutes the hot water became unbearably hot and there was no cold water. This was a one hundred-dollar room. Forty dollars would have been more than enough!

134. Going to Russia

At around ten o'clock at night I ordered food: coffee, french fries, chilled soup and plain salad. A black girl said, "Please tell me what kind of dressing you want."

I said, "I don't know. Any dressing."

Then she asked me, "How old are you?"

I said, "Fifty."

Then she said to me, "Grandpa, I am sending you Russian dressing. I will send you to Russia."

I said, "How I wish I could go to Russia!" This was our joke.

When I ordered, they told me that in half an hour they would send the food to my room. After an hour had passed I phoned and said, "Please cancel my order; it is getting late." But they said they had just sent it. Finally the food came, but unfortunately it was not good.

When they gave me the bill I just signed it without looking at it. In the morning I saw that it had come to 17.50 dollars! Why? There was a service charge.

135. Long legs

The next morning I went out to run at five o'clock. I was running right in front of the hotel. Seventy or eighty metres I ran. Then I stopped, and then again I ran. I did this seven times. The weather in Bermuda was like Chicago: very windy! At times you couldn't even walk, so how was I going to run?

There were about seven or eight taxis in front of the hotel. One taxi driver, an old man, was joking with me. He came very near me and was watching me. Then he said to me, "Champ, you have two long legs. Champ, you have long legs, long legs!" I was wearing shorts, although it was quite chilly. He was a gentleman, so he was wearing trousers.

It was so dangerous there. There was no proper sidewalk. I saw so many scooters. How fast they went! It reminded me of our vacation in Bermuda a few years ago.

136. The Waterloo Hotel

Later that morning I walked across the street to the Rosenden Hotel, because I didn't like the Princess. The Rosenden was a very, very nice place, and the man there was also very, very nice. I said, "All right, I shall take a room here." I told him that I would be back in an hour. I sincerely meant it!

Then while walking I passed the Waterloo Hotel, and I remembered that the previous time I had stayed at the Waterloo. I went inside and the old lady at the desk jumped up. Immediately she recognised me. She said, "I remember you! Your room near the water is unfortunately occupied." In that room I wrote fifty songs. "I shall show you another room. The regular price is 135 dollars, but now it is off-season so the price has come down to 90 dollars. Last time you didn't eat breakfast. If you don't eat breakfast, the price becomes 70 dollars, so the total with tax will be 80.50 dollars. Are you ready to take it?"

I said to myself, "How does she still remember that four years ago I didn't have breakfast?" I was very, very happy about the idea of going back to the Waterloo. It was only two blocks from the Princess. I said to myself, "Definitely I will take the Waterloo. Waterloo is so famous because of Napoleon!"

But, O God! The wind was so strong! While I was walking back to the Princess, it pushed me so hard – as if I were a cotton ball! It felt like I was running at a six-minute pace instead of just walking. When I reached the Princess Hotel, I couldn't move because the wind seemed to be all inside my back – it was so stiff! What could I do? The Princess Hotel was bad, and the other two places were so good. Still, instead of changing hotels, my decision was to come back home to Queens.

137. The phone call

Around nine o'clock that morning I tried to phone Alo in Mexico. The phone rang and rang but nobody answered at her hotel. The operator asked if she should keep ringing and I said, "I will be very grateful."

After twenty times I told her, "Let us stop."

She said, "Fine," and it was all over.

O God! At twelve o'clock, when I went to check out, the girl had put a telephone charge of twenty-seven dollars on my bill, and I hadn't even gotten the party on the phone! I said to myself, "How can it be?"

At the desk I asked a man, "If I didn't get the party, why did I get a bill? It is impossible! Is this a service charge?" He said, "No, no, for this we don't have a service charge." But God knows for how many other things they did have a service charge! Just to take food upstairs they charged seven or eight dollars.

I was arguing with him, saying that my call was never completed. I said, "I am going to miss my plane. For God's sake give me the phone and let me speak to the operator."

The man said, "The girl went upstairs and she has not come back."

I said, "Either ask the girl to come down or let me go up to ask her."

I was getting annoyed. I was not going to pay twenty-seven dollars when I didn't get the party on the phone. I went to speak to the manager, a black man. He said, "Hello! Do you recognise me? Do you recognise me?"

I said, "No."

He said, "I recognise you. Several years ago you were at the Sherwood Hotel with so many students. Charlie still remembers you. Now what has happened?" I said, "I did not get my party on the telephone, but they say I have to pay twenty-seven dollars for the call."

So he phoned the man at the desk and said, "What are you doing? Tell the truth! This is such an important person." What he heard from the man at the desk God alone knows, but to me he said, "Finished! You don't have to pay."

So the manager recognised me and said I was an important person. He used to come to the Sherwood Hotel. Now the name has changed. First it was the Eagle's Nest and now it is the Hamiltonian. Charlie still remembers me. He is the owner of the tennis store at that hotel – a tall, thin man. I do not remember seeing this manager, but he remembered me and he saved me twenty-seven dollars.

138. Dancing in the park

I went to the airport, but I had a two-hour wait, so I went to Georgetown. There I was watching the water and wondering how I was going to kill time. Right in front of me there were twenty elderly women in a park. All of a sudden, some kind of music came from a house and they all started dancing!

Then I went to a restaurant and waited, waited, waited. Instead of being at the airport, at least I was near some hotels.

139. The flat tyre

To go back to the airport I took a taxi. The taxi fare in Bermuda starts with eighty cents. I never look at the meter, but this time, after we had covered fifty metres, I happened to look at it. O God! It said 3.10 dollars. I said to the driver, "I just entered into the cab. How can it be 3.10 dollars already?"

He said, "Don't worry, don't worry, don't worry." Then he changed the meter back to eighty cents. We covered another two hundred metres and boom! We had a flat tire.

The driver, an old man, said, "You are a bad man; that is why we got a flat tire.

I said, "Either I am bad or you are bad or both of us are bad. What am I going to do?"

He asked me to give him a hand. What could I do? I could only get out of the taxi. I got out, but it took him such a long time. He was an old man, and he could barely get out of the car, but I could not give him any help. I just looked at him sympathetically.

I saw two or three taxis going from Georgetown towards the airport, but they would not stop. Nobody was sympathetic. After some time I raised my hand and one particular man stopped.

As soon as he saw us he started singing, "Flat tire!" He was amused.

I said, "Just take me to the airport for whatever you want to charge."

He said, "Three dollars."

I gave him three dollars, and he said, "It will take only five minutes. I also am going there."

140. *I don't blame you*

When I arrived back at the airport, the lady at the counter looked at my ticket. She saw that I was supposed to stay there for three days but I was leaving after one day. She said to me, "Why are you not staying here?"

I said, "I don't like this place at all." There was no sun, and it was dark and cloudy.

She said, "I don't blame you."

141. *Paying the penalty*

I didn't have to pay the telephone bill, but I did have to pay a penalty to the airline. The price of my ticket had been fifty dollars less because I was on a three-day excursion. When I changed my ticket, I had to pay fifty dollars extra. So twenty-seven dollars I saved, but fifty dollars I lost. Still, I was happy to come home because here at any time I can get heat – at least from the radiator.

In Bermuda it rains only twenty days a year, but one of those days was when I was there!

142. Rain in Bermuda

Another time I went to Bermuda for three days alone. The hotel was beautiful. It was near the water. But that time also it was raining heavily the whole time and I could not even go out. I only went across the street once to a Chinese restaurant. During those three days I wrote two hundred poems; that was my only consolation.

NOTES TO SALUTATIONS, BOOK 3

84–92. *(p. 71)* Sri Chinmoy made a short visit to Florida in November 1981.

93–119. *(p. 78)* During December 1981 and January 1982, Sri Chinmoy and a group of his disciples vistited Mexico for their Christmas holiday.

120–131. *(p. 90)* Sri Chinmoy visited Puerto Rico in December 1981, for the second annual Sri Chinmoy Marathon in San Juan [120–127]. He visited again in February 1982 [128–131].

132–142. *(p. 102)* Sri Chinmoy went to Bermuda in January 1982. The last story refers to an earlier trip.

PART II

I LOVE SHOPPING

BOOK 1

1. Upside down

When I was in Hawaii, I went to a cafeteria. I took a tray and went on line for some food. I came to the section where they have mashed potatoes. But instead of saying "mashed potatoes", I asked for "potatoes mashed". I thought I was saying it correctly and that the lady behind the counter had not heard me. I was very brave. When she asked me again what I wanted, I repeated it. Then she said, "Are you upside down?"

2. The polaroid camera

At one store in Hawaii the lady was so nice. I wanted to buy a Polaroid camera. It cost ten dollars. But the saleslady said, "Don't buy it unless you can get film for it. We are all out of film, but you can look around. If you find the film, then come back and buy the camera."

Ashrita went to four or five stores, but he couldn't get any film. He came back and told me. The lady said, "I told you! What is the use of buying a camera if you can't get film?" If it had been somewhere else, they would have said, "Buy the camera here and then look for film somewhere else."

3. Father, husband and brother

When I entered into another store, I saw an elderly lady who was about fifty or fifty-five years old. As soon as I opened the door, she came and stood behind me and started patting my back, saying, "You remind me of my father, husband and brother."

Immediately my heart surrendered to her. I asked her a few questions. She said she was Japanese and that her father, husband and brother had died in the Second World War. Her husband used to work in the post office.

While she was patting me, she said, "You are serene, pure and full of peace, peace, peace, peace." She said "peace" at least four or five times.

I bought from her store a suitcase with wheels on the bottom. It was nine dollars or something like that, and I gave her a twenty-dollar bill. She did not ring it up on the cash register. Instead she took the twenty-dollar bill from me and put it inside my bag. So I took it out of the bag and gave it to her again and said, "You have made a mistake."

At that time her daughter came over. She was very angry and upset and she rang up the sale on the register. The mother then took the exact amount out of her pocket and put it in the register.

The daughter was puzzled.

The mother said, "He reminds me of my father, husband and brother. Of late I am seeing my dear ones quite often."

What could I say? Inwardly I was telling her, "Perhaps your time has come to join them." But if I told her outwardly, her daughter would be mad. Since the lady was so nice, I wandered around and got a few more things. The lady said to me, "Had it been my store, I would not have charged you at all. But I am only an employee here."

Then, when I was leaving the store, she followed me out to the door in such an affectionate way. Tears were visible in her eyes.

4. *The stuffed animal*

In one store I saw a beautiful stuffed animal, but I could not figure out if it was a cow or a dog. It had a bell around the neck. I was going to buy it for Susan.

Before I bought it, I said to one of the salesladies, "I like it very much; it is white and very nice. But is it a cow?"

She laughed at me and said, "No, a dog!"
It was very beautiful, and it looked like a cow.

5. *I am sorry*

The other day I went shopping and I bought a few things. At one store I asked a saleslady for a shopping bag. She said I had to pay twenty cents extra.

I asked, "Are you Hawaiian or Japanese?"

She said, "I am Japanese, and I am sorry I asked you for twenty cents extra."

She gave me the bag and wouldn't take the twenty cents from me. Afterwards, I got a few more things. As I was going out, she followed me and said very fast, "I am sorry."

6. *The "thank you" business*

Three or four days ago I went to Woolworth's to buy a bag. I was standing in line behind a little girl around six or seven years old. She was with her brother, who was about four or five.

The little boy said to his sister, "Jeannie," – or something like that – "if you have ten cents, can you give it to me?"

She said, "No!"

Then the boy said, "Didn't you hear me say *if, if, if?* I said, '*If* you have, *if* you have!'"

Again she said, "No!"

Then he said, "Damn you!"

The girl bought a roll of thick string. It came to one dollar and thirty-six cents. She only had one dollar and thirty cents. So when she gave one dollar and thirty cents to the lady at the register, the lady at the register said, "O my God, O my God," looking at the manager. How could she give the girl the string when the actual price was six cents more?

Immediately I took out a dollar and gave it to the little girl, so she was very happy. The lady at the register said to her, "Say 'thank you' to the gentleman." But the girl didn't say anything. Then from the change I gave a dime to the little boy. He grabbed it from me. The woman behind the register, who was about twenty-three or twenty-five years old, said to him, "Little one, say 'thank you'." He also wouldn't say it. So the woman said to the little girl, "What kind of parents do you have? I am ashamed of you." Then she said to me, "On their behalf I am thanking you. It's a shame that parents don't teach their children the 'thank you' business!"

7. *In his own world*

We entered into a store to buy some prasad. There were so many posters with pictures of me there. In so many ways Sharon was trying to let the store owner know that I was the one on the poster, but he was in his own world. Just behind him was a poster where I was playing the esraj.

8. *Banana ice cream*

Saraswati has a divine enterprise that sells ice cream. The name is Amrita Kutir. When I went there, I was testing or examining the flavours. I liked the banana the best. Because in India I ate bananas millions of times, I don't have a liking for bananas. But the banana ice cream I liked the most.

9. The suspect

There is a bookstore in Jamaica where I like to buy things. The previous owner was very bad. He used to suspect everyone. Every time I would enter into the store, I had to leave my bag outside. You weren't allowed to bring your bags inside. The owner looked like President Truman. I would always say jokingly to myself, "Truman has incarnated again."

When I went into the store a few days ago, I left my bag outside as I always do. It was raining, but what could I do? Then I went inside. Half an hour I spent there. I bought a dictionary for a dollar. Then I saw Shakespeare's *Hamlet*. I wanted to buy the whole Shakespeare set. The man was so nice. He was looking for the other books, but he could not find them. He said he would have them ready for me the next time – thirty-eight volumes.

I said, "Next week I will come."

He said, "You will get the books."

He was looking at me. Then he said, "It seems you are Sri Chinmoy. I can feel the fragrance from your body." He was saying he was so honoured that I had come into his store.

Then I was looking for my bag. It was on the shelf inside. The man had taken it from outside and put it on the shelf. He said, "Why did you leave it outside?"

I said, "The previous owner used to suspect me." I told him how nice he was and how bad the previous owner was.

10. The sari store

There is a store where I go to buy saris. First I will buy things, and then the owner will bow down and touch my feet or knee because I am a religious man. He has a big picture of his Guru hanging in the store.

11. The same customer twice

Yesterday I went to see Alo off at the airport. She likes to read newspapers and magazines, so while she was standing at the ticket desk, I went to buy her *The New York Times, Newsweek* and *People* magazine. There was a teenager working at the counter. I gave her a twenty-dollar bill. My purchase came to over four dollars, so she gave me back three five-dollar bills and some change. Then she said very haughtily, "I don't have a ten-dollar bill!" She said it as if I had asked her to give me a ten-dollar bill.

I said, "It doesn't matter, so long as you have given me the proper change." Then I saw two cute writing pads that said "I love New York" with a heart sign. I said to myself, "I really love New York. It has given me shelter. No other place has given me shelter like this."

I went up to the girl with the pads. I was standing in front of her, and she was about to press the register. Suddenly I got the inspiration to buy cookies for Alo and Savyasachi. Then she got mad at me. Nobody was behind me. Only one other person was browsing in the store; that is all. I said, "What is the difference if I come back or if another customer comes? Can't you take me as another customer?"

She said to me, "Oh, I didn't think of it."

12. An encounter at Lucille's Diner

Last night after the public meditation at PS 86, I gave a flower arrangement to one of the seekers who came up for prasad. A few years ago that particular gentleman was taking a meditation course that Dhrubha was giving. He appreciated Dhrubha's course like anything. Poor Dhrubha, once in a blue moon he gets appreciation! So this man's appreciation was like a full moon.

About four days ago I went to Lucille's Diner with six or seven visiting disciples. When I sat down, this particular man wanted to come over and say hello to me. But Databir stood up and prevented him from approaching me. I looked at the man through the corner of my eye and saw that he was a very nice, very soulful man. So I approached him and said hello to him.

He was so moved. Immediately he showed me his key chain which had my picture on it. It was one of my smiling pictures. When he spoke to me, he addressed me as "Guru".

I asked him what he does for a living. He is a fire marshal. We exchanged just a few words, and I invited him to come to our Wednesday night meditations if it was at all possible. Afterwards, he talked to Databir for a few minutes, and then he left. I wasn't paying any attention when he left. We were just sitting and eating.

When the time came for me to pay the bill, the waitress informed me that the man had paid it. He had told her that he was very happy that he could take care of it. That is why last night, when he came to our Wednesday night public meditation, I gave him flowers. Now today I heard that after the meeting he said he would like to become a disciple.

13. Who is right?

The previous day there was another funny incident. There is a donut shop on Jamaica Avenue next to another store that has burned to the ground. It is near the Long Island Railroad station. They have four or five kinds of donuts there. I asked them for ten egg salad sandwiches. The man said to me, "Ten? Ten? How about five?"

While he was making everything, I asked another worker if she could give me a Tab and a donut. This is how I follow my diet! You won't believe it, but I have lost eight and a half pounds since the fifteen mile race. This is solid weight loss – not water weight. I ran and took exercise; I worked very hard. When I started, I was 146 1/2 pounds. When I got on the scale, I cried. Then, after running the fifteen mile race, I gained two and a half or three pounds, as usual. But now my weight is back down to 138, or even a little less. So it is possible for everyone to lose weight!

Anyway, I finished my food, and what did I see? A black man entered the store. He was wearing an expensive suit and was very well dressed. At that time it was around twelve-thirty or one o'clock. The man ordered something and ate it. He gave a ten-dollar bill to the owner, but he did not get as much change as he was expecting. The owner just pointed to the price list.

The customer said, "No, you have to give me more change!"

The owner said, "From six to eleven in the morning there is one price. After eleven, the price changes."

The customer said, "I would not have eaten if I had seen that."

The owner said, "You have to pay for what you have eaten."

A real argument started, and I was standing right between them. There was a container of milk on the counter. One of them accidentally struck it, and it spilled all over. Both the black man and I jumped away from the counter.

Then I said, "Please, please, I am ready to give the fifty cents."

The customer was so embarrassed that he said to the owner, "Hell with you!" and walked out.

The owner turned to me and said, "Please tell me who was right?"

I said, "You were right!"

The man grabbed my hand and with his other hand he grabbed two donuts and put them in my other hand.

He said, "You don't have to pay a cent for these."

I said, "I don't want the donuts." So he put them into my bag. This is how I got two donuts free. Of course, if the owner had asked me who was right while the other man was in the store, I would have said to him, "Do I understand your English?"

14. Honeybread

Today in the bakery I bought a loaf of bread. I don't appreciate bread at all, but some of my disciples like it. The sign said "honeybread", so I asked the girl behind the counter, "Is there honey inside, or is it just a name?"

The girl said, "I don't know." So she went to her boss, an elderly lady.

The boss said, "It has honey inside."

How they put honey inside the bread, God knows!

15. The bargainer

Yesterday we went to buy something. I remained in the car and Victor and Databir went inside as my representatives. The man said, "Four hundred dollars." I told them to go back inside and offer him three hundred. The message came back, "Four hundred!" This time I told them to say, "Two hundred." He said, "Three seventy-five." I said, "Two thirty-five."

Finally he told them, "I am not going to sell it for less than three fifty." So I said, "Then I am not going to buy it. We are going to another place." Then I felt sorry because I liked the thing so much. So I asked them to go back in and offer three hundred. He said, "No, three twenty-five."

So it started again. I was arguing for three hundred, but he wouldn't agree. Finally, he agreed and he sent his assistant, a black man, to talk to me. The man said, "It is very valuable."

I told Databir and Victor, "Let them hate me for bargaining. I always ask for half price, because they always ask for two or three hundred dollars extra." In India everyone always bargains. In America some shopkeepers say nasty things when you try to bargain. But they ask such an inflated price! Why give them so much money unnecessarily?

16. Sari bargaining

The other day I went to buy some saris for two disciples. They were thirty-six dollars each. I told the shopkeeper, "No, thirty." The man agreed. Right after that a lady came in and wanted the same sari. He quoted her the same price – thirty-six dollars.

She came in after me, but she wanted to be served before me, so she bought it for thirty-six dollars, and left while I was still standing there.

Then the shopkeeper said that he gave me a better price because I always buy more than one. And he added, "Also, she is an ugly woman. I don't see any beauty in her." That is why he sold the sari to her for thirty-six dollars.

17. The steam machine

I wanted to buy a steam machine to lose weight. Sanatan took me to Brooklyn, and he got lost going there, so we went to Manhattan on the way from Queens to Brooklyn. Then, once we got there I couldn't believe what a horrible place it was! It was full of old hospital things – everything used and secondhand. Sanatan wanted me to buy a machine that was very large and very old. I was ready to buy it, but then my mother's soul appeared and said, "This is a hospital. You don't have to come to a place like this."

I didn't like the machine at all, but I would have surrendered to Sanatan. But when my mother interfered, I did not buy it. This machine was three times as large as the one I eventually did buy.

18. English saves us

Five or six years ago I was in a restaurant in Paris. I was talking to them in English. Because I am an Indian, they also were talking to me in English. Everything was in English. But when an Englishman came in after me, although he was asking questions in English, he was getting the answers in French from them. So you see, they didn't like speaking English. The same thing sometimes happens in England. When a Frenchman comes and asks them questions, they pretend they don't know French even if they know it.

In India, Hindi is the official language, but even now many people do not know Hindi. In so many places they can't speak Hindi, but they do speak English. So English saves us.

19. Soul's connection

Yesterday we went to a shoe store in Brooklyn to buy running shoes. They know Thomas there, and they like him very much. The wife has a tremendous soul's connection with Pratibha, and the husband has a tremendous soul's connection with Kanan. While I was talking to them I was seeing their soul's connection with our disciples.

If you go there, you will see on the wall my picture in the New York Marathon. Thousands of people are ahead of me, but I am clearly visible.

20. The flute

I stopped in London on the way back from India. While I was there, I went to buy a Western flute. The man very politely said to me, "Do you play?" I said, "Yes, I play a little."

He said, "Do you want an expensive one or an inexpensive one?"

I said, "Inexpensive." The most inexpensive flutes were four hundred dollars; the others were twelve hundred and even two thousand or three thousand dollars.

Then he said to me, "If you know how to play, I advise you to go into our studio and play; then you can see if you like the flute. But if you don't know how to play, the best thing is for you to look at it in front of me here." He very nicely suspected me. After I had played for two seconds, he said, "You don't have to play here." Then he took me to the studio.

Whether it was his sincerity or flattery, God knows, but after I played for two or three minutes he said, "You are a concert flautist. You should not play this flute. You should use an open-hole flute."

Inwardly I said, "What is his intention? Those flutes are four thousand dollars. He may just be flattering me to get the money. Flattery sometimes makes you lose your sense of proportion." So I said, "I can't play that kind of flute."

The flute that I was going to buy was three hundred dollars. But he flattered me to such an extent that I decided to get one that cost about a thousand dollars. When I was about to pay the bill, Alo came into the store. She said, "A thousand dollars!"

But I said to myself, "I sell so many flute tapes. In two weeks I will be able to make this money back. I won't be wasting money. Now I will be able to make more tapes and sell them."

So I bought the expensive flute. Now I am practising on it, and I am already planning to make several more tapes.

21. The harmonium

When I was in London at a smaller-than-the-smallest shop, I saw a small harmonium. Just for the sake of fun and curiosity, I said, "Can I see the harmonium?"

The man said, "Certainly you can see it, but first you have to tell me if you have ever played one. If you have never played one, I can't allow you to play it. You have to listen to me play it. I will play, and you will hear what a wonderful sound it has."

I said, "Definitely I can play it. Please let me try." It was very small. After playing it I said, "I have four or five harmoniums and this one is infinitely worse than my worst!"

He kept quiet because he saw that I did know how to play.

22. The good-hearted Indian

While I was shopping in London, an Indian really proved to have a good heart. I was buying some saris, and I wanted to pay the owner in American dollars. I was telling him that to simplify things, I would say that two dollars equals a pound. The owner said, "Do you want to make me very rich?"

I said, "Why?"

He said, "It is a dollar eighty-five, and you want to give me two dollars. I don't want you to make me rich!"

Since I was offering, he could have easily agreed. Then he was begging me to drink some juice because it was very hot. I said no, because I had to leave.

He said, "At least take some handkerchiefs from me. Do you have any handkerchiefs?"

I said, "No, I don't have any handkerchiefs."

So he forced me to take three handkerchiefs.

23. Looking for shorts

In London I spent half an hour in Barkers looking for a pair of shorts. All the shorts were sizes thirty-two and thirty-four. A salesman went to look for my size, but after fifteen minutes he came back and said they did not even have one pair in size thirty. I was disappointed not to be able to get a pair of shorts, but secretly I was very happy to find that it is so rare for a man to have a size thirty waist!

24. The baked potato shop

There were over six hundred people at the concert I gave in Edinburgh the last time I was there. They were very receptive.

Afterwards I was very hungry, but I didn't want to eat much. Sabuj is the manager of a baked potato store, so we went there to eat. After I ate one baked potato, my hunger increased like anything, so I asked them to give me three or four items more. Even that was not enough, and again I asked for more. So this is how I diet when I am travelling.

25. The embarrassing question

After the seven mile race in Scotland, we went to a store where I bought a football for Tejiyan's team. In India I hadn't seen that kind of ball, so I bought it. Janaka and Janani were with me, browsing.

One of the workers came up to me and said, "I am embarrassed, but I would like to ask you something. You have no hair, yet you look so smart and strong. May I know your age?"

I said, "Fifty-one."

He said, "Fifty-one?"

The worker was much younger than me, but he was very fat. He couldn't believe I was over fifty. And he was not just flattering me because I bought the football. He said this to me long before I bought it.

26. Buying a flute

Before leaving for San Francisco, I went with Baoul to buy a new bow for my esraj. There were seven flutes in the store and I decided to buy the cheapest one, which was for beginners. The man said, "Do you want the one in the showcase or would you like to have a new one?" I took the old one, which cost 206 dollars. This was the cheapest beginner's flute. It is so useless that I can't play it.

27. The thirty-dollar meal

Many years ago I went to a restaurant alone. The waiter was wearing a tie and a black suit. He asked me if I had thirty dollars. He said, "Here the minimum is thirty dollars."

I had two hundred dollars or more in my wallet but I said, "I thank you," and went away.

The waiter probably thought that I didn't have thirty dollars. But although I *did* have it, I said to myself, "What am I going to eat for thirty dollars?" That is why I went away.

28. Losing one's appetite

Yesterday I went to a coffee shop after I had gone shopping. A lady came in after me and ordered some food. Then she said that she was going to make a phone call. When she came back to the counter the waitress said to her, "Here is your food."

The lady started screaming at the waitress and then went out of the coffee shop. The waitress followed her, also screaming, because the lady had ordered food and had gone away without paying for it. God knows what happened during her phone conversation, but she did not want to eat.

29. What else?

When I was in Maryland, I went to a candle shop and got four or five different items made of wax. At the cash register the shopkeeper asked, as usual, "What else, what else?"

Whenever I stand by the cash register, before they tell me how much I owe them, they always ask, "What else, what else?"

30. The King's admirers

I went to a bookstore today on Sutphin Boulevard, near Jamaica Avenue. Next to the bookstore is my most favourite Italian restaurant. For years I used to walk down there and bring pizza back to my house for any disciples who were working there. The owner's name is Mark. Always the people in that restaurant are so nice to me!

When I went into the bookstore today, a black man was reading Muhammad Ali's book, *I Am King*. In this book Ali did not say he was "the greatest". He said, "I am the King."

The man was very nice. He was showing such interest in the book. He said, "Would you like to buy this book?"

I said, "I am, like you, a great admirer of Muhammad Ali."

He said, "You are a great admirer of his?"

I said, "I have had quite a few interviews with him."

He couldn't believe his ears. He said, "Oh, you have met the King? You talked to him?"

I said, "I have talked with him for hours."

I took the man's name and address and said that I would send him the brochures with our interviews.

The man had with him a cage with a rabbit inside. The shopkeeper wouldn't let him bring it inside the bookstore.

31. The one-cent "discount"

After I finished talking to the black man, I bought a few books. The price came to five dollars and forty cents. Before I paid the man at the counter, I was talking to him for a while. I asked him if he was the new owner. He said, "Yes, I am."

So I said, "Good luck!" I said many other nice things to him also.

Then, when I reached into my pocket, I saw that I had a five-dollar bill, plus a quarter, a dime and four pennies. I said to him, "I have here five dollars and thirty-nine cents. If you do not want to accept it, I will give you a twenty-dollar bill."

He grabbed the twenty-dollar bill. He wanted to have the twenty, instead of five thirty-nine. Then when he was about to give me the change, he said, "Not worth it!" He returned the twenty, and took my five thirty-nine.

I said, "Fine!"

I should one day give him a hundred books free. His spiritual section is nothing – all rubbish novels.

32. Mistaken identity

Yesterday I went with Nirvik and Baoul to get a machine. In the store, Nirvik saw on the owner's desk two small paintings on a card. Nirvik is a great art lover. He brought the card to me and said, "Look, Guru, your paintings!" He was positive, a hundred per cent sure. I was ninety-five per cent certain that it was my painting. But when we turned the card over, there was somebody else's name on it. I looked at it and said, "How can it be?" Baoul also felt it was my painting, but somebody else's name was written on the card.

33. Buying the Post

Last week I went to a candy store and bought the *Post*. It was not the *Enquirer* so luckily I was saved! My disciples always tell me I should not be seen buying the *Enquirer*, although reading it always amuses me. As I was buying the paper, a man with a moustache and beard asked me, "Are you Sri Chinmoy?"

I smiled at him.

He continued, "Are you really? I have come to your meditations at PS 86 on Parsons Boulevard."

I was carrying a bag over my shoulder, so he said "Now you are carrying a bag."

I said, "Now you see the difference from the way I am at meditation."

He said, "No difference!"

While I was paying for the newspaper, he was telling the shopkeeper, "He is Sri Chinmoy."

When I was coming out of the store, he was still gazing at me.

34. An important person

The other day I was in a store shopping for something for Alo. A very, very fat lady came into the same store to buy something for herself. The lady had her hand on a garment when she saw me. She kept her hand on the garment and started looking at me with such awe. Then she said, "Are you Sri Chinmoy?"

So I smiled at her. Then the owner started asking her, "Who is he?"

I have been at that clothing store on Jamaica Avenue at least sixty or seventy times, but the owner thinks that I am an ordinary person. After talking to the lady, the owner realised that I am an "important person". So that is how I became an important person overnight!

35. Filled with saris

When I was in Japan, I went into a shop that was completely filled with saris. In every nook and corner there were saris. It was difficult even to walk inside the store. They knew how to keep as many saris as possible inside a small space!

36. The little girl who wouldn't move

I went to Dan Lurie's exercise store with Dhanu to buy some exercise equipment. A black gentleman came up to me, practically with folded hands, and asked with such respect, "Are you Sri Chinmoy?"

I said, "Yes."

He was so excited. He was telling his six- or seven-year-old daughter, "That is Sri Chinmoy! That is Guru Sri Chinmoy!"

His daughter felt shy, so she stayed in one corner of the store while I was taking exercise on an exercise machine. After ten minutes she came over to watch me. Then she wouldn't move. She was standing so near me, looking and looking at my eyes for ten minutes, with her eyes wide open. Dhanu couldn't figure out why she wouldn't move.

37. A mentor

Yesterday I went to an old bookstore and bought *Mystics as a Force for Change* by Sisir Kumar Ghose. He is a Bengali who lives in Shantiniketan. He happens to be a very close friend of mine, plus one of my great mentors. He is extremely fond of me, and I am extremely fond of him.

I LOVE SHOPPING

I know him so well. He has been going to the ashram for the last thirty years. We used to walk along the shores of the Bay of Bengal together in the evening. Eighteen years ago he came to America to give lectures at Mississippi University. Some nice pictures of us together were taken while he was here. He brought me a beautiful small statue of Lord Buddha and other gifts. I remember them – especially a peculiar ballpoint from Shantiniketan.

For most of the articles in the book that I bought, I had served as his messenger boy. During that time I was unofficial sub-editor of *Mother India,* and I used to take his articles to the editor. Also, I made arrangements for him to have an interview with _ Mother India._

I was so delighted and excited to see the book. It was 2.95 dollars. So I bought it and started reading it. I truly admire Sisir Kumar Ghose. He was such a nice, kind mentor. I am really grateful to him. My immediate offering of gratitude to this supremely noble soul can only be felt and never be described. Many, many things one day I will tell about him.

But after I had bought his book the funniest thing happened. That same afternoon I received a letter from Vidagdha saying that Sisir Kumar Ghose of Shantiniketan had been one of the examiners of her doctoral thesis on my poetry. Melbourne University had submitted her thesis to various places, but the professors didn't want to examine it because they didn't know anything about the subject. Finally, Sisir Ghose accepted. He is head of the English section of the university at Shantiniketan. According to him, Vidagdha should have also said something about my Bengali poems.

38. Such a nice man

I was at a fruit stand on 147th Street, beyond Jamaica Avenue. The Japanese girl there said to me, "Hi! I have not seen you for a long time."

I said, "I have also not seen you for a long time."

Then I got seven or eight items. I came to her and she added it up on the cash register. It came to thirteen dollars. I said, "It is wrong. Are you sure?"

She said, "Do you think I am overcharging you?"

I said, "No, it seems to me that you have not charged me for all the items."

Then she took the receipt out of the cash register and checked each item to show me that it was all right. I was wrong.

Then she said, "You are such a nice man!"

39. A brother named Sri Chinmoy

Yesterday I went to a grocery store nearby. When I went to pay, the man behind the counter said to me, "Do you have a brother named Sri Chinmoy?"

I said, "Why?"

He said, "You look exactly like him."

Then he looked at me again and dropped his bag of plantain chips and said, "Sri Chinmoy! Sri Chinmoy!"

He told me, "Two or three years ago I went to one of your meetings in Manhattan. There I saw you meditating." He couldn't believe that I would be shopping in a grocery store. He came from the Dominican Republic.

He was so excited. He told his friend, "Sri Chinmoy is in my store! Sri Chinmoy is in my store!"

40. *The disciple*

Another day I was looking at wristwatches. On that day I was carrying two heavy bags.

Baoul was waiting for me in the car at a particular place. I could see him, but he didn't see me, so I had to carry the bags myself.

A man came up to me and asked, "Are you Sri Chinmoy?"

I said, "Yes."

He said, "I came to one of your Wednesday meetings. It was so powerful." Then he started telling me all about his Guru while I was standing holding the heavy bags.

He said, "I was initiated by my Guru. Now he has passed away."

I said, "Your Guru has left successors. You should follow his successors."

He said, "My Guru taught me Kundalini Yoga. But I don't get anything from his successors."

I said, "I don't teach Kundalini Yoga."

He said, "Do you think you could take me faster?"

I said, "You have been initiated by your Guru. Now he is the one to take you."

For ten minutes I talked to him, all the time holding my heavy bags. Finally I said, "Your Guru is the right Guru for you."

Then I carried the bags to Baoul's car.

41. The St. Thomas restaurant

In St. Thomas I was eating in a restaurant when a young man – one of the waiters – came up to me and asked, "Are you the same guy that I saw in the newspaper?"

I said, "I am the same guy."

Then somebody passing by said, "Yes, he is the same gentleman."

The first man said, "Oh, he is a great man!" Then he disappeared.

42. The philosopher

I went to a bookstore yesterday. First I was reading religious books and then I got inspired to read some jokes. So I went to another shelf that had joke books. I was the only customer, so the owner was watching me. He said, "What are you doing? This moment you are reading religious books, and the next moment jokes!"

I told him, "When I want to get joy in this world I read joke books, and when I want to get joy in the inner world I read spiritual books."

So he said, "Are you a philosopher?"

I said, "Yes."

Then I continued reading the joke books.

43. Twelve donuts

After I left the bookstore, I went to a donut store and ordered a dozen. I could not tell whether the person behind the counter was a man or a woman. The voice was like a man's, but the hair and everything was like a woman's.

When I asked for a dozen, he or she couldn't understand me. So I said, "Twelve."

Then the worker started putting the donuts in a brown paper bag. Another worker came over and said, "No, put them in a box." So he started putting them in a box.

Then a young Puerto Rican woman came and said, "Twelve? Do you know how much they cost? Fifty cents each!"

I looked at them and said, "I have the money."

They were warning me that it was so expensive, as if I couldn't buy twelve donuts. This store changes hands quite often. Six months ago when I went there to buy five or six donuts, the owner gave me three or four extra for free. Always when I used to go there he would pat me on the shoulder and say, "You are a nice man." Now he is no longer there.

NOTES TO I LOVE SHOPPING, BOOK I

1. *(p. 115)* 1 January 1980.
2. *(p. 115)* 1 January 1980.
3. *(p. 115)* 1 January 1980.
4. *(p. 116)* 4 January 1980.
5. *(p. 117)* 8 January 1980.
6. *(p. 117)* 30 January 1980.
7. *(p. 118)* 16 February 1980.
8. *(p. 118)* 2 September 1980.
9. *(p. 119)* 28 February 1981.
10. *(p. 120)* 28 February 1981.
11. *(p. 120)* 17 September 1981.
12. *(p. 121)* 8 October 1981.
13. *(p. 122)* 8 October 1981.
14. *(p. 123)* 8 October 1981.
15. *(p. 124)* 17 October 1981.
16. *(p. 124)* 17 October 1981.
17. *(p. 125)* 1 November 1981.
18. *(p. 125)* 31 December 1981.
19. *(p. 126)* 21 February 1982.
20. *(p. 126)* 28 March 1982.
21. *(p. 127)* 28 March 1982.
22. *(p. 128)* 20 May 1982.
23. *(p. 128)* 20 May 1982.
24. *(p. 129)* 20 May 1982.
25. *(p. 129)* 20 May 1982.
26. *(p. 130)* 5 June 1982.
27. *(p. 130)* 13 June 1982.
28. *(p. 130)* 13 June 1982.
29. *(p. 131)* 26 June 1982.
30. *(p. 131)* 21 July 1982.

31. *(p. 132)* 21 July 1982.
32. *(p. 132)* 24 July 1982.
33. *(p. 133)* 7 August 1982.
34. *(p. 133)* 11 September 1982.
35. *(p. 134)* 13 September 1982.
36. *(p. 134)* 14 October 1982.
37. *(p. 134)* 28 October 1982.
38. *(p. 136)* 31 October 1982.
39. *(p. 136)* 31 October 1982.
40. *(p. 137)* 31 October 1982.
41. *(p. 138)* 22 November 1982.
42. *(p. 138)* 11 December 1982.
43. *(p. 138)* 11 December 1982.

I LOVE SHOPPING

BOOK 2

44. Buying a chair

We all know that the Japanese are very honest by nature. But I had a very un-Japanese kind of experience in Kyoto while we were buying a chair. In one shop the man said, "It is on sale, so I won't be able to reduce the price. This is the cheapest price in Japan, and you won't get this chair at a better price anywhere else." Kirit was the translator.

I looked at the man and then said to Kirit, "Let us go to some other store."

Right across the street we found another chair that was just like the one in the first store, but it also had a footrest. In spite of that, it was six or seven thousand yen less than the first one. It was a better price and, in addition, it had a footrest! Kirit was so excited.

Later I told Kirit's mother, "Your son is a very, very good boy. I am very proud of him." But unfortunately, not all Japanese are like him.

45. Lowering the price

In Kyoto I bargained with the shopkeepers. In one place I wanted to buy a particular game. As soon as I went there, they lowered the price. Even when you agree to pay the quoted price, they lower it.

It is the same in Okinawa. Today I bought a watch. As I was buying it, the man brought the price down five thousand yen. I am shameless. I said, "You have lowered it, but can you not lower it another two thousand?"

So altogether he lowered it seven thousand yen. He was such a nice man.

46. The old lady

Then I bought something for Alo. The old lady in the store was very greedy! She quoted a price and wrote it down. Then I wrote down what I wanted to pay, and she agreed to it. I opened my wallet in front of her, and she started pointing to a large bill that she wanted me to give her. Something within me said not to give her so much, so I gave her some smaller bills. She was grumbling. When she wanted me to give her more, I said, "No, no, no!" Finally she agreed to take what I offered.

Chidananda was watching, and he was quite amused. He saw his Guru's bargaining capacity with the old lady.

47. The hair tonic

While I was out shopping with Nirvik, we saw hair tonic that was supposed to make your hair grow. He said, "That is for Sharon. Whenever I clean out her drain, I see that she is losing all her hair."

I said, "No, I need it, since I have already lost mine. Sharon still has excellent hair."

48. Incorrect English

Can you imagine! The Japanese have printed something totally incorrect on a T-shirt which is being sold in the stores. It says, "If you have freedom, then practical what you say."

Chidananda was reading it out, and he was automatically saying "practise". He did not realise that they had written "practical".

49. Buying "sunglasses"

Today I went to a store where they have very beautiful glasses. I asked if they were sunglasses, and the man in the store said, "Yes."

As soon as I put the first pair on, the man said, "Very nice, now you can read."

I said, "I don't need glasses to read."

Then immediately my eyes started burning. I said, "They are very powerful. I don't need these."

The second pair also started giving me pain, so the man said, "You should go to an eye specialist."

If they had been sunglasses, they would not have burned my eyes!

50. Who's who

I went to a bookstore and saw a book called *Who's Who in America*. My name is in a book called *Who's Who Among Indians in America*, so I was looking for my name in this one.

A very fat lady was looking for books to help her fight fatness. She said to me in a sarcastic way, "I'm sure your name is there!"

I didn't have the heart to enter into conversation with her, so I just gave her a smile.

Thomas Chinmoy or somebody was mentioned in the book, but my name was not there. They didn't have anything under Ghose or Chinmoy. So I gave up.

51. The Christian bookstore

I always have problems when I go shopping. The last time I went to a Christian bookstore to buy an inspirational book, the book that I wanted cost 50 cents. I don't like to carry much change with me because it makes my pockets very heavy. So I had a quarter and three dimes. I gave the man 55 cents for the book, and he said, "Thank you very much." He was thanking me for the extra nickel I gave him.

This time, in the same store, I wanted to buy a book called *Flying with the Birds*. It is about people who follow birds in a boat. You can't imagine how hard they work, according to the book. Some people don't care for God-realisation; they are only crying for the birds.

The price of the book was 50 cents. This time I had three quarters in my pocket, so I gave the exact amount. The lady took my 50 cents, but this time I didn't even get a "thank you".

52. The false sign

Once I was running in Florida in the early morning when I saw a store that advertised "All T-shirts $2.99". They even mentioned some very good brands. But the store was not yet open.

In the afternoon I went there again to run. This time the store was open. I said to myself, "Let me buy quite a few T-shirts for 2.99 dollars." Then I thought, "I have to run. Why take so many T-shirts? I will buy one now and send Savyasachi back for more later."

I gave the saleslady 5 dollars and stood waiting for my change. She was looking at me like I was an idiot.

I said, "It is $2.99."

She said, "No, that is a very old sign."

As I was going out, I saw some old men looking at the sign – $2.99. I did not have the heart to tell them that the sign was false.

I was so disgusted that I ran home very fast!

53. Kailash of India

On my previous visit to Florida, I had seen a store called Kailash of India on the same street as my hotel. The following morning I ran past it, but the store was closed. Then at noon I went there again. O God! I entered only to come out immediately! All unbearable women's things! All these things they put in a store called Kailash of India. Kailash is the most sacred Mount Everest!

54. Cash only

In Florida, Savyasachi and I went to a famous bird store, but I have more of a variety in my house. They had only six or eight kinds of birds, but of each kind they had hundreds. What shall I do with number? I was looking for variety.

The lady asked, "Do you have cash? We take only cash."

Savyasachi said, "Yes, we have cash."

Then the lady said, "If you don't buy at least 300 dollars worth, you have to pay a penalty of 25 dollars." Now, am I stupid enough to buy 300 dollars worth of birds just to save 25 dollars?

We saw some beautiful lovebirds. I wanted to buy one or two. The lady said again, "Mind you, it is cash!"

Then I got disgusted and said, "I am not going to buy it."

The lady looked at me as though to say, "I was right. You don't have cash!" She didn't know it was because I was disgusted with her.

55. The koala bear

In one area of a variety store I saw a chandelier for 10 dollars, and nearby was a very tiny koala bear. There was no price anywhere on the koala bear, but since it was in the same place as the chandelier, I thought perhaps everything in that area was 10 dollars. So I decided to buy the koala bear, and I gave the lady 10 dollars.

She said, "It is 13 dollars. Can't you see the price?"

I said, "It doesn't have a price." I really got disgusted. She was so rude.

She looked at me and said, "All right, you can have it for 11 dollars."

I said to myself, "I am not going to get it," and I walked away. But then I thought, "These are very old people. Perhaps they are senile." So I went back again.

When I went back in, the lady said to her husband, "There! I told you he was going to come back."

Again I got disgusted. I said, "I am only going to buy the chandelier, not the koala bear."

56. The handkerchiefs

In one store in Florida I was looking at handkerchiefs. I liked them so much. I started buying dozen after dozen. The lady was looking at me. It came to over a hundred dollars.

She said, "Oh, gentleman, please come back again."

The last time I was in Florida, in the same shop, a young salesman asked me if I could afford the thing I was looking at, which cost nineteen dollars. This time I spent a hundred and thirty dollars or even more. I will sign the handkerchiefs and give them to the disciples.

57. Two jokers

Once I was browsing in front of a bookstore. A Muslim saw me and recognised that I was a Hindu. Because my back was hurting, I placed my hand on my back. By way of joke he said, "Krishna, Krishna, Krishna!"

Then I started chanting, "Allah, Allah!"

He was invoking Krishna to save me and I was invoking Allah. We Indians are all jokers. Even when we suffer, we have to joke!

58. The shopkeeper's kick

Let me tell you a juicy story that happened in Hong Kong. It is not wise to waste precious time in a shop – not your precious time, but the precious time of the shopkeepers.

In Hong Kong it was drizzling outside, so I went into a shop. I started looking at a translating machine that had a few cards with different words. If you put the cards into the machine, it will translate the words from English into Spanish, Italian and French. I was curious, so I tried using it. But when I saw that there were only forty words in each language, and that those words perhaps I already knew, I did not want it. Curiosity always brings punishment.

The worker who was helping me happened to be Chinese. When he realised that I was not going to buy the machine, right in the shin bone he kicked me very nicely. He could have said that it was unintentional, but it was definitely intentional. He did not even apologise. Instead of crying, I laughed. I didn't feel like leaving just then, so I walked away a few steps and continued browsing.

There were also other customers in the store. One of them was a tall, stout man who seemed to be Scandinavian. His English was not very good. He was also browsing. Suddenly, I saw the

Chinese worker do the same trick to that man also. But this time he picked the wrong person! The shopkeeper himself got a smart slap from the tall man.

Then the Chinese man started screaming, "I am calling the police!"

The Scandinavian man followed him to the telephone, saying, "Yes, call the police."

The worker was not dialing; he was only screaming that he would call the police, and I was enjoying it like anything!

I could have left after I was kicked, but God wanted me to stay there and see this.

59. *Looking at flutes*

Whenever I see an Indian flute, I always like to play it. In a store in Delhi I was playing a wooden flute. The price was ten rupees. In India I always offer them half the price, so I said, "Five rupees."

He said, "It is not even cost price. Cost price is seven rupees."

I said, "I am not going to take it."

Then he followed me two or three blocks, flattering me. He said that five minutes ago I had played so well.

Who can resist flattery? Because he flattered me so shamelessly, I gave him seven rupees and got the flute.

A few hours later I saw some reed flutes in another store. These flutes were not good at all, and the price was also very high. But I have a bad habit. Whenever I go into a store, I try to play the flutes. The salesman was annoyed that I was trying all the flutes and I could not make any sound. So he said, "The flute talks only to nice people."

I said, "It is true – it talks only to nice people." Since the flute didn't talk to me, I didn't have to buy it. So if you are not a nice man, you save money!

60. The first customer

In India, no matter which hour of the day you go into a store, you are always the first customer. If you go at eleven o'clock or twelve o'clock or even in the afternoon, the owner will say you are the first customer, and that is why he is lowering the price for you.

When I passed by one store, from a distance I could see that there were customers inside. The store was selling T-shirts. I thought that perhaps people were buying because they were quite cheap, so fifteen minutes later I went into the store. The salesman immediately told me that he would give me a very good price, since I was his first customer.

61. The tabla book

In a store in a Delhi hotel I saw a tabla book and I thought of Sahishnu. A few months ago I had said nice things about his tabla playing. So I said, "Now let me get him a book."

I was browsing through the book. I did not know the cost, but I made up my mind to buy it. I asked the owner, "How late do you stay open?"

He said, "9:30."

I said, "I will come back again." I was really hungry, so I went to eat.

Around three o'clock I came back. Their afternoon siesta is wonderful. Their lunch break is three hours, and the store was closed. So I came back again at 8 o'clock. Can you imagine? That book was sold. The shopkeeper said, "Do you expect opportunity to come again and again?"

I said, "Tell me the truth. How many months have you had that book here?"

He said, "Months? It has been here for two years."

So look at Sahishnu's luck. Nobody had bought the book for two years, but that day somebody had to come and buy the book. It was my stupidity. I should have bought it the first time.

62. The overpayment

The owner of an Army and Navy store in Jamaica likes me very much. The other day when I was in the store I asked him, "Do you have a medium jacket?"

He said, "Medium? For whom?"

I said, "For me!"

He said, "Extra large, extra large!"

I said, "Extra large for whom?"

He said, "Extra large for me."

I said, "You are the owner. Why do I have to get one for you?"

He said, "Can you not buy one for your old age?"

I said, "I am already old."

Then he looked around and found a medium. The jacket cost forty-six dollars, but he reduced the price to forty, and said he wouldn't charge me tax. I gave him the money and smiled, and then went out of the door. Suddenly he started shouting and shouting.

I thought, "What, have I not given him enough money?" So I turned around.

He said, "Man, you have given me fifty dollars!"

I had counted it, but I hadn't noticed that two ten-dollar bills were stuck together. If he himself had trusted me and not counted it again, then he would not have known that I had given him too much. But for him to call me back was really something!

63. Sincere people do exist

After overpaying for the jacket, I went to a bakery. I told the lady to give me a dozen cookies. She said, "I am sorry. We only have eleven."

I said, "Fine, then give me eleven!"

She could have easily pretended that she had given me twelve. Who is counting? But some sincere people do exist. That is why we are still alive.

Eight or nine months ago I drank some tea in that bakery. The lady still remembers. She always says, "You don't want tea?"

This is that famous shop that always burns down. Previously there was another owner. He used to shake hands with me and give me everything half-price. Whatever the item was, he used to give me half for free.

64. The great man

Yesterday on my way back from the United Nations I went to an Indian restaurant in Manhattan called Curry in a Hurry. A young man came up to me and said, "Are you Sri Chinmoy? I am so happy to see you. I interview great men like you." Then he gave me a brochure about a book he had written on an Indian mental giant.

The man who was serving the food was looking at me with such admiration when he saw the other man talking to me, so I asked him, "Where do you come from?" First he said, "Bangladesh." Then he said, "Chittagong." Previously, whenever someone said he came from Bangladesh, it was always from some other district.

Here, for the first time, I heard "Chittagong," which is my own district. And then he said the name of a village which is only four and a half miles away from my village. For seven or eight years he had been in Cairo.

Thousands of miles from Chittagong we met. So is this not destiny? If the other man hadn't come up to me and said that I was a great man, I would probably not have spoken to the man who was serving. But if somebody says you are a great man, immediately ten persons look at you.

65. *A spiritual guy*

The other day, as I was coming back from shopping, I saw a teenage black girl.

She said to me, "Are you the same guy who teaches meditation?"

I smiled at her. Then she continued across the street. All of a sudden she came back to me and said, "I am sorry I called you 'guy'. You are a spiritual teacher."

66. *The egg salad sandwich*

In Victoria, while the running portion of our triathlon was going on, we went into a restaurant and I asked for an egg salad sandwich.

In the sandwich there were small pieces of cabbage and a lot of mayonnaise, but very little egg. I showed it to Alo and said, "Look! I told them to give me egg salad, and there is hardly any egg here."

Alo said, "This is better than what they give you at Annam Brahma."

I said, "What is wrong with Annam Brahma?"

She said, "Once, after John became the manager of Annam Brahma about twelve years ago, he gave Robert an egg salad sandwich. Robert said, 'I asked for egg salad. There is no egg in this!'

"John said, 'Don't you know? Inside the mayonnaise is the egg.'"

Alo was justifying her Canada by saying that at least there was a little bit of egg in my sandwich.

67. *The good side of Canada*

In Victoria we went to another restaurant and I asked for a grilled cheese sandwich. I paid for it with an American ten-dollar bill, and the lady at the cash register gave me the change. As soon as I got it, I put it in my pocket and left.

After I had gone half a block, the cashier came running up to me and said, "I'm sorry, I didn't give you the correct amount of change. You gave me ten American dollars, but I gave you change for ten Canadian dollars."

So this is the good side of Canada; the bad side is that when you ask for egg salad you get mayonnaise.

68. *Honouring McEnroe*

I went into a shoe store the other day. They had a big poster of John McEnroe right at the cash register. But the owner had put a piece of tape over the mouth. On the one hand, they were honouring him with a very big poster. On the other hand, they had taped his mouth shut.

69. *Buying* rasgulla

I went to buy *rasgulla* today to give for prasad. It used to be my favourite Indian sweet. I also wanted eight or ten *samosas*. The people at the store were shylocks. They charged me 75.83 dollars for the sweets. When I gave the lady 75 dollars, she said, "Eighty-three cents more."

I said, "Eighty-three cents?"

She said, "My boss will not allow me to give any discount."

I said to myself, "They do not deserve it!" So I took back the 75 dollars and turned to go out of the store.

Then the lady said, "Oh, have a nice day. Please come!" Then she gave it to me for 75 dollars.

Can you imagine what her name was? Amita! I couldn't believe it. Amita is a Bengali name. How did she get it, since she was Gujarati?

The Korean store is far better. In the morning I got some hair and food items from the Koreans. I bought quite a few things from them. There the bill came to 65 dollars. I didn't bargain with them because they had already given me a discount.

When I gave them 65 dollars, they said, "We will only charge you 64 dollars, and no tax."

I said, "You keep the dollar."

The Koreans were far better.

70. *I can't take money from you!*

As you know, I always like shopping in Indian stores. One evening Baoul took me to Elmhurst to look for ladies' *punjabi* outfits. I went browsing in two or three stores. Outside, it was drizzling.

When I was near a store called Sari Palace, an Indian lady saw me and became very excited. She came outside and pointed me out to an Indian man who was passing by. She did not say anything to him; she only pointed at me.

Then I wanted to go into Popular Fabrics. Baoul said I wouldn't be able to get punjabi outfits there, but I said I was in the mood to go in.

When I entered into the store, a young Gujarati lady was talking to a Gujarati customer. They were bargaining and having an argument. The man was saying that she was charging too much. Finally, he got very mad and went away without buying anything.

When I went towards the counter, I noticed that my transcendental picture was hanging up along with other pictures of Indian cosmic gods and goddesses and spiritual Masters. There were Lakshmi, Krishna, Kali and others, as well as some spiritual Masters. The lady did not recognise me, and I said to myself, "Who wants to tell her?"

I asked the lady for punjabi outfits. She said, "We don't have them ready-made."

I said, "You don't? Are you sure?"

She said, "No, but you can buy the material to make them. It is 4.99 dollars a yard. We don't have special *dupatta* material, but you can buy six-and-a-half-yard lengths of material and make the whole outfit, including the dupatta."

I asked, "Can you not speak Hindi?"

"No, I do not speak it," she answered.

I told her, "Well, your English is perfect." So perfect English we used.

I like bargaining, so I asked, "Can you not reduce the price? I will buy at least five different kinds of material."

She said, "4 dollars a yard."

I said, "Very good! I won't ask you to come down any more."

While I was looking at the material, she was telling me, "This is very beautiful, that is very beautiful."

Then, to my wide surprise, a middle-aged man suddenly appeared and fell flat at my feet. He was not bowing his head a little in the usual civilised way. No, he was lying flat on the ground, showing his respect according to the traditional Indian custom.

The lady was startled. She said, "He is my boss! Sushil! Sushil!" She couldn't believe that her boss was lying down flat on the floor. He had not been there when I entered into the store, but when he saw me, he was so happy and excited that I was in his shop.

When he stood up, he said to me, "You don't have to think of the price. Just take whatever you want. I will take care of it."

I said, "This material was 4.99 dollars. Now she has reduced it to 4 dollars. I am satisfied. I don't want her to reduce it any more."

I continued browsing, and Sushil remained near me. He said to me, "Miss Ghose came here today." He meant that Ranjana had been in the store earlier that day. Then he said, "I come from the Punjab, and my assistant comes from Gujarat."

When I had made my selection, the assistant cut six and a half yards from each roll of material, and put it all in a bag for me. When she was finished, I saw that the owner was not going towards the cash register. I said to myself, "What is the matter with him?" I calculated in my head that the material would cost 156.00 dollars. I opened my wallet, took out the exact amount and was about to give the owner the money.

Suddenly he was lying down flat on the ground at my feet! It was the same scene as before.

I said, "What are you doing?"

He said, "You have blessed me. This store is here all by your grace. I first saw you when you came to my store on Canal Street. Then I got another store in Manhattan, and you came there twice. Now, for the first time, you have come here to bless me. I can't take money from you. Everything here is yours."

I said, "You are really embarrassing me! At least take 100 dollars."

He said, "How can I take money from you? Especially now, in Diwali festival time, how can I take your money? Absolutely, I can't take anything! Everything I have is all due to your grace." He was trembling with joy and delight. He couldn't believe that I was there in his store.

I said, "Next time I come, you have to charge me. Otherwise, I will not come to your store again to bless you."

He said, "Yes, next time."

Eight or nine years ago, in Manhattan, the same kind of thing happened: a shopkeeper wouldn't take money from me. When I was picking out things, the man pretended he didn't recognise me. Then, afterwards, he wouldn't take money from me. I had selected 86 dollars worth of things from his store, but he said, "Just give me a ten-dollar bill and sign your name on it, so I can treasure it and preserve it always."

His friend had been a disciple in Connecticut for a short time, but the shopkeeper felt that he could not become a disciple because he was not pure enough.

71. *The Christian preacher*

A few days ago I went to a bookstore. I didn't buy any books, but I bought a few tapes because I wanted to hear what is required to be a "first-class Christian". I was eager to hear the sermon of the great preacher, so I played the tape while I was taking exercise.

I couldn't believe how he was criticising Indian spiritual Masters. He said that those who practised Indian-type meditation are possessed by Satan. In fifteen minutes you heard Satan's name more than God's Name. "Satan" came in every sentence – not God.

Transcendental Meditation in particular he attacked like anything. He said, "If meditation is something worthwhile, why are they not practising it in India? Why do they have to come to the West?"

So, while listening, I was answering his rhetorical questions. I was saying, "You fool! The Christian missionaries came to us in India to teach us. We were their favourite students. Why did they not stay in the West with their religion? You felt you had something worthwhile to teach us, and we learned devotedly. Now, whatever we have that is worthwhile, we have come here to teach you. So what is wrong?"

Like that I talked to him. The Christian evangelists forget that they also go to distant lands to spread their light! The Transcendental Meditation people should hear this tape!

I never learn! One tape was not enough. I started listening to another tape. There also the preacher had nothing else to do but attack the Indian meditation teachers. Perhaps we *are* the culprits. We have probably taken some of his people into our fold. So what else can he do? Now he has to use his preaching power to take away some of the passengers from *our* boats.

Two or three years ago when I went to that bookstore, the owner, an old man, was very unkind to me. I used to go with a shopping bag, but he wouldn't allow me to carry the shopping bag inside the room. I had to leave it at the door. Always he believed I was going to steal something.

Now I have got a promotion. The new owner is very nice to me, although he doesn't know who I am. When I left my shopping bag at the door, he said, "No, you can take it in."

So I bought sixteen dollars worth of tapes.

I LOVE SHOPPING

72. Bargaining in Maracaibo

As you know, I like bargaining. Here in Maracaibo it is quite possible to bargain. Today I wanted to buy something, but I don't speak Spanish, so I wrote down the price I wanted to pay. The storekeeper wrote down something else. Then what a battle we had! He wrote down 460 bolivars. I wrote down 350.

He said something very emphatic which, fortunately, I couldn't understand.

Then I wrote down 360. He wrote down 400. I said to myself, "No, I am not giving four!" and I started to leave.

So I got it for 370.

73. Exchanging dollars

I was in another store. I had only four bolivars left, so I wanted to change some American dollars. The shopkeeper said he would give me 11.30 per dollar. I knew the rate was higher, so I said, "12.30, or I am not going to buy!"

He said he would raise it to 12, but I insisted on 12.30, and finally he agreed.

You may ask, "Is it good to do that kind of thing?" But with these people it is good, because they are such rogues! I never take those shopkeepers seriously! They say "fixed price", but you have to bargain with them if you want a grain of satisfaction.

74. The twenty dolls

It took two hours for me to buy twenty dolls for Tanima's and Sarah's groups. I lost in bargaining to a lady in one store, so I had to go back to the first store and pay the higher price. But all together there were only twenty dolls, and I needed twenty-two.

What could I do? I said, "For the leaders, let me buy something else."

So Tanima and Sarah got stuffed animals instead of dolls.

75. A restaurant musician

The day we had our first concert in Caracas we went to a restaurant to eat afterwards. The music was so loud! After an hour and forty minutes, it still went on. When we were about to get dessert, I got the inspiration to play on the flute. For just a minute or so I played. The noise in the restaurant was unbearable, so no one heard me, but they saw me playing my flute and they showed me such respect! All the musicians stopped playing and they were asking me to play. So I started again. All the musicians remained silent while I played. God knows for how many hours they had been playing. So probably they needed rest!

76. A discount for big shots

In Puerto la Cruz we went to buy a chair. We saw a chair like the one I have in New York, but I didn't like the price. I wanted to bargain the price down, but the lady in the store wouldn't bargain, so we went to another store. There I liked a chair which was from Italy.

Shubhra said to the saleslady, "Can you lower the price?" Then Shubhra said, "This morning we were with President Lusinchi in Caracas."

The lady immediately lowered the price. She told us that when Saraswati and Savyasachi had been in another store they showed a pamphlet of me with some big shots. She happened to have been in that other store at that time. So she lowered the price even lower than Shubhra asked because I was a big shot.

77. A helpful lady

I am fond of bargaining. Whether I am an expert or not is a different matter.

I have all kinds of belts to liberate me from my back pain – white, blue, black, green – it is endless. Two days ago I saw a belt in a store window. I was about to enter into the store when a middle-aged lady came rushing up to me and said in English, "I see you will have trouble. Let me help you."

How did she know that I didn't speak Spanish? All right, very good! Then both of us entered into the store and she started talking to the lady there in English. She was so excited about trying to help me that instead of speaking Spanish, she started speaking English.

I said, "What are you doing? You are speaking in English!"

Then she started speaking Spanish, and she really helped me.

78. Buying a notebook

I went to the store in our hotel in Puerto La Cruz to buy a small notebook. The owner said, "The price is forty bolivars, but that is too much. You give me twenty. It is not even worth twenty, but I have to charge you twenty."

I said, "Fine," since I liked the cute notebook.

Then he said, "Are you the same gentleman that I see on the ring the ladies wear?"

I said, "Yes."

He said, "Oh, I saw you in the newspaper with the President."

I said, "I have seen all three presidents – the present one, the future one and the previous one."

The man said, "I am so happy and so honoured to meet you. Please tell me how your people support themselves if they always go around with you."

I said, "No, only for one month they have come here."

Then he asked me the significance of the sari. He said, "It is very beautiful. Where does it come from?"

I said, "India. I am Indian, and I like this Indian form of dress."

He said, "You have Indian skin, but your face is not Indian. You don't look like an Indian."

He was so happy, and he was shaking my hand. I wanted to buy two T-shirts for some disciples who had stayed home, so he said, "My hands are dirty. You please take them yourself."

79. The Italian restaurant

Yesterday I went to an Italian restaurant with Pahar and Tejiyan. The owner recognised me from the newspapers and showed me such respect. He didn't speak English, and Pahar's Spanish was really something! So we could not understand each other.

I asked for coffee with milk. He could not understand, and gave me coffee without milk. So Pahar and Tejiyan went outside and bought milk from a store. They said, "Leche," but their pronunciation! When the owner saw our milk he grabbed it and said, "No good!" Then he brought warm milk for the coffee.

The music was so loud! We said, "Can you not turn it down?" Then his worker went and turned it down. The owner came to our table two or three times to ask if the food was good. Then he kept staring at me; he was so curious! He couldn't speak to us and we couldn't speak to him, but he was so happy to have us in his restaurant.

80. Ketan's gift

At one place Bipin bought a T-shirt to give to Ketan. It had a picture of a toucan on it. I said, "It is so beautiful! I want to give it to Ketan." So Bipin bought it and I gave it!

81. Buying gold dumbbells

Savyasachi and I went to a sports store in Florida. Right at the counter were some 15-pound dumbbells. The man said they cost 36 dollars.

I asked, "Don't you have 25 pounds?"

The man said, "I don't now, but tomorrow I will be able to get them." He said they would cost 56 dollars.

The next day we did not go, but the day after that we went to see if they had gotten the 25-pound dumbbells. The man who had previously waited on me was not there. Another man came and said, "I will see if we have 25 pounds in stock." When he brought them, we asked the price. The man said, "It is 36 dollars for 25 pounds." We thought it was a mistake.

Then the other man came and said, "No, 56 dollars!" Then they had a serious argument. The nice man said, "I will take the responsibility." Luckily he was in charge, so we paid only 36 dollars for the 25-pound dumbbells.

82. Overpriced bookmarks

While I was shopping in Ft. Lauderdale, I saw a bookmark. It was a most ordinary-looking card that only said, "Dear God, I like you", but it cost 1.25 dollars. Then I saw another card that cost 2.25 dollars. It said, "Dear God, do You really care for me?"

I don't think even sincere God-seekers who believe in God will spend so much money for a bookmark, unless they live in the depression-world.

83. *God's exercise book*

While I was in a bookstore in Florida, I saw an exercise book by "God", telling how you can live for 100 years. It was written by George Burns, who played God in several movies.

In the bookstore I read and read quite a few pages. Unfortunately, I was not able to agree with "God's" recommendations, so I could not buy the book. Otherwise, I really wanted to buy the book by God telling how to live for 100 years.

84. *Shopping for a cello*

Kodanda took me to a music store to buy a cello. The owner of the store was an old man. He was very nice, but he was so old that I was afraid his soul had actually left the body. He looked as if his soul was in Heaven but his body was still here on earth.

I played on ten or twelve different cellos – cellos for 3,000 dollars, 4,000 dollars, 8,000 dollars, 10,000 dollars and 16,000 dollars. First the man said one particular cello was 6,000 dollars; then he said it was 8,000 dollars. So he was saying anything he wanted to say. I played on the 16,000 dollars cello secretly. Otherwise, I thought that perhaps it might not be allowed.

There were four or five that were not as good as the one that I have. Three or four were good. There was a little difference between the ones for 8,000 dollars and 16,000 dollars. You could hear that the higher-priced ones were sweeter.

Kodanda said later that to be in a room with me without any disciples made it the happiest day in his life. He was giving me the different instruments to try. He was the only boss.

85. The fabric store

I went to a fabric store this afternoon. As soon as I entered into the store, the owner showed me that he had *Silence Speaks,* my daily meditations, in his store. He said he was so happy to have *Silence Speaks* in his store, and I also was so happy.

He told Pahar that in one *Silence Speaks* picture – where I am feeding the lamb – I am more visible, while in the other pictures I am not at all visible. He showed me two pictures and said, "Here I recognise you, but there you are barely visible." For me it was all the same, but fortunately the right person was hearing it, since Pahar is the printer.

86. The Bengali film

I went to an Indian store and asked, "Do you have Bengali films?"

The man said, "Yes, we have one." I could tell that he came from South India.

I asked, "What is the name?"

He said, "Pohari."

I said, "There is no such word in Bengali."

He said, "Yes!"

I said, "I am Bengali."

He insisted, "There is that word."

So Baoul and I looked for *Pohari.* Finally Baoul found one called *Prahari.* "Prahari" means "guard".

I said to the man, "This is not your mother tongue, so it is easy to make a mistake."

He said, "I asked a Bengali about it."

I said, "I am sure he said 'Prahari', but perhaps he did not pronounce it carefully."

Then he was counting things in Tamil. I was amused, and I also started counting in that language. He looked at me, surprised. Then I told him that I had stayed in South India for twenty years.

87. The Lotus Inn

Yesterday I went to the Lotus Inn to eat. On the counter they have my *Silence Speaks*. The people recognised me immediately, and they came up to talk to me. They were extremely nice and respectful. Plus, they served us very quickly.

88. I care a lot

Yesterday I went to a stationery store. I saw a cute duck and I thought I would buy it for Chandika. I asked the man, "Is it a pin?"

The man said, "No, it is a magnet." Then he said, "This one is 2.45 dollars and the other one is 4.47 dollars."

I looked at him. He was a joker. I said, "Which one do you want me to buy?"

He said, "It depends on how much you care for the person. Do you care a lot?"

I said, "I care a lot."

He said, "Then buy the one for 4.47 dollars!" and he put it in my bag. Both were cute. The bigger one was just a little bigger, but it was 2 dollars more. To me it looked like a pin, but it was a magnet.

89. *The French flute*

The other day I was in Sam Ash Music Store here on Queens Boulevard. For the first time I saw a flute with holes in the keys. Of course, immediately I wanted to try it. The salesman asked me how many years I had been playing. I said, "Five years."

He laughed and said, "Five years is not enough. The French flute is much more difficult to play than an ordinary flute."

For a few minutes I struggled and struggled, and he laughed and laughed. Then he went to the other side of his store. In two or three minutes he came back again to the counter, and he saw that I was playing the flute. He couldn't believe his eyes and ears!

I played for five or ten minutes. He was so moved and he asked many questions about me. Then he asked for my autograph. He also had back trouble. Once when he bent down to get something, he could not get up. He was holding the counter and pressing with his arms to get up.

Leonard Bernstein once signed an autograph for him. He was so proud of Leonard Bernstein's autograph. I told him I had met with Leonard Bernstein. When I told him I had also had an interview with Pablo Casals, he couldn't believe it!

90. *Alap's tape*

I entered into a music store with Kalika in Washington to buy the music from the *Gandhi* film. The shopkeeper immediately came up to me to show me Alap's tape. That means not only did he recognise me, but also he knew that Alap is my student.

91. The five-dollar bill

In Los Angeles I went into a shop owned by some oriental people to buy a shaver. A little girl happened to be there. While I was giving the money to the shopkeeper, she was looking at me; she was so curious. Then I dropped a dime. The little girl picked up the dime and put it into a tiny wallet she had. She was so happy to take the dime.

Her mother asked her to return the money to me. I smiled and said, "Let her take it."

The mother said, "Yes. You are saying that just because it is only a dime! If it had been a dollar bill, would you have let her keep it?"

I said, "Whether it was a dollar bill or a five-dollar bill, I would let her keep it." Then I dropped a five-dollar bill, and the little girl took it.

I was looking at her mother, but she didn't ask the child to return it. When it was a dime, the mother asked her to return it. But when it was five dollars, the mother didn't say anything.

Still I have not been able to decide who was greater: the fool in me or the rogue in the little girl's mother!

44. *(p. 145)* 19 December 1982.
45. *(p. 145)* 29 December 1982.
46. *(p. 146)* 29 December 1982.
47. *(p. 146)* 29 December 1982.
48. *(p. 146)* 29 December 1982.
49. *(p. 147)* 4 January 1983.
50. *(p. 147)* 29 January 1983.
51. *(p. 148)* 12 February 1983.
52. *(p. 148)* 12 February 1983.
53. *(p. 149)* 12 February 1983.
54. *(p. 149)* 12 February 1983.
55. *(p. 150)* 12 February 1983.
56. *(p. 150)* 19 February 1983.
57. *(p. 151)* 6 March 1983.
58. *(p. 151)* 31 March 1983.
59. *(p. 152)* 2 April 1983.
60. *(p. 153)* 2 April 1983.
61. *(p. 153)* 2 April 1983.
62. *(p. 154)* 12 May 1983.
63. *(p. 155)* 12 May 1983.
64. *(p. 155)* 6 July 1983.
65. *(p. 156)* 6 July 1983.
66. *(p. 156)* 3 August 1983.
67. *(p. 157)* 3 August 1983.
68. *(p. 157)* 3 August 1983.
69. *(p. 158)* 19 September 1983.
70. *(p. 158)* 3 November 1983.
71. *(p. 161)* 5 November 1983.
72. *(p. 163)* 20 December 1983.
73. *(p. 163)* 20 December 1983.

74. *(p.163)* 31 December 1983.
75. *(p.164)* 31 December 1983.
76. *(p.164)* 2 January 1984.
77. *(p.165)* 7 January 1984.
78. *(p.165)* 8 January 1984.
79. *(p.166)* 8 January 1984.
80. *(p.167)* 14 January 1984.
81. *(p.167)* 26 January 1984.
82. *(p.167)* 27 January 1984.
83. *(p.168)* 29 January 1984.
84. *(p.168)* 31 January 1984.
85. *(p.169)* 3 February 1984.
86. *(p.169)* 3 February 1984.
87. *(p.170)* 26 February 1984.
88. *(p.170)* 17 March 1984.
89. *(p.171)* 3 May 1984.
90. *(p.171)* 27 May 1984.
91. *(p.172)* 5 August 1984.

I LOVE SHOPPING

BOOK 3

92. Advice from a fellow shopper

This afternoon I went to Woolworth's and bought a book that had answers to all kinds of questions. While I was in the store, a man came up to me and said, "Are you Sri Chinmoy?"

I said, "Yes," and I smiled at him.

He said, "I wish to give you a piece of advice: you run too much! I always see you running on 150th Street, on the Grand Central Service Road and at other places. At our age we should walk.

"I saw you the other day while I was walking. I tried to catch up with you to tell you not to run, but you ran ahead. I know you are not going to accept my advice. So keep up what you are doing."

What could I do? I thanked him profusely.

93. The jackfruit

In Australia, Kishore and Prashanta were running here and there looking for my favourite fruit – jackfruit. Finally Prashanta came and told me that they had found some. So I said, "Let me go and see."

When I saw the jackfruit, I wanted to buy some, but the store manager didn't want to sell any. Instead, he gave us three times as much as we wanted – free!

While we were eating the fruit, the manager came with three pieces of another kind of fruit, which he said was even more delicious than jackfruit. That also the manager wanted to give us free.

Then Kishore told him who I was, but the man said he already knew.

94. Meeting a friend

After I finished shopping on Jamaica Avenue, one of the boys was supposed to come and collect me. I waited and waited for the car, but it did not come. Finally, I started walking home, carrying a huge bag.

The manager of Marine Midland Bank noticed me walking by and knocked on the window, waving for me to come in. So I went into the bank and we talked. He told me his daughter is studying yoga in Sarama's class.

95. What do you want?

The other day I was in the White Plains Galleria with Victor. A man came up to me and said he had seen my picture in a Greenwich restaurant.

I told him, "The restaurant owner is my student."

Then the man said, "I understand you do many things for peace. What do you actually want for the world?"

I said, "I do not want or expect anything from the world. Only I want to become a better person."

Then I smiled and he also smiled. He looked like Nayak.

96. A German consciousness

I went into a store in Spain. A boy said, "Are you an Indian?"

I told him, "Yes!" Then I used my intuitive capacities and said, "And you have a German consciousness."

He said, "I was born in Cologne."

Then I asked him to write down Cologne the way they write it in German. He said his parents are from Spain, but his father worked in Germany for a few years and that is where he was born. He knew a little bit of German, and he started saying things in German.

I went out to search for some of our German boys who could talk to him, but by the time I found them, this little fellow had disappeared.

97. Mistaken identity

We went into a music shop in Essouira, Morocco. The man thought that I came from Morocco. Savyasachi said, "He is from India."

The man said, "No, he is Moroccan." Then he asked me, "Are you Muslim?"

I said, "No, I am Hindu."

He said, "Oh no, you are Muslim. I can see you are an Arab."

Then he asked me how old I was, and I told him. He told me that his father was 105 years old and showed us his picture. The father had been married five times and had twenty-one children.

Based on what he told us, the man in the store would be over forty years old. So jokingly I asked him, "Are you twenty-nine years old?"

He said, "Twenty-nine!" Then he took off his hat and showed me his bald head.

He was so nice to us. He was showing us all his instruments. He explained how one skin instrument immediately changes for the better when exposed to fire. Then he set fire to a piece of wood and put it over the skin frame, and it sounded so much better.

98. The football player

When I was shopping in the Souk, the market-place in Marrakesh, I was wearing a shirt of the national football team. Two times children placed footballs right in front of my feet, but I didn't have the heart to kick them. They thought I was a great football player.

99. Pulak's gift

Today on a street in Marrakesh, a lady was trying to sell Pulak a necklace. He said he didn't need it.

She said, "You need it. Please buy it as a gift."

So he paid her two dirham and took the necklace. Then he said, "This is now mine. So I want to give it to you." Then he gave her back the necklace.

This is how he got rid of the lady who was bothering him.

100. The Indian rogues

This morning I went to buy *jalabee* for Ranjana's birthday. At the counter they had broken pieces, while in one corner they had good ones. I said, "I would like to buy five pounds of the whole ones."

Whatever the price was, I gave it to the man. Then he wanted to give me the broken ones.

I said, "But I want the whole ones."

He said, "Oh, the taste is the same."

I said, "But my eyes won't appreciate them."

Then he looked at me and asked, "Are these for you or for somebody else?"

I said, "They are for somebody else."

He said, "Why didn't you tell me? All right, I will bring the other kind."

101. Bargaining for an exerciser

You know I like bargaining. While I was in Florida, we were buying an exerciser that cost around 139 dollars, but the man came down to 109 dollars.

I said, "Since you are so kind, can you not come down to 100 dollars?"

Then he said, "I am better than you – 99 dollars."

What an experience!

Then his wife said, "Please take your picture now, and when you lose weight with the help of our exerciser, send us another picture. Then we will keep both pictures here in our store so that people can see how much weight they can lose."

I was so amused, but I didn't have a camera with me.

102. Exploding into light

While I was in a music store, a young man came up to me and said, "Sri Chinmoy, a few years ago I went to one of your concerts and you played one Indian instrument very intensely. Afterwards, you chanted *Aum* five times. When you chanted Aum the fifth time, you exploded into white light. Later I told my experience to Fred Lebow, but he didn't believe me."

The young man asked me about the United Nations. He was speaking with such respect.

Then he admitted to me that he cannot tune any of his instruments. He said his workers tune them.

I said to him, "I can't tune my instruments either."

103. Pretending to cook

In Australia, Alo, Kishore and I went to an Indian restaurant. From the window we could see that all the food was already cooked.

When we went inside, they drew a screen around the kitchen so they could tell us that everything was being cooked fresh. They were delaying like anything – just pretending they were making it fresh.

After ten minutes I told them that we had already seen the food cooked and to please give it to us. They didn't deny it; they just laughed and gave us the food. Otherwise, they would have kept us waiting an hour, pretending that they were cooking it.

104. Projjwal's violin

In Germany, Projjwal and I went into a music store looking for a violin. They had one for 300 dollars, but it was very bad. I said, "Since the expensive one is so bad, show us one that is quite cheap."

The lady brought us one that cost 65 dollars. I liked it so much. I asked, "Can you give us an expensive bow?"

She said, "You don't get a bow." Then she gave me a rotten bow.

At first she couldn't find the case. Buy a violin, but there is no case! Finally she found one.

She knew English well, but all the time she was talking in German. Just as we were ready to go, she started speaking English. For four or five minutes she had to speak to us in English!

So this is how we got the violin that Projjwal bought me on his birthday.

105. Money does not talk

The next day we went to another music store and saw four or five most expensive violins. One that I was playing cost 1,200 dollars, but I was sorry I heard it.

I said, "This is as bad as my eighth-class disciples." The one Projjwal got me on his birthday was much better.

So money does not talk here!

106. Not for you, Swamiji!

I went into a video store and said, "I would like to buy a nice, spiritual Hindi movie."

The shopkeeper said, "For you, it will be free."

I said, "I don't take anything free."

He said, "We sell it for 12 dollars. For you, 10 dollars."

I said, "Fine."

There was one movie named *Trishul*. I said, "I have a student named Trishul, so I will take this one."

The man said, "Oh no, Swamiji. That is not for you!"

See how nice the shopkeeper was. He knew that it was a romantic movie. He was sincere.

107. Taking out the ghost

The last time I was in Germany, I went to a store to buy a French flute.

A man was playing a saxophone very loudly in the store. He was taking everybody's ghost out of the body!

108. Converting Canadian money

I went down to the lobby of our hotel in Quebec City to do some shopping. I bought lots of things, and it came to 115 dollars. I asked the lady, "Do you accept American money?"

She said, "Oh, sure."

I asked her to convert the total cost from Canadian dollars into American dollars.

She said, "It is 165 dollars."

I said, "How can it be?"

She said, "This is what the register says."

I was laughing, and she was getting mad at me. She asked me to wait for her supervisor.

I said, "I am ready to wait for your supervisor."

When he came, the supervisor apologised to me. He said, "She has just joined us. She doesn't know the difference between Canadian and American money."

Then, when the supervisor converted the cost, it became 85 dollars.

109. The taster

I went to a restaurant in Hawaii that lets you take whatever you want for a fixed price of 4.75 dollars. They had twenty items to choose from.

When I got to the cash register, the lady placed her hand on my shoulder and asked, "Are you going to pile your plate still higher?"

The plate was so small! Out of twenty items, I won't take a little of each?

Saraswati was behind me, but she didn't have the heart to insult the lady.

110. I am ready to pay!

At a bookstore in Hawaii, I wanted to buy so many books, including one of my own. The owner touched the register and said, "You please tell me what I should do. If I take money from you for your own book, I will be able to buy two more of your books. But if you don't pay me, I will not be able to buy those books."

I said, "Yes, I am ready to pay!"

Then he told me that I have a very big heart.

I bought 70 dollars or 80 dollars worth of books, and he had to tell me that only if I paid for my book would he be able to buy two more of my books!

111. Ten dollars for advice

In Hawaii I went to buy a dumbbell. The owner gave me advice for an hour and a half, so I gave him 10 dollars.

He asked me, "Why are you giving me this?"

I said, "You gave me advice for so long."

Then Savyasachi told him, "It is an Indian custom. The first customer gives money to the shopkeeper."

Afterwards, I told Savyasachi that it is just the opposite: it is the shopkeeper who gives a good price to the first customer of the day for good luck. In India you can go into a store at three or four o'clock in the afternoon, and they still say you are the first customer.

112. The broken clock

About a month ago I was in a store on 148th Street. The Spanish-speaking owner of the shop was trying to sell me a clock, but the clock was not working. He was telling me, "It will work at home."

I said, "Here it does not work, but it will work at home?"

He said, "Here I have not tried to fix it. But you have many people who can fix it for you. Then it will work."

I said, "No, I won't buy it if it is not working."

He said, "Then don't come into my shop anymore!"

I said, "Fine, I will not come into your shop."

Four or five days ago I happened to pass him on the street. He invited me to come into his shop, but I said no.

113. A toy for your children

It was raining heavily and I entered a little Chinese store where they sell all kinds of things. The owners were an old man and woman from Shanghai, who spoke broken English.

I was browsing and buying presents for some people. Then I stood on line to pay. Ahead of me were a few people.

A tall, young black man was standing by the register; his charge came to around 17 dollars. He handed the lady a bill and said very abruptly, "Keep the change." Then he quickly left the store.

The lady looked at the bill and saw that it was only a ten-dollar bill, not a twenty-dollar bill, so she came from behind the counter and ran after him, shouting and screaming in Chinese. Her husband also ran after him. But the man had his car right outside, and he just jumped in and drove away.

Everybody felt very sad. When I came up to the cash register, my charge came to 93 dollars. I wanted to give the old woman 7 dollars extra to make up for what the black man had done, but she did not want to take it.

I said, "But you are not charging me tax."

She said, "Oh no, I can't."

I insisted and finally she took it. Then she pushed a little toy car across the counter and said, "This is for your children."

So I was nice to her, and she was nice to me.

114. Jumping up like a young man

In Florida, I was buying a Chinese flute. The man asked for 80 dollars. When I looked at him, I felt that he would not live much longer – not even one month. So I gave him 100 dollars. Then he jumped up like a young man!

115. Sudden inspiration

Yesterday afternoon I was in a sports store in Japan, trying out weights and bowing down to the people in the store. Suddenly I got inspiration to write a new song about Japan.

Agraha and Kirit were the witnesses; those two gave me inspiration.

116. Faster than the fastest

Sudarshana was born in Kamakura. The first time I came to Japan, when she was a little girl, I took her to a shopping area. How fast she walked! She was a little girl, but she did everything faster than the fastest.

117. The cute monkey toy

At a store in Beppu, I saw a cute monkey toy which had a very good consciousness. I wanted to buy it, but there was nobody in the store. At least ten minutes I waited, but nobody came. The shop was wide open. Finally, I left without being able to get the toy.

118. The smiling girls

While shopping today in Oita, which is about an hour away from Beppu, I saw three young girls selling sticky candy. God knows what those girls saw in me, but they started smiling and smiling at me. They would put two or three candies inside the package, and then they would look at me and smile.

They didn't know English and I didn't know Japanese, but they were saying so many things to me!

119. Department store music

In a department store in Fukuyama, they were playing music on the ground floor. I did not like the music they were playing, so I said, "Let me go to another floor."

I kept going from floor to floor thinking that that particular floor wouldn't have music. But there was music on each floor. I am such a fool!

120. The nice shopkeeper

In one store in Beppu, the man was so nice that I bought something even though I didn't want it. In American stores, sometimes the people are so rude that even if you want something, you don't buy it!

I went to that store three or four times to buy different things because the man was so nice.

121. The laughing shopkeeper

In an instrument store in Kyoto, I was looking at an expensive trumpet. The shopkeeper was laughing at me because I couldn't play it. Usually the Japanese don't laugh like that!

Then I went away and came back again. As soon as he saw me, the man started laughing again. I said, "I am going to get the sound." Finally I made some sound and he was so happy. Then I bought it.

122. The Bengali film

I went into a video store in Queens. The owner was a Gujarati who had lived in Calcutta for many years. So we talked in Bengali about many, many things. Then I asked him if he had any Bengali films. He said, "Many, many!"

I said, "Please give me a spiritual one."

He gave me one about Lord Shiva's sacred place in the Himalayas. I believed him when he said it was in perfect Bengali, so I bought it.

When I watched the film, it was not in Bengali at all. It was in Hindi – and with a silly actor whom I do not like.

Vinaya went and got another one, but it was very undivine. And this was from the same man that I was talking to about spiritual things!

123. Kakali's change

While driving from Dhaka to Chittagong, we stopped in the town where Chittagong's greatest poet was born. We went to a restaurant named Kakali, which means "the chirping of the birds".

The price of the meal came to 55 rupees. I didn't have a five-rupee or a ten-rupee note; I had only fifty-rupee notes.

I said, "I have only fifty-rupee notes. Here are two fifty-rupee notes."

The man saw that I gave him 100 rupees. Then he went to the cashier, only five metres away, and brought me back a five-rupee note as change.

I was so surprised and shocked. I said, "I gave you 100 rupees. You should give me 45 rupees change."

He said, "No, you gave me sixty rupees, one fifty and one ten."

Then I told him in pure Bengali that I had given him 100.

124. The half-priced lassi

In Calcutta I went to a restaurant and asked for a *lassi*. On the bill the waiter gave me, it said "5 Rs."

So I went to the owner and said, "Five rupees for one glass?"

The owner said, "Who has given you this?"

I pointed to the waiter. The man said, "Oh, he cannot have been mistaken. He has been working here for fifty years."

In Bengali the words for fifty and fifteen are very different, so definitely the man said fifty years.

Then I looked at the waiter and said, "Tell me how old you are."

The waiter said, "I am twenty-one."

I said, "You are twenty-one, but you have been working here for fifty years! You deserve five rupees."

As I was coming out of the restaurant, the owner called me and said, "Since I was mistaken, you have to give me only half the price." Then he gave me three rupees back.

125. The two owners

At one place I wanted to buy three saris. They had their price and I had my own figure. They were asking for 300 rupees and I said, "130!"

They said that in their lifetime they had never sold any sari for 130 rupees.

I said, "Then do it this time. You will remember it."

We were talking in Bengali. Then the old man I was talking to came down to 240. Inwardly I was hesitating a little, but outwardly, in my eyes, he could not see my hesitation. I said, "No, I don't want it!"

Finally, he said, "All right." Then one of his workers got mad at him for coming down so drastically. The other man said, "He is not the owner. I am the owner."

Then the old man said, "No, I am the owner!"

At the time, I was thinking that maybe I would go up to 140 or 170. But when the giggling started, I decided I was not going to go up in price because their egos were fighting.

Finally I went to another store and began browsing. The old man from the first store came up to me and said, "I am the owner."

I said, "What difference does it make if you can't sell the saris at the price we agreed on?"

He said, "No, I will be able to sell them to you at that price."

We went back to his store. I thought that the other man would be furious, but he said, "This fellow is telling me that he has agreed to sell you these saris for 130 rupees. So what can I do?"

So I got the saris for 130 rupees.

126. *Sympathy defeats temptation*

In Calcutta a young man about twenty years old was selling handkerchiefs on the street right behind our hotel. He said, "If you buy a dozen, I will give you one free."

I asked him, "If I buy five dozen, will you give me five free?"

He said, "Of course." He was insulting me in Bengali as if I didn't know Bengali.

He counted out twelve and then started counting out the second dozen. I said, "I won't get one free?"

He said, "No, let me first count out five dozen."

After he had counted out the second dozen, he felt sorry for me and he added one extra to the pile.

I said, "Now you are supposed to give me two."

Again he said, "No, I will give them to you later."

After he had counted out five dozen, I said, "Now you have to give me four more."

He said, "No, I was just tempting you! I will give you only one extra."

I said, "Then I don't want any."

He said, "No, you should feel sympathy for me because it took such a long time to count out five dozen."

So sympathy won over temptation, and I got only one extra.

I LOVE SHOPPING

127. The short two metres

This is a story about Calcutta deception. I went to a store to buy cloth to be made into trousers. I selected four or five materials and said, "Please give me two metres of each one."

Then I went browsing in the store. When I was ready to pay, I asked again if they had cut off two metres and they said that they had.

The following day when I took the material to a tailor in Pondicherry, he said, "How can I make trousers for you? This material is not even one metre seventy-five centimetres."

128. The friendly discount

In Pondicherry I went to a sari store whose owner had been my classmate in the ashram. We had studied together for five or six months.

He immediately recognised me when I came in. Then he started insulting his workers mercilessly so that he could show me who was the boss. He was insulting them without rhyme or reason!

Suddenly he got a phone call from his house about some emergency, and he went away on his motorbike.

After I finished shopping, the bill came to 1,100 rupees. My friend's assistant said, "Since you two are good friends, I am sure the boss will reduce the price. So do not fill in the amount on the cheque. Just take the material and tomorrow I will ask him what discount to give you."

I said to myself, "I didn't ask for a discount. He is such a nice fellow."

The following day I was shopping in the same area, so I went into the store and asked the assistant if he had spoken to the boss.

He said, "My boss didn't come back to work. But you don't have to worry. He knows your brother Chitta so well."

I said, "For God's sake, take the 1,100 rupees. Then I don't have to worry." But he insisted that I not fill in the amount on the cheque.

Two hours later, while still shopping in the area, I saw my friend on his motorbike. I shouted to him, "For God's sake, tell me the reduction on the things I have got from your store so that I can pay."

He said, "I already told them this morning."

When I got home, I said to my brother, "This fellow is such a liar. Now you have to go there."

So my brother went to the store with 1,100 rupees. When he saw that they were going to give me a reduction of only 23 rupees, he got mad. He said, "You keep your 23 rupees. We will not take any reduction at all."

There the story does not end. Afterwards, my brother said, "I tell you, you will definitely get the same saris much cheaper in other stores."

So I took one of the saris I had bought and found almost the identical sari for less than half the price at another store. At my friend's store I paid 89 rupees, and in this store it was only 43. I couldn't believe that I had bought so many saris from my friend for twice the amount that other stores were selling them for.

129. *The rickshaw driver*

In Pondicherry, a rickshaw driver became my friend. He lived near our family's house, and each day he would take me around for an hour or two when I went shopping. I told him, "You have Mother's picture on your rickshaw, so you can't deceive me."

When I go out, usually I leave my bag with my passport and all my American money inside the house. On one particular day, a new maid was working in the house and my sister had to go somewhere. Since the lock on the safe is not satisfactory, she took out the bag and went looking for me. I said, "Since the lock is not good, let me take the bag with me while I go shopping."

So I went shopping for saris. Then I realised that I didn't have the bag with me. I had left it in the rickshaw!

The driver and I had agreed to meet at a fixed place. But, O God, when I came to that place, the rickshaw driver was nowhere to be found! I was looking this side and that side for him. Finally, I saw him sleeping on the front of the rickshaw, waiting in the shade about seventy or eighty metres away.

I asked him, "Where is my bag?"

He answered, "It is on the seat in the back. You didn't take it with you."

Since he had been fast asleep, somebody easily could have come and taken the bag out of the rickshaw, or out of curiosity the driver could have looked in the bag. But when I looked inside the bag, everything was just as I had left it.

Rickshaw drivers get two rupees per hour, so I was supposed to give him three or four rupees. Instead I gave him a fifty-rupee note. He couldn't believe it.

130. Encounter with an old teacher

One day, while I was shopping in the Pondicherry market, an elderly lady placed her hand on my shoulder and said, "Hi, Chinmoy!"

O my God, I was so embarrassed. I didn't recognise her at all.

She was so surprised that I didn't recognise her. She said, "I am Coo-Coo's mother."

Coo-Coo is the nickname for Vinay Verma, the Deputy Ambassador of India to the United Nations. We were brought up together and for a year his mother had taught me English.

She said she was able to recognise me because Vinay Verma had sent her a picture taken of the two of us at our recent meeting in Queens. So she recognised me, but I could not recognise her.

Then she begged me to come to her house. I wanted to go, but as usual, five or ten people were at our house waiting for me. Always so many people come to our house when I am there. I have so many things to tell them and they have so many things to tell me – endless stories!

131. The undivine son

In Bombay I went to buy more handkerchiefs. While in the store, I told the shopkeeper about the man who tempted me with extra handkerchiefs in Calcutta.

The Bombay shopkeeper used undivine words about the fellow in that story. Then he asked me where I came from. I said, "I am from Bengal, but I live in America."

He said, "My son lives in Manhattan."

I said, "Tell me your son's name. In Manhattan many people know me."

He said, "My son is not leading a good life, so I do not want to give you his name."

I said, "You can tell him about me."

He said, "You seem to be a very nice man. I don't want to tell you his name, and I don't want to tell him your name."

Then I bought the handkerchiefs from him. The price was cheaper than what I had paid the man in Calcutta who gave me only one extra.

132. Surrendering to insults

In Bombay I was buying picture frames. For two or three frames I was bargaining and bargaining. God knows, the man insulted me with his price, and I insulted him with my price!

Finally I had to surrender to his insults because I liked the picture frames so much.

133. Airport deception

Always I go to the airport early to buy things or to eat. On the trip to India, I ate so much and gained four or five pounds. This time I went to a restaurant in the Bombay airport to have a little juice and some Horlicks, a hot drink.

The man told me the price – five dollars. Indian rupees they do not accept – only American dollars or British pounds. I had Indian currency, but the only American currency I thought I had was a hundred-dollar bill. So before I ate, I asked the man if he would be able to give me change.

The man said, "Yes, easily!"

When it was time to pay, I looked in my bag and found both a hundred-dollar and a twenty-dollar bill. I said, "I can give you a twenty-dollar bill."

The man said, "No, you give me the hundred-dollar bill. I will be able to give you change."

He took the hundred-dollar bill, and then he gave me a ten-dollar bill in return. He was looking for more money, but be had only three one-dollar bills.

I said, "Give me back my hundred-dollar bill and take my twenty-dollar bill."

What kind of rogue God created! He said I hadn't given him a hundred-dollar bill. He said I had only given him the twenty.

My blood boiled! I said, "I am calling the police!" and started to walk away.

Then he gave me my hundred dollars back. I had got thirteen dollars from him in change, and he was supposed to give me two more dollars, but I just called him a rogue and threw my twenty dollars at him.

Then I left the place, absolutely furious. Even now when I tell the story, I feel such disgust for rogues like this.

134. The problem sweater

Since there were no shops open in Berlin when I went out walking this morning, I went into the hotel shop when I came back. I bought a magazine.

Then I saw a sweater that cost 1,000 marks. I said, "Expensive!"

The saleslady said, "First of all, it is expensive. Second, it is for ladies!"

The sweater was not in the men's section.

135. The garlic bread

Yesterday I went to a Greek deli and asked for garlic bread.

The man asked, "Where do you come from?"

I said, "From India."

He said, "That's why you speak like that."

Then I asked him, "Where do you come from?"

He said, "From Greece."

So I said, "We are brothers, we are brothers!"

He was finding fault with my pronunciation of "garlic". But he himself was speaking broken English.

When I first came to America, I used to feel a little sad when people could not understand me. But now I don't have to repeat words like "magnificent" and "table" because people understand me. Americans may criticise me, but the British – even children – don't have any problem understanding me.

In Scotland I find it very difficult to understand the people. Three or four times I have to ask them what they are saying. It is too much, too much!

NOTES TO I LOVE SHOPPING, BOOK 3

92. *(p. 177)* 19 July 1984.
93. *(p. 177)* 6 October 1984.
94. *(p. 178)* 4 November 1984.
95. *(p. 178)* 1 December 1984.
96. *(p. 178)* 19 December 1984.
97. *(p. 179)* 31 December 1984.
98. *(p. 180)* 7 January 1985.
99. *(p. 180)* 9 January 1985.
100. *(p. 180)* 1 February 1985.
101. *(p. 181)* 19 February 1985.
102. *(p. 181)* 18 March 1985.
103. *(p. 182)* 23 March 1985.
104. *(p. 182)* 2 April 1985.
105. *(p. 183)* 2 April 1985.
106. *(p. 183)* 19 May 1985.
107. *(p. 183)* 25 May 1985.
108. *(p. 184)* 9 June 1985.
109. *(p. 184)* 8 July 1985.
110. *(p. 185)* 8 July 1985.
111. *(p. 185)* 8 July 1985.
112. *(p. 186)* 3 August 1985.
113. *(p. 186)* 3 August 1985.
114. *(p. 187)* 29 October 1985.
115. *(p. 187)* 17 December 1985.
116. *(p. 187)* 17 December 1985.
117. *(p. 188)* 22 December 1985.
118. *(p. 188)* 27 December 1985.
119. *(p. 188)* 29 December 1985.
120. *(p. 189)* 29 December 1985.
121. *(p. 189)* 13 January 1986.

122. *(p. 189)* 4 February 1986.
123. *(p. 190)* 1 March 1986.
124. *(p. 190)* 1 March 1986.
125. *(p. 191)* 2 March 1986.
126. *(p. 192)* 1 March 1986.
127. *(p. 193)* 1 March 1986.
128. *(p. 193)* 2 March 1986.
129. *(p. 194)* 2 March 1986.
130. *(p. 195)* 2 March 1986.
131. *(p. 196)* 2 March 1986.
132. *(p. 197)* 2 March 1986.
133. *(p. 197)* 2 March 1986.
134. *(p. 198)* 7 June 1986.
135. *(p. 198)* 2 November 1986.

I LOVE SHOPPING

BOOK 4

136. Woodstock flutes

There is a lady in Woodstock who has so many little, little crafts in her store. She also sells super-excellent flutes. After trying out two flutes, I told her the one I liked. Then she said, "I have a special surprise for you. It is a gift." She told me that Tanima had given her money to get a flute for me, and she had kept it aside. After I played on Tanima's flute, I saw that it was the best.

Anupadi had also gotten me a gift from that store. So I wanted to give the lady some money so that Tanima and Anupadi could get gifts for themselves the next time they came in.

I trusted the lady, but she insisted on giving me a receipt.

137. Saral's brother

Yesterday I went to a store in Santiago, Chile, and bought an umbrella. The man in the store talked and looked so much like Saral that I couldn't believe it. He was showing me such devotion – just like Saral.

He was one hundred per cent Saral's brother!

138. Tanima's jacket

Yesterday I was shopping in Valdivia, Chile. I was looking at a jacket in a store window when all of a sudden Tanima's soul came to me and said, "Pretty!"

I asked her soul, "Is it the right size?"

The soul didn't know. So I went inside the store and saw the price was 5,500. I always bargain; it is an Indian tradition. But how could I bargain, since I didn't speak Spanish? So I wrote down 5,500 on a piece of paper, then crossed out the first 5 and wrote in 4. So it went on. The owner smiled at me and I smiled at her. Finally I bought the jacket.

139. The broken wristwatch

I found a store in Valdivia that had a very peculiar and funny wristwatch. I said, "I will buy it for Victor."

But the wristwatch did not work. I knew that I could ask Dhanu to fix it, but the man did not want to sell me a broken wristwatch.

140. The yogurt lover

It takes such a long time to buy things in Chile because you have to write down what you want. I went into a restaurant to buy 100 cups of yogurt, but they thought I wanted only twenty cups.

I tried to show them that I wanted five times twenty, but they thought I wanted just five.

Finally I took out the eighteen or nineteen yogurts that were there and then asked for more. Then at last they understood.

141. The soundless flute

I went into a music store in Lima to buy a flute. I was trying a particular flute, but I could not make any sound.

Then the saleslady said she would show me how to play it. She was so happy and proud to show me, but she could not make any sound either.

142. Lost in Lima

I was told by a disciple that there is a particular street in Lima that sells lots of musical instruments. So Agraha, Savyasachi and I went looking for it. When we came to a one-way street, Agraha and I got out of the car, and I told Savyasachi to drive around and meet us from the other direction.

After walking a few blocks, Agraha asked someone in Spanish if there were some music stores on that side of the block. The person said it was on the other side of the block and in the other direction – on Emancipation Street.

I decided to walk three or four blocks in that direction while Agraha continued looking in the original direction. After six or eight blocks my legs were hurting, so I turned around and started coming back.

After going several blocks, something within me instigated me to look across the street at a pastry shop, even though I had no inclination to eat. As soon as I looked, I saw Emancipation Street. It was only half a block away from where I had started fifteen or twenty minutes before!

But there were no instrument stores there. I wanted to go back to the hotel, but no taxi would stop for me. Finally, when one did stop and ask me where I wanted to go, I didn't know the name of our hotel. I said, "Miramar," but the driver said there was no such hotel. I told him I would give him directions, but he didn't trust me. So he wouldn't take me.

Suddenly I saw Agraha and Savyasachi, so I was saved.

When you are lost, each minute is torture. How many taxis passed by without stopping! And when one did stop, I couldn't tell the driver the destination.

143. Language problems

I went into one store just as it was about to close. I was pointing to what I wanted to buy, but I could not speak Spanish and the shopkeeper could not understand me. Such an expensive thing I would have bought, but she could not help me. What could I do?

144. Savyasachi's compassion

I was at the Indian market in Lima for such a long time. The shopkeepers would say one price and I would say another.

Savyasachi has more compassion than I do. I wanted to buy something, but I could not get the price I wanted. So I went away without buying it. But Savyasachi thought I liked it, so he went back and got it for me.

145. Flattery pays off

In another store I wanted to buy a pillow case. The lady said 65 and I said 40.

Then I flattered her and said, "You speak such good English!"

The lady was so happy that she gave me the pillow case for 40.

146. So nice!

In one store Saraswati and I looked around but didn't buy anything. Then we went out.

After we had walked about a block, the owner of the store came running after us to tell us that there was another place that might have what we wanted. She was so nice!

147. The llamas with beautiful eyes

In one store they had toy llamas with such beautiful eyes. The two small ones had such compassion. I looked at them and meditated and meditated. Then I felt sorry for the llamas, so I bought six.

148. Buying gifts

Since Mahasamrat has a connection with Peru, I got him a huge jacket. From small they went to large; medium sizes they didn't have.

I also got a nice sweater for myself. The price was 350. I liked it and didn't want to waste time bargaining. So I said 300 and just took it.

I bought so many presents for people who didn't come on the Trip.

149. The coffee shop

It seems that everywhere I go, people recognise me. Today I went into Manhattan with Vinaya to buy some saris. Garima was also with us. At one point we went into a coffee shop, and I asked Garima to get me a grilled cheese and a piece of pizza.

The restaurant was worse than the worst, darker than the darkest. We only stopped there because I was so hungry. The first floor was very narrow and seated only three or four persons, so I went upstairs to see if there were any empty seats.

Two young girls were eating there. As soon as they saw me, one of them said, "Sri Chinmoy is here."

The other girl said, "Oh, Sri Chinmoy wouldn't come here!"

I smiled at the one who recognised me.

The grilled cheese Garima got was very bad, and the pizza she didn't buy because she didn't understand my English. So we went across the street to an Indian restaurant, Delhi Palace. They were so fast. It didn't take them ten minutes to bring our food.

150. *A Heavenly majesty*

Recently I went to a store in Queens. The owner, who is an Indian, said, "I saw you playing music in Vancouver at the end of last year."

I was wearing my track suit, so I said, "Now I am in this uniform."

He said, "No matter what you wear, you have a Heavenly majesty."

151. *Unknown in Jamaica*

On our Christmas Trip in South America, people often recognised me on the street. In one store, the owner said, "My friend, I saw you on television." But his wife didn't believe that I was his friend.

On another occasion, I went looking for flutes with Saraswati. She went into one shop and when she came back to the car, a young girl came running out of the shop just to see me.

But at an Indian store here in Jamaica, the saleslady did not know me at all. When I went inside, she asked me, "Are you with the Hare Krishna movement?"

I said, "No, I have my own."

She said, "You?"

I told her my name but she had not heard it before. She said, "Oh no, I know only about Hare Krishna."

The store was right here in Jamaica, and she did not know me! Databir was one hundred per cent sure that he had a brochure about me in his car, but he could not find it. So what could I do?

152. You are so blessed

Many years ago in Puerto Rico, I was looking at Bhakti Vedanta's picture on the wall of his students' restaurant. God knows why, but I had to tell the lady at the register that I knew him well.

She said, "You are so blessed." Then she called over the other workers and said, "He saw our Master. He is so blessed."

Bhakti Vedanta used to come to the Indian Consulate when I was working there.

153. Buying one fish

When I was in St. Louis, I wanted to get Nilima a present because she did not come on the Trip. I saw two fish, but one was black, so I took only the other one to the counter.

The man said to me, "They are a set. You have to buy both of them."

I said, "No, I don't want the other one because it is black."

The man said, "They are salt and pepper shakers. You don't want to use both salt and pepper?"

I said, "No, I am not going to use it for that."

He asked, "What will you use it for?"

I told him, "I am going to use it as an incense burner."

The man said, "You will have to pay the full price even if you only take one."

So I said I would pay. But when I took out my money, he said, "All right, I'll charge you only for one."

154. Now you are so strong!

Two days ago I went to buy some birds at a pet store in Queens. A few years ago I used to go to that store very often, but I have not been there recently.

While I was looking at two birds, Databir told the owner about my 7,000-pound one-arm lift and gave the man a poster.

Finally, I bought the two birds. When I came up to the man to pay, he said, "You look twenty years younger than when I last saw you. Now you are so strong!"

155. The affectionate dog

Victor, Vinaya and I went to a store. There was a very nice dog in the store, but it didn't pay any attention to either Victor or me. It immediately went over to Vinaya and started licking his feet very affectionately.

156. Trying to buy sushi

Today I went to buy sushi for Lucy's birthday. It took fifteen minutes to make them understand what I wanted. My Indian English they didn't understand. What could I do?

157. Buying an instrument in Japan

In Japan, Maral told me that he had found an instrument that he thought I might like. He said, "Guru, it is very expensive, but if you like it, I will buy it for you." But I didn't like the instrument, so I told him not to buy it.

The store also had some Western flutes. I said, "I would like to buy one," but the man wouldn't allow me to try the flutes because they were too expensive.

I said, "Without examining the flute or playing it, how can I buy it?"

The man said, "No, good musicians don't need to play the flutes. I won't allow it."

We had pamphlets that said I play the flute at my concerts, but the man couldn't read English. So we went to another store and found a Yamaha keyboard. I said, "Maral, just buy it."

Then I left the place and Maral bought it.

158. The advantage of being short

Two days ago Victor and I went shopping. At one spot, they were unloading things from a truck, and there was a rail blocking the sidewalk. I was about to go out into the street to walk around the rail.

Victor was smiling at me. Then he just walked right under the rail.

I said, "See, there is an advantage to being short!"

159. Two nice persons

Yesterday I went to a store that sells medallions and trophies. This was my second visit there. The owner knows all about us because we always buy prizes for our marathons from him. His name is Joe.

I bought seven or eight trophies and some small medallions. I also bought a trophy for Databir because he had stood first in our tennis competition.

The bill came to 45 dollars. I said, "How can it be so low? I could never buy so many things from any other store for this price!"

Joe said, "It is because I have a soft heart for Sri Chinmoy."

I said, "All right, your soft heart has touched my soft heart." So instead of 45 dollars, I gave him 70 dollars, since seven is one of my lucky numbers.

The man wanted to know how I could jump from 45 dollars to 70 dollars, but I forced him to take the 70 dollars. Then he told me that since he is Catholic, one of the disciples had promised to give him a picture of me with the Pope. I said, "I will make sure that he keeps his promise."

See how two persons can be nice!

160. *The Pope's picture*

The manager of the Marine Midland Bank told his wife that I had met the Pope and that I was going to present him with an autographed picture.

His wife didn't believe that I would sign the picture for him.

The manager begged me to autograph the picture so he could prove to his wife that we are friends.

161. *The author*

I often go to a bookstore across from the Jamaica Savings Bank. The owner has known me for a long time, but to him I was just a customer. He had never been particularly interested in me.

Today when I went there, right on the front of his desk I saw *Beyond Within* and *Eastern Light for the Western Mind*.

I said, "These are my books."

He said, "Heh!"

I said, "Yes."

He asked, "You are the author?"

I was wearing shorts and he was looking at me as though he didn't believe me.

Then he started asking me questions, and we talked for ten minutes.

I told him I wanted a daily prayer book. He found one and gave it to me. He said, "I will give you a little discount. I will sell it to you for eleven dollars."

So I took out a ten-dollar bill and a single, but he gave me the one back and said, "Please come back again and again. I like to talk to you!."

I have been there so many times, but this is the first time that this has happened.

162. Memories of Bloomingdale's

I went shopping with Databir today at Bloomingdale's in Manhattan. When I used to work at the Indian Consulate, every day I would go to a small post office in Bloomingdale's to mail passports for the Consulate. There was a black man who worked there, and each time he saw me he used to beg me to come to his church and listen to the sermon of his minister. He was very nice to me, but unfortunately I never went to his church.

163. The proof

About two or three months ago, on the way back from the airport, Nishtha took me to a store that only sells books about the Bible. A black lady came into the store and said that she knew me. In order to prove it, she showed me an aphorism that she had taken from Annam Brahma and was keeping in her bag. She said, "Here is the proof that I know you."

164. Another George Bernard Shaw

I went into a bookstore that sold many spiritual books. I was very happy to see some books written by friends of mine in India, so I got four or five books.

At the counter I appreciated the bookstore like anything. Then I had to become another George Bernard Shaw: I had to ask if they had any books by Sri Chinmoy.

The man at the counter said, "Yes, there are many books by Sri Chinmoy." Then he took me to one of the shelves, but none of my books were there. He said, "Definitely they were there."

He said they sell my books, but that they were out of stock. He told me they get my books from India.

Then I introduced myself and said, "You don't get them from India. Our Aum Publications sells them."

They were so moved to meet me and asked for my autograph.

165. The bookstore owner

After I left the spiritual bookstore, I went downstairs to a musical instrument store. I was playing on a violin when an elderly lady came up to me with folded hands. I asked her if she wanted anything.

She said, "I did not see you when you were upstairs. I am the owner of the bookstore. I came here from down the street to see you."

It was raining so heavily outside, but she had come into the music store just to see me. For her to go out in such weather was really something! She was standing in front of me so devotedly with folded hands.

166. The little bargainer

In Singapore I went into a camera shop to buy a camera case. A little girl about nine or ten was taking care of me. I asked her the price of one bag. She said it was 28 Singapore dollars, so I said, "Fine."

Then she said to me, "No, it is 25 dollars." I did not pay any attention to her because I was looking at other bags. Suddenly she said to me, "Why are you not buying the first bag? It is only 27 dollars."

I looked at her and thought I had made a mistake. Perhaps she had not told me that it was 25 dollars. Otherwise, how could it be 27 dollars now? I continued browsing, looking at other bags.

She said, "No, these other bags are very expensive. You take this one. It is 28 dollars."

Finally I said, "Am I deaf? How could the price go up?"

The little girl said, "Did I tell you 25 dollars?"

I said, "You told me 25 dollars, 27 dollars and 28 dollars."

She said, "All right, if I said 25 dollars, then you can have it for 25 dollars."

Then, when I gave her 25 dollars, she gave me back a dollar in change. She was great!

167. Three becomes four

In another store in Singapore, I was looking at some shirts imported from Hawaii. After I had selected three shirts, a little boy came up to me and said, "You will be sorry."

I said, "Why?"

He said, "You need extra-large, not large."

I said, "No, I am a large."

But he took the trouble of getting the same shirts that I had selected – only in extra-large.

I asked, "Is there no place for me to try on these shirts to see which size fits me?"

He replied, "Yes, you can go there. But take both sizes."

So I took one large and one extra-large to try on. The large size fit me perfectly. It was even a little long. I came back and told him, "The large fits me."

The boy said, "Now that you have won, will you not buy one more shirt?"

I said, "Definitely I will buy one more." Originally I had selected three shirts; but because I won, it became four.

168. Shopping video

While I was shopping in Padang, Indonesia, Niriha was following me and recording everything on her video camera. In five or six stores she took video. In the last store she took video of me bargaining. In the beginning the price was 200, but in the end it came down to 100.

Then, when I went into an Indian music store to buy two flutes, Niriha disappeared. I suspected that the owners were Tamil. Then all of a sudden the wife spoke to her husband in Tamil, asking him to give Agraha and me a chair.

Immediately I started speaking my Tamil. If Niriha had stayed to video, she could have got my Tamil voice. We were looking for Niriha, but that was the time she was missing!

169. Fighting in the store

Today I was bargaining in one store in Bukittinggi. The saleslady held up her hand twice, and I thought she wanted two times 500 or 1,000 rupiah. I said, "No, 200."

I said to myself, "I will fight!"

Finally I said, "I will pay 500 rupiah," and I gave the lady 500. Then she returned 200 to me.

At first I thought I may have given her 5,000 rupiah by mistake, but it was 500. So I was fighting for more than she was asking for!

170. Vijali's immediate luck

In Bukittinggi, I was bargaining to buy a synthesizer. The man in the store was coming down only 2,500 rupiah, so I did not want to get it.

I told Savyasachi to take Vijali there to bargain with them some more. She has immediate luck.

The synthesizer has one setting that sounds like a violin and another that sounds like a harpsichord. With my Yamaha, I have to push several buttons in order to make these sounds.

171. The silent Brahma

In some stores the people are nice; they are ready to bargain. In other stores, whatever price they say is all they will take – finished!

In one store I was bargaining and bargaining. The man in the store would write down one price, but I did not understand his writing, so I would write down another price. It never ended. Finally I bought two items and left.

Then I decided to go back and buy a third item – a T-shirt for Raghu. I said to myself, "I am not going to bargain this time. Whatever price the man asks for, I will give."

The man said, "5,000 rupiah."

I became the silent Brahma and said, "All right."

The man couldn't believe his ears. When I gave him 5,000, he returned 2,000 to me. That was a nice experience.

172. Special greeting

Every day when I am on my way to the shopping area in Bukittinggi, some little boys see me. They greet me by saying, "Good morning, Air India!"

173. A great performance

When I went into a flute store in Bukittinggi, Dhanu and a few other disciples also came in the store, and they were listening while I was trying out different flutes. Dhanu was supplying me with flutes, and I was trying to see which ones were good.

The owner was also selecting flutes for me. He wanted to show me how they sounded, so he was playing as loudly as possible. Meanwhile, I was trying to play in my civilised way. So the owner and I were giving a great performance!

Finally I selected two flutes. The man used two Hindi words, so I started talking to him in Hindi. But he could not speak Hindi; he knew only two words and used them because I was an Indian.

The man asked for 10,000 rupiah for the two flutes, and I offered 5,000. The man said 7,000 and I was a little bit disappointed. Then Dhanu took out 5,000 from his wallet. I could see that the man was ready to accept 5,000, but he was not taking it. Finally, he agreed and took the money.

I thought the transaction was over, so I took out 10,000 rupiah to pay Dhanu back. When the man saw my 10,000 rupiah, he thought it was for him. Then he didn't want to sell the flutes for 5,000 and started asking for 10,000 again. What kind of problems I created!

Finally, I said that I wouldn't pay more than 5,000, and Dhanu asked for his money back. Then the man accepted our price.

NOTES TO I LOVE SHOPPING, BOOK 4

136. *(p. 205)* 11 December 1986.
137. *(p. 205)* 23 December 1986.
138. *(p. 205)* 2 January 1987.
139. *(p. 206)* 2 January 1987.
140. *(p. 206)* 3 January 1987.
141. *(p. 206)* 7 January 1987.
142. *(p. 207)* 7 January 1987.
143. *(p. 208)* 8 January 1987.
144. *(p. 208)* 13 January 1987.
145. *(p. 208)* 13 January 1987.
146. *(p. 208)* 13 January 1987.
147. *(p. 209)* 13 January 1987.
148. *(p. 209)* 13 January 1987.
149. *(p. 209)* 12 February 1987.
150. *(p. 210)* 5 March 1987.
151. *(p. 210)* 12 June 1987.
152. *(p. 211)* 2 July 1987.
153. *(p. 211)* 2 July 1987.
154. *(p. 212)* 4 July 1987.
155. *(p. 212)* 18 September 1987.
156. *(p. 212)* 18 September 1987.
157. *(p. 212)* 30 October 1987.
158. *(p. 213)* 30 October 1987.
159. *(p. 213)* 30 October 1987.
160. *(p. 214)* 30 October 1987.
161. *(p. 214)* 18 November 1987.
162. *(p. 215)* 18 November 1987.
163. *(p. 215)* 18 November 1987.
164. *(p. 216)* 4 December 1987.
165. *(p. 216)* 4 December 1987.

166. *(p. 217)* 20 December 1987.
167. *(p. 217)* 20 December 1987.
168. *(p. 218)* 30 December 1987.
169. *(p. 219)* 1 January 1988.
170. *(p. 219)* 2 January 1988.
171. *(p. 219)* 2 January 1988.
172. *(p. 220)* 2 January 1988.
173. *(p. 220)* 2 January 1988.

I LOVE SHOPPING

BOOK 5

174. The same smile

In Yogyakarta I wanted to buy a fan. The lady in the store smiled at me and said 500 rupiah.

I said 200, and she gave me the same smile. She gave me the same smile even when I bought the fan for only 200 rupiah.

175. Talking soul to soul

In Bali I went into a music store to buy an instrument. The owner said, "80,000 rupiah," and I said, "No, 60,000." We were haggling for such a long time. Finally, he agreed to 70,000.

Then I saw two bamboo flutes on his desk. I examined the flutes, and one of them I liked very much. But the man said, "I am not going to sell this flute, because it is my personal flute. I play this one every day, so I don't want to sell it."

His soul was very open to me, and it was telling me to take that flute, but the man did not want to give it to me. He said, "Take the other one – the smaller one."

To myself I said, "The physical plane and the spiritual plane will never go together."

Because his soul was telling me to take the flute, I said to the man, "You have to give it to me. During the day there is no moon, but the moon will beg you to give it to me."

Then I asked, "What is your name?"

He said, "Madhu Chandra."

I said, "Are you a Hindu?"

"I am a Hindu," he replied.

Then I took the flute I wanted and said, "I will break the flute over your head if you don't give it to me."

Savyasachi just looked at me.

Finally the man said, "All right. The flute has a fixed price of 1,000 rupiah. You are getting the instrument for 70,000, plus 1,000, so it is 71,000 rupiah."

Then I gave him 70,000 and another 10,000 by mistake. I thought I had given him only 1,000. He looked at me and said that I had made a mistake and gave me the change.

Then he started helping Savyasachi with the big instrument. Savyasachi told him that I was a great musician, and the man was very happy that he had met a great musician.

His soul wanted me to have the flute, but his mind would not give it to me. So I said to myself, "The only way to get the flute is to threaten to break his head."

Bali is the land of simplicity. Otherwise, would I ever dare talk to anybody like that? It was just soul to soul that we were talking. He was such a sweet soul!

176. *How could he go shopping?*

I was in an Indian sweet shop in Bayside yesterday buying *jalabee* for prasad. A young man recognised me and was so surprised. He said, "Oh boy!"

Then he saw Databir and asked, "How could Sri Chinmoy come here and go shopping?"

He has come twice to our meditations at P.S. 86 and is used to seeing me in my high meditative consciousness. He couldn't believe that I was standing in front of the counter buying *jalabee*.

177. *Maybe she believed me!*

On my first piano anniversary, Sarah blessed me with a cake, and Chetana also blessed me with a cake. Then I went to a store to get three more cakes.

The lady asked, "The cakes are for whom?"

I answered, "They are for me, because I play the piano."

She asked, "When are you going to play at Carnegie Hall?"

I said, "I have already played there."

She did not believe me.

Then I said that I have also played at the Royal Albert Hall in London and the Sydney Opera House. In the beginning she did not believe me at all. After I mentioned five or six places, maybe she believed me. Or perhaps she herself had never heard of those places!

178. *How much talking I do!*

Databir brought me to a mall and left me there, and I was nicely shopping. When I went inside one store, the shopkeeper asked me, "Are you from India?"

I answered, "Yes."

He said, "That's why you have such a tan."

Perhaps he thought I was tanned because I had just come from India. He was very white.

I said, "Yesterday spring started."

He said, "You are wrong. Today spring started."

I said, "All right, yesterday or today spring started, but it is still very cold."

He said something like "Bad luck!" Then he said, "Why are you not taking this item? If you don't like it, you will be able to return it."

I said, "I am not coming back here to return it."

When I go shopping, how much talking I do with these people!

179. The wise guy

This morning I went shopping in a mall. Databir drove me there, and Victor was the distinguished back-seater.

In one store I was browsing through a book called *How to Become a U.S. Citizen*. My soul was telling me not to waste my time because it does not want me to become a U.S. citizen. The book had so many facts that had to be learned if someone wanted to become a U.S. citizen: what was the capital of this state; how many members there are in the Senate and Congress; and so forth. How do people remember all these things?

An elderly woman about seventy years old asked me, "Where do you come from?"

I answered, "India."

She said, "Do you have a green card?"

I said, "Yes, I have a green card."

She asked, "Now you want to become a citizen?"

"No, no," I replied.

Then I turned around and started looking at books in the religion section. I bought some books about Socrates, Buddha and the Christ. I also saw a tiny booklet by Thomas Merton. Vidagdha had written her Master's thesis on him.

The lady was still watching me. I saw one of my booklets, *The Fountain-Heart of Wisdom*. The price sticker was over the word "Wisdom", and I was trying to read the title behind the sticker. The lady saw me trying to read the title and she said, "Wisdom". Then she said, "By Sri Chinmoy – wise guy Sri Chinmoy."

I was quite amused and just smiled at her. I didn't have the heart to tell her I was that wise guy.

180. *Buying* prasad

Today I went to a bakery to buy heart-shaped cookies for prasad. I have been to that store so many times, and usually they are very nice, but this time they didn't pay any attention to me.

While I was there, a young boy of fourteen or fifteen years took an ice cream cone from the display case and started eating it without paying. The lady went inside to inform the manager. Then a stout man came out.

The boy did not run away. He just walked out with no fear. He was so daring. There were two or three other customers, but they just watched.

For another five minutes they did not serve me. Finally I said, "I need about 200 of these cookies."

They said they had no time to count them. Then I asked for a quarter pound.

They asked, "Why do you want a quarter pound?"

I replied, "I will be able to count how many are in a quarter pound, and then I will know how many pounds I have to buy in order to get 200."

They said, "We don't understand."

Finally I got my 200 heart cookies.

181. *The misplaced glasses*

While I am standing on a line, if I hear the word "credit card", I go away! Today I was so lucky! The old lady in front of me said, "Cash!"

While the cashier was taking care of her, the poor lady removed her glasses and put them into her glasses case. She forgot to put the case back in her purse and went away without it. I saw what had happened, so I took the glasses and tried to find her. But I am lame and cannot walk very fast, and I didn't know in which direction to go. I was praying to God that I could find her.

Then I saw her browsing only five or six metres away. I was a little doubtful that it was the right lady, so I asked, "Are these yours?"

She was so happy. She said, "I do this thing all the time. I am so grateful to you."

182. The Taj Mahal shopping bag

When I was waiting to pay in one store, I saw a shopping bag with "India Day" written on it. It also had a picture of India's Taj Mahal.

The saleslady said to me, "Do you come from India?"

I answered, "Yes."

Then she said, "Oh, here is your Taj Mahal," and gave me the bag.

183. The wrong change

I bought a white coat that cost 165.08 dollars. I gave the man at the cash register 166 dollars. While he was taking care of me, a young man came up and started talking to him. What keys they press on the cash register, God knows!

When the man left, the cashier gave me back one dollar and some change. I asked him, "Why did you give me the dollar?"

He said, "Why not? That's what the computer says."

I said, "They might fine you."

"They will fire me?"

I said, "No, I said they might *fine* you."

He said, "The world needs honest people like you. All right, then let me just give you the change."

I said, "You already gave it to me. The change is in my pocket."

When I went to Vinaya's car, I saw that the change he had given me was only 58 cents instead of 92 cents. He had not meant to deceive me; he had wanted to give me more change.

184. The free battery

Today I bought a little clock for 20 dollars. It had only one battery, which was smaller than the smallest. The man at the counter said to me, "Are you ready to pay an extra 50 cents for the battery?"

Then the man's wife came up and scolded him. "What are you doing?" she said. So I got the battery free.

185. American bargaining

At Main Street, near my four-mile mark, there is a shopping mall. From outside you can't tell that it is a mall, but once you enter, you see all the stores.

Yesterday Databir took me to that mall and I was buying something. The man said, "60 dollars."

I said, "40 dollars."

Then the man said, "Come here." He was very rough.

I said to myself, "Physically I know we won't fight, so why do I have to worry?" So I went towards him very powerfully.

He said, "I said 60 dollars, and you have to say 40 dollars?"

I said, "You don't have to sell it."

Then he said, "Can you not go higher?"

I said, "I am not going higher."

He said, "Just yesterday I sold one like this for 55 dollars."

So I said, "No, I can't go higher," and I walked away. Later, when I was passing by him again, he said, "Hey! Why do you have to act like that?" Then he said something that was insulting. This time I did not go near him.

Then he said, "55 dollars."

I said, "I won't give you more than 50 dollars."

Then he said, "All right, take it. Just because it is the last one, I am giving it to you for 50 dollars."

Sometimes people treat you so mercilessly, but I enjoy their talk! When I go shopping, I become part and parcel of the shopping world and all my headaches go away. It is great fun! This is the only way I can mix with people at their own level.

186. The egg rolls

While I was shopping, I wanted to buy some Chinese egg rolls. The lady didn't understand my English, and I didn't understand her English. I said, "No meat, no fish – only vegetables."

She understood "vegetables".

Outside in the display case the egg rolls had meat, fish and God knows what inside them, so she brought me egg rolls from inside. She repeated the words, "No meat, no fish!"

She was so simple and humble, but I suspected her. I said, "Can you cut one for me?"

When she cut it, I saw that it was full of fish. See how she wanted to deceive me!

I said, "I was going to get them, but now I don't trust you." Then I started going away.

She said, "Please wait for a few minutes. I will make special ones for you."

I sat there waiting for five or six minutes. I said to myself, "This time I hope she will be sincere." When she brought the egg rolls, I didn't have the heart to ask her to cut them again. When I brought them home, I saw they were all vegetables.

I go shopping and bring back a Mahabharata of stories!

187. The sales tax

In one store I was about to buy something for 20 dollars, but the lady said, "21 dollars."

I said, "It is written here – 20 dollars."
She said, "There is tax!"
Then she asked, "Where do you come from?"
I said, "India."
She said, "In India there is no tax?"
I said, "Yes, there is."
She asked, "Then why are you surprised?"
I said, "But this is on sale."
She said, "When something is on sale, there will always be sales tax."

188. Indian devotion

Some Indian shopkeepers show me such devotion! In one store I gave an Indian man 10 dollars, and he was supposed to give me 5 dollars change. But I said, "I don't need the change. You keep it."

He followed me outside to the car with folded hands to give me back the money. He wanted to give me the full 10 dollars back. I wouldn't take it, but later we found that he had slipped the ten-dollar bill inside the car.

189. The same book

In my room I keep a book that contains difficult English words. Many times I have looked at that book, marking words here and there.

Today I went to a bookstore and bought another copy of the same book. I thought it would give me inspiration.

I didn't see any other book in the bookstore that I wanted, so just because I wanted to buy something, I bought a book I knew was in my room!

190. *A small world*

The day before yesterday I was in a boutique in Woodstock, which is my most favourite town. As soon as I entered the store, the young girl in charge said with wide eyes, "Sri Chinmoy? Sri Chinmoy? I know you! I saw you for the first time when I was three years old in Flatbush. My mother lives in Brooklyn, and she has come to your meditations many times."

She gave me the store card and asked me to autograph it.

I said, "What is your name?"

She said, "You don't have to write down my name. Just write your name."

I said, "Yes, but I would like to know your name."

She said, "Ayesha."

So I wrote, "Dear Ayesha, with my good wishes", and I signed it. She was so happy.

This world is so small. She used to live in the Flatbush area. I also used to live there. Now she is sixteen or seventeen years old and lives in Woodstock, which I have visited so many times over the past twenty-four years.

191. *Nicholas is your best admirer!*

Today I went shopping in a Chinese store where the lady likes me. As I was paying, her husband came up to me and grabbed my shoulder. He was smiling.

He said, "7,000!" and raised his arm. On his wall was the picture of my 7,000-pound lift.

He has a sixteen-year-old son named Nick. He said, "Nicholas looks at your picture every day. He is your best admirer!"

192. The "far-off" milk shake

In Seoul, Korea, I went into a 24-hour restaurant and ordered a milk shake. I asked how long it would take. The man behind the counter said, "Twenty-five minutes."

I said, "It will take such a long time?"

He corrected my English and said, "It is not too far, not too far."

I was thinking, "What will happen if I fall asleep? Let me see how much time it will take."

I set my watch and saw that it took not even eleven minutes. Such a language barrier!

193. He will come on my deathbed!

In Korea, I bought a beautiful swan pin for Tanima. As I was paying, right behind me I saw an Indian man and woman. The man was dressed in Indian dress and the lady was wearing a sari.

They were speaking in Bengali, so I asked if they were Bengali, and we started talking in Bengali.

The man asked me, "Do you live here?"

I said, "No, I come from America."

He told me that he had been living in Korea for six years. He said he was a famous engineer.

Then he asked me what part of Bangladesh I came from.

I said, "I come from Chittagong."

He said, "I come from a place you do not know."

When he told me the name, I said, "It is a very famous place. So many great Bengali writers were born there."

The man did not know the names of the writers that I mentioned.

Then his wife said, "Please come to our house to give us the dust of your feet." That is the Bengali way of saying, "Just come and eat."

I said, "I am here with so many people. I will not be able to come."

She said, "Just come for a few minutes. You are such a wise man." But the husband did not want me to come and got very mad. He and his wife started fighting. The man said, "He will come on my deathbed!"

I said, "I don't want you to die." Then I disappeared.

194. *Indian-style bargaining*

In another store in Korea, I saw something I liked and asked the elderly lady at the counter how much it cost.

The lady said, "13 dollars." I had bought a few things already from her, so I said, "No, 10 dollars!" and gave her 10 dollars.

She said, "No, you have to give me three more." Since I was bargaining, I told the lady I had no more money.

I thought that all my money was in my left pocket and that only some papers were in my right pocket. To show the lady that I had no more money, I pulled all the papers out of my right pocket. O God, so much money came out!

The shopkeeper said, "You have money."

What was I going to do? I smiled at her very soulfully and offered her the other three dollars, but she didn't take it. She gave me the item for 10 dollars.

When I said I had no money, I was not telling a lie. I was just bargaining in my Indian manner. But after she saw all my money, I smiled at her and she became so nice!

195. Why buy such a stupid thing?

I went to another store in Korea and was looking at a dirty wallet. The owner asked me, "Are you Japanese?"

I said, "No, I am Indian."

He said the wallet cost 10,000, but after I took one step out of the store he said, "Since you are an Indian, I will give it to you for 3,000."

I went back into the store, but when I was about to buy the wallet, he said, "No, the price is 5,000."

So I didn't buy it. I said to myself, "For 5,000, why should I buy such a stupid thing?"

196. You have to be an Indian

I was buying T-shirts in a store. The owner said, "It is 2,500 for one." After I bargained with the lady, she agreed to sell me six shirts for 12,000.

While I was paying, a man came up to me and said, "Are you free?"

I asked, "Why?"

He said, "I want to ask you what price you are paying."

As soon as he asked me the price, the lady immediately said, "2,500." I was not trying to hide the amount that I was paying, but he did not see how much it was.

He was an American, so he did not bargain. I did not have the heart to tell him what I was paying. I didn't want to get into a fight with the shopkeeper.

You have to be an Indian to bargain!

197. Buying yo-yos

I had such a fight while trying to buy yo-yos. The yo-yos had a light in them and were so nice. I wanted to buy them for the young singing girls.

I said one price, but the man wouldn't come down. Then I said another price, but still he wouldn't come down. I tried a third time, but then I had to surrender. After failing three times, I had to buy at his price.

198. The key-ring

As soon as I see something I like, I try to think who can use it. One key-ring I saw was so beautiful; it had two deer. Mahasamrat's wife is very fond of deer. As soon as I saw the key-ring, I immediately thought that she was the right person.

I don't think of the person first. Only after I see something that I like do I ask myself who I can buy it for.

199. A warning in Greece

In Greece everything had a fixed price. On the street they were selling very cheap things, but all for a fixed price. The items they were selling were so bad – worse than useless.

I wanted to enter into a shop to see if they had anything different. At the entrance to the shop were two English-speaking ladies. One of them touched my hand to stop me from going in.

The lady said, "These people are rogues. They have cheated us. You must not go in there."

So I didn't go inside.

200. Two doubters

Vinaya and I went to buy potatoes with broccoli. We ordered sixteen. The man at the window said, "Are you kidding?" He didn't believe we wanted sixteen potatoes.

We paid him and asked how long it would take. He said it would take two minutes. Then we didn't believe him!

First he didn't believe us; then we didn't believe him. So we went away to do something else. When we came back in five or six minutes, our order was already waiting for us.

201. Two sincere bargainers

I was buying a gift in Bangkok. The price was 250 bahts. I offered the lady 150.

She said, "200."

I said, "No, 160." She didn't say anything, so I went up to 170. But there was still no sign that she would give it to me. After I said 180, I was about to go away.

Then she said, "Yes, you can have it."

I gave her 200 bahts, and she returned 30 to me. I said, "Why are you giving me 30? The price was 180."

She said, "No, I decided in my mind to sell when you said 170."

I said, "No, I agreed to pay 180," and I returned 10. She started jumping with joy and giggling. She was so happy that I gave her back 10 bahts.

202. The garlands

I wanted to buy two small garlands for Ranjana. I thought that the little girl who was selling them said that they were five bahts, but then she said, "No, that is for the shorter ones."

Then Savyasachi helped her by saying, "These are a little larger."

I wanted to buy two for five bahts, but she said, "No, five for each."

Finally I said to myself, "I have to buy them." So I gave her 10 bahts. Then she started giggling because she had gotten such a high price.

203. The advantages of knowing Tamil

Sometimes when I speak Tamil, it is all wrong, but the owners of one store in Singapore were very pleased with my Tamil.

I wanted to buy something, so I asked, "Can you not reduce the price?"

They said, "Of course we shall reduce it."

They reduced it and I asked, "You won't reduce it any more?"

They said, "Oh, no, no!"

Then an elderly lady, the aunt, said, "If you can say correctly the total price in Tamil, then we shall reduce it more."

I was very happy and I said the price correctly. So when the total figure came, the old lady said to reduce it by three Singapore dollars.

The younger one, who was around fourteen or fifteen years old, said, "No, Auntie, he speaks Tamil, so please give him a five-dollar reduction."

So I got a five-dollar reduction by knowing Tamil.

204. Time to visit the ear specialist

People can be so kind! I was buying a garment for Alo at a store in Kuching, Borneo. The man said, "90 dollars," but I said the price was too high. Then he came down to 70 dollars.

I said, "50 dollars."

After some time he said, "Yes, yes!"

Then I gave him 50 dollars and left with the garment to go to another store.

While I was in the second store, the fellow from the first store came running up to me and gave me 35 dollars.

I asked, "Why?"

He said, "You gave me 50 dollars, but the price we agreed on was only 15 dollars!"

From the beginning he was saying 19 dollars, whereas I thought he was saying 90 dollars. Then when he said 17 dollars, I thought he was saying 70 dollars.

So he came running after me to give me 35 dollars back. I looked at him and gave him a ten-dollar tip. He was so happy with that 10 dollars.

How nice he was! He could easily have kept the 35 dollars.

While giving him the 10 dollars, I said, "It is time for me to visit the ear specialist!"

205. The Tamil bookstore

I bought quite a few Indian books in a Tamil bookstore in Kuala Lumpur. The bill came to 57 Malaysian dollars. They told me there was a five-dollar discount, so it became 52 dollars.

I said, "Can you not give it to me for 50 dollars?"

One manager and two assistants were there. The manager said, "Already we have given you a discount. We will not go any lower." She was showing off, and then she went away.

The two assistants were very sad that I was not going to buy the books. They were speaking together in Tamil.

As soon as she left, I took 50 dollars out of my wallet and gave it to them. In Tamil I said, "It is sufficient."

O God, the manager overheard me speaking Tamil. She practically came running over and grabbed the bill from her assistant. She smiled at me and said, "You speak Tamil?"

I said, "For twenty years I lived in South India!"

Then she gave me the books for 50 dollars.

NOTES TO I LOVE SHOPPING, BOOK 5

174. *(p. 227)* 8 January 1988.
175. *(p. 227)* 12 January 1988.
176. *(p. 228)* 4 February 1988.
177. *(p. 229)* 18 February 1988.
178. *(p. 229)* 21 March 1988.
179. *(p. 230)* 27 March 1988.
180. *(p. 231)* 30 April 1988.
181. *(p. 231)* 28 May 1988.
182. *(p. 232)* 28 May 1988.
183. *(p. 232)* 28 May 1988.
184. *(p. 233)* 28 May 1988.
185. *(p. 233)* 28 May 1988.
186. *(p. 234)* 28 May 1988.
187. *(p. 235)* 28 May 1988.
188. *(p. 235)* 28 May 1988.
189. *(p. 235)* 28 May 1988.
190. *(p. 236)* 5 June 1988.
191. *(p. 236)* 13 July 1988.
192. *(p. 237)* 23 September 1988.
193. *(p. 237)* 26 September 1988.
194. *(p. 238)* 26 September 1988.
195. *(p. 239)* 26 September 1988.
196. *(p. 239)* 26 September 1988.
197. *(p. 240)* 26 September 1988.
198. *(p. 240)* 26 September 1988.
199. *(p. 240)* 8 October 1988.
200. *(p. 241)* 13 October 1988.
201. *(p. 241)* 18 December 1988.
202. *(p. 242)* 22 December 1988.
203. *(p. 242)* 28 December 1988.

204. *(p. 243)* 30 December 1988.
205. *(p. 243)* 4 January 1989.

PART III

THE WORLD-EXPERIENCE-TREE-CLIMBER

BOOK 1

1. You know how to fool everyone

As I was coming out of the plane at the Eugene, Oregon airport, there was an old man with a cane right in front of me. With his right hand he was holding the rail, and he was dragging his legs. I was behind him doing the same because of all my back pain and leg pain. He turned around, mad, and said, "What are you doing?" He thought I was mocking him. He said he was seventy-six years old. I said that I was not mocking him, only I had leg pain. He believed me.

When I got to the motel, I went to the gift shop to buy some candy. The saleslady started to talk to me. She was saying, "How are you? Did you have a nice day?" and other things. Salespeople like to talk to everyone, so I didn't think she was talking to me because she knew who I was. I only smiled at her.

When I gave her a dollar for the candy, she gave me back a quarter. Then she said that she had gone to one of my meditations once, and had seen me meditating in my *dhoti*. Now I was in western clothes. So she said, "You know how to fool everyone."

2. You have to carry two bags?

When I arrived at the airport in New York from Puerto Rico, I was carrying two small bags, one on each shoulder. Lucy and Ranjana were watching me from the other side of the glass partition. I saw them, but they could not come inside.

One of the porters recognised me, saying, "Sri Chinmoy, you are such a great man! You have to carry two bags?" He wanted to carry my bags for me, but they were such tiny bags! He was not a runner, I am sure, since he was quite fat, so I don't think he knew me from our races. I was looking at my shirt to see if

"Sri Chinmoy" was mentioned anywhere, but it wasn't. How did he recognise me? God alone knows!

3. Thank you

This morning I had to telephone someone. I could not dial directly from here, so I had to take help from the telephone operator. She was an elderly lady who was very, very kind to me. When I gave her the number, she said to me, "Thank you."
 So I said to her, "Thank you."
 Then she said to me very affectionately, in a motherly way, "When someone says 'Thank you', you are not supposed to say 'Thank you'! You are supposed to say, 'You are welcome'!"
 I thanked her for telling me that, and then she started laughing and laughing.

4. The Philippines airport

At the airport in the Philippines, I had three pieces of luggage – two suitcases and a carry-on. Three boys took them away, but they were not going in the same direction. I told a policeman and he laughed, but he made the boys come back. I said that I needed only one fellow. Afterwards I found out that when you give the porters money, it goes to the police.

5. Italian experiences

On this trip the Italians were so bad to me! It started at the airport, where all my luggage was missing. Even when I was in a taxi on the way to see the Pope, the taxi driver took me out of my way. The Vatican was in sight, but the driver, thinking I wouldn't recognise it, went somewhere else. The ride never ended!

In Italy the churches are very beautiful. But when you go to a church, five or six photographers will take your picture and then try to sell you the photographs.

6. Rainy Bermuda

Once I went to Bermuda for three days alone. The hotel I stayed in was near the water. It was very beautiful. But it rained heavily the whole time I was there. I could not even go out. It rained cats and dogs. Only once I went across the street to a Chinese restaurant. My only consolation was that I wrote two hundred poems while I was there. But I was not able to go out walking or running at all!

7. Unfortunate experiences in France

I have many good things to say about France, but each time I go there, I have to lose something – or perhaps I should say they have to steal something! Once they stole my harmonium and another time they took my tape recorder. I had left a tape recorder right on the dresser in my room. As soon as we reached the airport, only fifteen minutes later, I called the hotel and said that one of my students was coming back for the tape recorder. The manager said he would send someone up to see if it was there. After a few minutes he said that there was nothing on the dresser in my room – as if my mind would go blank in fifteen minutes!

8. Indian hotels

In India, the hotel people show you a room and say that all the rooms are the same. So you pay for a room, leave your bags in the car and go out for two or three hours. When you come back, O God, the room they take you to is unbelievable. Compared to the room they showed you, it is the difference between Heaven and hell. It is on the same floor as the other room, but there is such a difference!

9. Indian drivers

In Agra, the drivers take two hours to go to the Taj Mahal, although it is only twenty minutes away. God knows where they take you! Then, in the hope of a little more money, for four blocks they will follow you like a faithful dog. If you throw them something – even the smallest coin – then when they go to pick it up, you can gain some ground on them and escape.

10. Airport encounters

At the Calcutta airport, quite unexpectedly Mother Teresa and I met face to face. For me to recognise her was a very easy task. But she didn't give any sign of recognising me. For a fleeting second she looked at me and I looked at her. We were only three metres from each other. She was travelling with only three attendants, and they were all wearing saris. Usually I have quite a few attendants around me, although this time I had nobody.

Then again at the Delhi airport we passed by each other. But it happened so quickly that I barely noticed her. Then I saw three or four people come up to her for her autograph.

11. A letter to the editor

As you know, a very nice article came out about me in *The Illustrated Weekly of India,* which is like America's *Time* magazine. The following week an Indian wrote four or five lines highly appreciating that article. It came out as a letter to the editor. I saw it when I was in India.

12. The deceitful taxi driver

Indian taxi drivers are notorious for deceiving people. On this trip deception started at the Bombay airport. From the airport to the hotel is a very short distance. The taxi ride normally costs only seven rupees, but the driver asked for two hundred rupees. I started arguing with him in Hindi. Perhaps I made some grammatical mistakes, but he understood me perfectly. From two hundred he finally came down to sixty. So I gave him sixty rupees. What could I do? The following morning, when I went from the hotel to the airport, another driver charged me the correct amount – seven rupees. So you can see what a rogue the first driver was!

13. The missing notebook

The following day, while I was waiting to board the plane to Madras, I was writing poems. After some time I put my notebook on the seat next to me and began meditating. Suddenly I noticed that my notebook had disappeared. I started asking myself, "Where did it go?"

I looked for the notebook in my blue bag, but it was not there. Then I started looking around me. There were about seventy or eighty people waiting to get on the plane, and it was almost boarding time. Then I saw that somebody was holding the notebook. He was not reading the poems; he was only appreciating the beautiful parrot that was on the cover.

I said to him, "Excuse me, this is my book."

He said, "Your book? I found it on a seat. Nobody was sitting there, so I took it because I liked the bird."

Fortunately I got my notebook back at the last minute. Otherwise, ninety-nine poems would have been lost.

14. The lightning call

When I arrived in Calcutta after leaving Pondicherry, I wanted to phone my family. My sisters and brothers had driven me to the Madras airport, and then they had to make the three-and-a-half-hour drive back to Pondicherry. So I was worried about them. I felt sorry, because going and coming back came to seven hours of driving altogether. For me, it was only an hour-and-a-half plane ride from Madras to Calcutta. So after about three hours I started phoning Pondicherry to see if they had gotten back all right.

The operator said that the Pondicherry line was out of order and that it could be that way for two or three more days. Quite often when I try to call from New York, the operator says that the Pondicherry line is out of order. The first day I believed the operator. The second day when I tried to call, again the operator said that it was out of order. I said, "O God, what does the government do if it has to make an urgent call?"

The operator said, "Oh, the government has a special line that is used only for lightning calls. If you make a lightning call, you have to pay eight times more."

I said, "Look here, I am willing to pay eight times more."

The operator said, "Eight times more? Are you sure?"

I said, "I have the money, so please do it."

THE WORLD-EXPERIENCE-TREE-CLIMBER

So the operator made the lightning call around one-thirty in the morning, but nobody answered. My mind was worried that perhaps something had gone wrong. One is allowed to try a lightning call only twice, and then the call is cancelled. They made the second call half an hour later and still there was no answer. What had happened was this: the Calcutta hotel operator had put through the lightning call, but the rogues in Madras had used a wrong number. All the time I thought that something had gone wrong with my family's phone. It turned out that our phone was all right, but the Madras operator was putting me through to a wrong number.

The following day I tried to make another lightning call two times, but again it didn't go through. Whenever the call does not go through, you don't have to pay; but you always get a scolding from the operator. The operator barks at you because a lightning call is only supposed to be made by very rich or great people. They did not feel that I was rich or great enough.

My family couldn't call me because they didn't know at which hotel I was staying. Finally, I called my house in New York. Since nobody there had heard from my brothers and sisters, I said, "That means that everything is all right. If anything had gone wrong, they would have called New York." From New York one of the girls tried calling Pondicherry, but she had the same fate. She could not get through. Finally, she sent a telegram to my family asking if everyone was all right.

The next day I told the operator that I had been trying to call Pondicherry for three days. She put in another lightning call, and in two minutes the call went through. My brother answered the phone and I immediately said to him, "Why have you not been answering the phone?"

At the same time he said to me, "Where is your concern for us? Why have you not called us for four days? One of us has always been near the phone, worrying."

I said, "I have tried to make lightning calls twenty times."

So everything was all right. The first day when they didn't answer, I felt that perhaps my sister was tired and exhausted from travelling, and therefore she didn't hear the phone ringing. It turned out that my brother was there, but the phone line was not working at all. For three days the Pondicherry line was not working. I said, "What kind of worries the telephone can create!" I was blessing the telephone like anything.

I was so happy that I finally got through to Pondicherry that I called the hotel telephone operator. I had heard her say her name, Mrs. Dasgupta. She was Bengali, but we started talking in English because telephone operators always prefer to speak English. She told me, "You asked for a lightning call, but I did not make a lightning call. I have a friend in Madras and I told her to make it a special call without saying it was a lightning call." It would have cost me six hundred rupees, but now I had to pay only one hundred and ten rupees. So I was very grateful to her.

I put a hundred rupees in an envelope to give her, and then I went downstairs to the hotel telephone office. The place was so dirty! I stood at the door and said, "I would like to speak to Mrs. Dasgupta." So many people were working there. How could I go in and give her the envelope when there were so many other girls around? I said to the guard, "Can you ask her to come here?"

The guard came back and said, "They are asking you to come in."

I said to myself, "I am in trouble now. I can't just give her this envelope in front of everyone."

So I gave her a copy of the small *Galaxy of Luminaries*. When she saw my picture with the Pope, she could not believe it. She said to me "Where do you come from?"

I said, "I am Bengali. Why?"

She said, "But when you talked to your family, it was not in Bengali."

I said, "I come from Chittagong."

She said she could not understand a word of our Chittagong dialect.

I said, "This is what you do? You listen to people's private conversations?"

She said, "Oh no, I just wanted to see if you got through to your party. Then I heard something very peculiar." Then she added, "You don't have a Chittagong accent."

I said to myself, "Not in vain did I stay at the Sri Aurobindo Ashram. There I spoke real Bengali."

Then she started appreciating my Bengali. I didn't have the heart to tell her how many books, poems and songs I have written in Bengali. Then she said, "Is your mother alive?"

I said, "No."

She said, "The person who would have been the happiest to see this picture is not alive."

I said, "I lost her when I was quite young."

She said, "I am so sorry that you have lost your mother. She would have been the happiest person."

I said, "There is something called Heaven, so she can be proud of her son from Heaven."

She was very moved. Then I gave her the envelope and said, "This is a gift."

I thought she would show false modesty and say, "No", and I would have to insist. But she just took it and thanked me. Inwardly I said, "You deserve it! You saved me from paying for a lightning call."

15. The flight to London

What an adventure this trip to Scotland was! So many things went wrong in the airport, on the plane and in the hotels.

After the disciples saw me off at Kennedy airport, I went to the British Airways lounge. Can you imagine? About forty people were standing because there were no seats left in the lounge.

Finally we entered into the plane. An orthodox Jewish man was sitting in the seat beside mine. He had a little cap and a long beard. His seat was on the aisle and mine was at the window. When I came and stood in front of him, he didn't want to move or get up so that I could get to my seat. It was only with greatest difficulty that I was able to sit down.

After ten or fifteen minutes I thought, "Let me start writing poems." But I could not find even one ballpoint. I had put six ballpoints into my bag, but at that time I could not find even one. I searched here and there. I said to myself, "How can I ask this man for a ballpoint? God doesn't want me to write poems." So I read for hours on the plane and I didn't write even one poem.

Towards the end of the trip, the stewardess gave out immigration cards for us to fill out. I could have asked the stewardess for a ballpoint, but often it is so hard to get their attention that you lose all your inspiration. I said to myself, "At the airport I will fill it out!"

THE WORLD-EXPERIENCE-TREE-CLIMBER

16. The drink

During the plane ride the steward came to me and said, "What would you like to drink?"

I said, "Tomato juice."

In ten minutes' time he brought me something that looked like tomato juice, but it smelled like wine. I was half in the dream world, but I asked myself, "How could it be tomato juice? Definitely this smells like wine."

Fortunately I smelled it first before drinking it.

I said to the steward, "This can't be tomato juice. I asked you for tomato juice."

He said, "Oh no, you asked me for...." and he said the name of a drink that started with the letter "T". He said the name at least twice, but still I didn't know what he was saying. He didn't say, "Sorry!" or apologise in any way. He acted as if it was my fault. Finally, though, he did bring me some tomato juice.

17. Begging for a ballpoint

In the London airport hundreds of people were standing in a queue. I saw one of the airport people sitting at an empty desk reading a newspaper. He had three ballpoints in his shirt pocket. I said to him, "Excuse me, may I use your ballpoint for a minute?"

He said abruptly, "I don't have one!" And I was looking at the pens in his pocket when he said it. I have never seen such a rogue.

There was such a big line; at least a hundred and fifty people were in front of me. I thought, "When I get to the front of the line, they will want to see this card filled out. Since I am wasting my time here, let me ask someone else." I asked another employee who was nearby, but he said, "When you get to the front of the line there will be someone to give you a ballpoint." I could see that he also had three or four, but he didn't want to give me one.

After fifteen minutes I reached the front of the line. I said to the lady who told you which booth to go to, "I don't have a ballpoint." She answered, "I am sorry, I don't have one. Otherwise, I would give you one." In her case, I saw that she really didn't have a ballpoint.

Then I saw a middle-aged Indian man sitting with his head in his hands. He was just a passenger waiting for someone. As you know, I have told many stories about Indians who acted like perfect rogues. But my Indian brothers can be of help to me also. I asked this man, "May I borrow a ballpoint?"

He said, "Of course, of course!"

He had a huge bag with so many clothes in it, and he started searching and searching through all his things. It took him two or three minutes to find one. So this is the difference between Englishmen and Indians. I said to myself, "Indians quarrel and fight, but in the time of need they will always try to come to each other's rescue with a big heart." I used the pen and returned it to him and thanked him. Inwardly I felt sorry that he was still brooding.

When people at the airport or other places are mean to me, I forgive them and God forgives them. It is just human nature. Then when I tell the stories, I get joy. I tell them in a cheerful way.

18. Looking for Terminal 3

After I gave the customs people my immigration card, I put my things on a trolley and went to the place where they check tickets. The lady looked at my ticket and said, "Wrong place!" There were two airlines whose names started with the word "British", and I had gone to the wrong one. But the lady wouldn't tell me where to go. She was so rude! Then one of the porters grabbed my shoulder very affectionately and said, "Do you see the bookstore over there? Just behind it is the booth that you want."

I went there and showed the lady my ticket. She told me which terminal to go to, but I couldn't hear her. So I said, "Excuse me, sorry, but I could not get what you said."

The lady said, "I told you!" and she wouldn't speak to me again.

Another porter happened to be nearby. He told me, "She said Terminal 3." He was so nice to me.

You can either take a taxi or walk to Terminal 3. I walked. The route was all zigzag, like a serpent, and it took me ten or fifteen minutes to get there.

19. The new disciple

When I was about to enter the plane – I was only ten or twelve metres from the door – a young girl looked at me, smiling, and said, "Guru!"

I couldn't imagine who she was. She said, "I am a new disciple."

I said, "You are a new disciple?"

She said, "I have been your disciple for only three weeks. I am a Zurich disciple. My name is Emily." She grabbed my instrument case and wanted to take my bag also. She spoke

English fluently. She works for Air France, and she was taking the same flight to Scotland. She carried my bags right to my seat. She was going on standby. But she told me that she would have no trouble getting on the plane.

20. *The plane ride to Scotland*

In the airport I had gone to a bookstore and bought three ballpoints so I wouldn't have to be a beggar anymore. On the plane one of the stewards asked me to fill out a form that I would need to enter Scotland. Emily was five or six metres behind me. When she heard that I was supposed to write something, she came running with a ballpoint even before I could get my own out of my bag. So this is the difference between disciples and non-disciples!

Hannelore, Robert and four or five other German disciples were also on the plane, but they didn't know beforehand that I would be on the same flight. The disciples were so happy and delighted to be on the plane with me. Emily sat behind me and the other disciples had seats near me, although no one sat right beside me. None of the disciples talked. They were absolutely silent, sitting and meditating. The American girls, on the other hand, will talk about their breakfast, their running, their shopping – everything – when they fly with me.

21. *The missing tote-a-tune*

Around three o'clock in the afternoon we were supposed to leave for the concert in Dundee; Shantishri was going to drive. I was sitting downstairs in the hotel waiting for Janaka and Janani, who were late. As soon as I saw them, I jumped up. I had a blue bag and a tote-a-tune with me, but because I was in a terrible rush, I left the tote-a-tune.

Shantishri had been driving for only three or four minutes when I realised that my tote-a-tune was missing. She drove back to the hotel and I went to the chair where I had been sitting. But the tote-a-tune was gone. One of the porters said, "I saw it," and gave me a full description. But he said that he had not taken it. What could we do? It was getting late, so we had to leave for the concert. Then Shantishri had to drive seventy or eighty miles per hour because we were so late.

The following day the police came and searched everywhere, but they could not find the tote-a-tune.

22. The chambermaid's test

The next day before I went running, I left a fifty-pence coin and two ten-pence coins in my room to see if the chambermaid was honest. I did this deliberately to test her. When I came back from running, I saw that the fifty-pence coin was gone, but the two ten-pence coins were left. So deliberately I did it and deliberately I got a slap.

23. The silver ballpoints

When I first got to Scotland, I told the disciples my stories about not having a ballpoint. I told them how bad the British are and how good the Indians are. They all felt miserable. They said, "Those people were not disciples. What can you expect from them?"

After the last concert, the British disciples performed scenes from *The Son* for the other disciples. They brought down the actual atmosphere of the play – even the Christ's consciousness and Mary's consciousness. No other performers have done it so perfectly. The director was Charana. Their costumes were also excellent. At the end of the play I appreciated them like anything.

Afterwards, Charana presented me with a set of three silver ballpoints. He said, "We have heard your ballpoint stories, so we are presenting you with these."

Then I entered into a small room near the stage to speak with two disciples for a few minutes. When I left the room, I very nicely left the ballpoints in the room. Later I realised that I didn't have them, but I did not remember where I had left them. I said to myself, "The ballpoint story will never end!"

Fortunately, the disciples found them. They were not supposed to go into that room, but after I left they went there to see if I had left anything. The following day they brought the ballpoints to me.

24. *The kilt*

I knew that Alo would be sad if I didn't wear my kilt during the trip. She had given it to Mangal to bring to me. So after the Christ play I said, "In five minutes I will put on the kilt." I put it on very nicely on top of my *dhoti*. I wore the top also, and it looked very nice. My dhoti was hidden underneath the kilt.

25. *The forgotten gifts*

When I was packing to leave Glasgow for London, the two zippers on my bag broke. The disciples put my things in a garbage bag, but not everything fit. So I took out some expensive, very nicely wrapped candies that I had bought as gifts. I had already eaten a few.

Shantishri drove me to the airport, and again we were in a terrible rush. It was a fifteen-minute or half-hour drive. Then I realised that I had left behind a wristwatch that I had bought for Victor. It had a football game on it. So I asked Shantishri to go back to the hotel to get the wristwatch.

When she reached the hotel, forty minutes after we had left, everything was still in my room. Not only did she find my wristwatch and the expensive candies but also many other gifts that I had bought for people. I knew that I had forgotten the wristwatch and the candies, but I had no idea about the other things. There was a football that I had bought for Tejiyan's group and some other items. I had left my door open, but nothing was taken.

26. *The Indian taxi drivers*

In London I went shopping in the Indian district. When I was finished, the store owner called a taxi company to send a taxi for me. The taxi came and I saw that the driver was a real rogue. He and his friend, who was another rogue, were sitting in the front seat. I told the driver where I was going, and then I said, "It has to be a flat rate," because they looked like such rogues.

Immediately they said, "Five and a half pounds."

I said, "When I came to this store from the hotel with an English taxi driver, it said seven pounds on the meter. Why are you asking for only five and a half pounds?"

The driver said, "Because you are an Indian and you look like a saintly person. Otherwise if you had not been an Indian, we would have asked for twelve pounds and driven here, there, everywhere."

I said, "I will give you seven pounds. But definitely you are going to take me to the right place? Are you sure you know the place?"

They said, "Yes, we know the place. We have been driving for so many years."

The whole way there they were talking about their relatives in America. They did bring me to the right hotel and let me off at the right place. I had told them that I would give them seven pounds, but when they stopped in front of the hotel I gave them eight pounds.

I said, "You people can be nice and I can also be nice." Then I told them, "Don't deceive people anymore!"

They said they would try, and they will.

Sarada Devi had this kind of experience with a *dacoit* [robber] once. When she called him "Father", the dacoit became like her father. The following day he let her go.

27. *The missing porters*

When I was leaving the Kensington Royal Gardens Hotel to catch the famous plane, the Concorde, I waited for the porters for fifteen minutes. The porters were not coming, so I had to bring down three heavy suitcases myself. As soon as I came down, two or three porters came running towards me to help me take them to the car. But before that, when I really needed them, they never appeared.

28. *The fat taxi driver*

On the way to the airport, the taxi driver started talking about this and that. I asked him about his father, who was in the army. Then I said, "During the Second World War, where were you?"

He said, "I was not born."

I looked at him. He was so huge. Everything about him was bulging, but he was fifteen years my junior.

He said, "My father was in the army in Germany, Hungary and Austria – but not in India. My parents waited until after the war to have children because they felt that if they had children during the war, the children would be defective. So I was born in 1946."

I was saying silently, "True, you are not defective but you are very fat!" He was extremely nice, though. He drove very fast to save me, since I had been delayed at the hotel.

29. The Concorde

The Concorde is quite small. The windows are very small and there are only two seats in each row. A middle-aged man was sitting beside me. As soon as he sat down, he said, "I hope you do not mind if I put my legs a little bit on your side." Throughout the trip he was sitting with his foot on his knee, and his leg bent towards my seat. Then he turned on the light and went to sleep with his hands over his eyes. He turned on the light, and then he wouldn't open his eyes! He wouldn't eat anything. After an hour I turned out the light. All of a sudden he woke up and said, "Where did I lose my ballpoint?"

Everywhere there are ballpoint problems! He was telling the stewardess that he had a silver pen. The stewardess was begging the person behind him to look for it. Then they found that it had rolled two seats behind. So the man got back his pen and he was very happy.

When we were about to get out of the plane, the man started looking for his passport. He couldn't find it, so he said, "That is interesting." He was banging everything around, searching here and there. Everybody was standing up in the aisle, waiting for him to find his passport. He was blocking everybody.

30. *Flight technicalities*

In the beginning the pilot started talking to us. He said, "I know it does not make any sense, but we have to do our duty." Then he started telling all about our speed, our altitude, and so on. But he was right. It was too technical.

The plane was going 1,320 miles per hour or even 1,500 miles per hour. The flight usually takes three hours and twenty-five minutes, but this time it took only three hours and five minutes.

When the plane is stopping, it goes 225 miles per hour. At that time you can appreciate that it was going 1,300. But when it is going at the fastest speed, you are not aware of it; you cannot see anything. The plane was flying at twice the height of Mount Everest.

Because it was such a short flight, I didn't get any leg pain. Even going to Puerto Rico, which is often a three-and-a-half-hour trip, I get cramps in my legs. But after the Concorde ride, when I stood up, there was no pain. Now I will go to California, and it will take five and a half hours!

From now on when I go to India, how I wish I could go to London on the Concorde. Otherwise, it is such a long trip, I suffer so much. But it is really expensive! I am not a millionaire and my disciples are not millionaires, so this was perhaps my first and last time flying on the Concorde.

31. *Concorde souvenirs*

On the plane everyone got a souvenir ballpoint saying that they had been on the Concorde. They said that anyone who wanted could come up for a certificate. A few ladies went up to get one. When the last lady went up, the certificates were all used up. The stewardess apologised and said to her, "Hope to see you again."

The lady replied, "I can't afford to see you again."

Right from the beginning of the ride, the flight attendants came and asked, "Do you want anything?" They meant well, but they didn't have enough people to give us excellent service. They should have more attendants helping.

32. Getting ahead

When I was waiting on line in the immigration area here at Kennedy airport, a young girl behind me gave me a smile and started talking to me. She said, "Do you mind? I am behind you but I am very tired, very exhausted. Can I go before you?"

She was a young girl of twenty-three or twenty-four years, and I am an old man. She was not an American, because we were both in the alien area, but I thought perhaps she was a French girl. There were many people on line, but she asked only to go ahead of me. After me, she couldn't go forward anymore because I was at the front of the line. I didn't see if she was actually behind me on line to start with. Perhaps this is how she got to the front of the line from somewhere near the back.

33. Harmonium experiences

Before I left for California, Vinaya ordered a case for my new big harmonium. I gave him the money and he bought it, only to discover it was too big – three times larger than the instrument itself. And he had measured the harmonium first!

I said, "Vinaya, you have bought my coffin!"

That particular harmonium is by far the best, so I wanted to take it to San Francisco. Two weeks earlier I had received it from India. The last time I was in Calcutta I played it in the store and I liked it so much. The people in the store were kind enough to send me the same one.

The first time I went to Japan I went via San Francisco. In San Francisco I liked a particular harmonium and I bought it. They said, "Oh, we will ship it to New York," and I believed them. When I got back to New York there was a harmonium, but not the one I had bought.

34. God on the flute

A woman who came to our concert in Davies Hall was so moved by my singing and playing. Afterwards she wrote a long letter to our music store saying how happy she was to have been able to come because it was so worthwhile. Then, in the last line she said, "I have never heard God play on the flute before."

This time San Francisco gave me two "God" experiences. The other one occurred on the plane on the way home.

35. Morning Star memories

Chandika's brother helped arrange my first trip to California. I will never forget that unique experience when I went to see him in the Morning Star commune near Santa Cruz. There were cockroaches and other insects all over. Nobody has asked me so many questions in this incarnation as he did.

36. Progress at Berkeley

The first time I went to Berkeley, it was not at all a good experience. One person would ask me a question and six others would stand up to answer it. I could not answer a question before two or three others also started answering the question. Then, while I was speaking, people in the audience were whistling.

But they have made progress at Berkeley. This time when I came they were silent, and they were kind enough to clap after the meditation.

37. Encounter in Chinatown

In San Francisco's Chinatown a man recognised me in the street. He said, "It's Sri Chinmoy! I can't believe this! I went to your concert last night. It was so beautiful." He was so happy and excited to see me.

The man was with a friend. He asked me to bless a coin that he had. So I put the coin in my right palm and meditated on it – not for one second, but very seriously, very powerfully I blessed his coin. He was so moved and grateful.

When he saw me on the stage I was wearing my Indian clothes. In Chinatown I was wearing a track suit, but he still recognised me. This man was very nice. When people are nice to me, I try to be nice to them.

38. I can feel it

When I was standing in my hotel lobby, a Japanese lady came up to me and said, "What are you doing?"

I said, "I am meditating and bringing down peace and joy."

The lady said, "I can feel it, I can feel it."

39. The smartest-looking guy

In the elevator a lady said to me, "You're the smartest-looking guy I ever saw." I had on my white track suit and my Tiger running shoes, which matched the track suit.

Her husband said to her, "Don't forget, you're married to me."

The wife said, "Correction! You're married to me!"

40. The fattest man

At the Guinness Museum we saw a 455-pound man. Previously, he and his brother had both weighed the same, but recently his brother died.

His wife weighs only ninety-five pounds. He said that his wife is thin but his brother's wife is fat. Everybody was curious to know his brother's wife's weight. It is 125 pounds!

When I saw his thigh, I couldn't believe it. Of course, he has custom-made trousers. Then we saw the tallest woman and the tallest man – he is eight feet something.

41. Flying ambassador class

For my flight to San Francisco, Sandhani the great got me a discount. I almost never fly first class, but economy class is real torture for me because there is no room to stretch out and after three hours my legs give way. I get such pain! And San Francisco takes practically six hours' flying.

Garima is always kind to me. When I said that I always have knee trouble because of the lack of room in economy, she wanted to change my ticket from economy to ambassador class for the return trip. She was asking me to let her change my ticket because she said the ambassador-class seats are very wide. She was begging me to let her pay the difference.

So I agreed, and Garima had to pay the difference, first between super-saver and economy, and then between economy and ambassador.

42. Let God enter first

At the airport the plane was an hour and a half late. I was chatting with the disciples in the lounge, cutting jokes and just killing time. As usual, the disciples were looking at me with affection, love and devotion, as though they were all about to realise God in the next second.

One middle-aged man was observing us. When it came time to board, strangely enough the disciples were allowed to come very near the entrance to the plane. So that man got mad. He came up to me and said, "Who do you think you are – God? These people are worshipping you as if you were God. Since you are God, you enter first!"

I said, "I am not blocking your way. You please go first."

Standing in front of him were Agraha and Brad. Immediately they wanted to go with me into the plane to protect me, but I said it was not necessary.

43. A pillow for God

Once I entered into the plane, I took my seat in the ambassador-class section and was getting ready to write poems. In five minutes' time the same man came to me with a pillow and a blanket and said, "God, take this!"

Previously he was mad at me, but this time he was joking. I didn't say anything to him. I just smiled. God didn't accept his offering, but God was grateful to him.

Then he put the pillow and blanket on the seat next to me.

44. Sue the airline

Then the man said, "You should sue the airline. You are paying for ambassador class, but the seats are so narrow! They are gypping you."

I also felt that the seats were unbearably narrow, but I didn't want to make a fuss. I just thought that I would cut jokes with Garima afterwards, saying that this was her ambassador class – extra cost, but no extra room! Then I said to myself, "Perhaps I should sue Snigdha; she works for that airline."

When my friend started complaining, a stewardess came and said I would get a full refund. Some of the planes have the new ambassador-class seats, but this particular plane had not yet been remodelled.

45. Eight refunds

As I was filling out the form for a refund, the head stewardess came by and said, "Where did you get this?" She was absolutely furious.

The first stewardess said, "I am giving him a refund. Otherwise, these people are going to sue the airline. We have taken money from them for ambassador class, but these are not ambassador-class seats."

There were only eight of us in the ambassador class, although there were about forty seats. So the head stewardess went to get refund forms for the other seven passengers as well. First she was angry at the stewardess who gave me the refund form. Perhaps she had wanted to deceive us. But then she herself went to all the other ambassador-class passengers and gave them forms.

It was all because of the man who called me "God" that eight people got refunds. The other ambassador-class passengers were fools like me. If that man had not spoken up, the stewardess would have kept silent about the fact that they were not ambassador-class seats.

My only thanks to that man came through my smiling. The man was very pleased when I smiled at him. Then he went away.

After some time I got up to look for my friend, because I wanted to thank him. I walked all around the economy section, going to this side and that side, but I could not find him.

First this man was angry at me. Then his heart came forward and he brought a little pillow and blanket for God. Then he saw that God was suffering, so he wanted to sue the airline. Because of him eight people got refunds.

46. *The dancing man*

As soon as the plane was in the air, a young man got the inspiration to dance. He would stand in front of someone and then start his dancing.

When I saw him coming near me, immediately I pretended to fall asleep. When he saw that I was sleeping, he went past me.

47. *The economy-class sleepers*

In two hours' time at least ten or twelve people from economy class came to lie down in the ambassador-class seats. These people didn't pay anything for ambassador class; they just came and were sleeping there. The stewardesses didn't ask them to move. If it had really been ambassador class, they wouldn't have allowed people from the economy section to occupy the seats.

48. Thin man

When I finished eating, I got up to go to the back of the plane to use the bathroom. Since we were only in the ambassador class, we were not allowed to go forward to the first-class bathrooms.

The stewardesses were still serving, and they had their trolleys in the aisles. Ahead of me there were two ladies who also wanted to go to the bathroom, but they couldn't move because the trolleys were blocking their way. One of the stewardesses said to me, "You are thin. You can pass by. But they can't." She put her hand on my back and said, "You can try, but those two can't even try."

Then she turned the trolley in such a way that there was a tiny space. I went through, and immediately she turned the trolley straight. As I was coming back, I saw that those two women were still waiting to get through.

NOTES TO THE WORLD-EXPERIENCE-TREE-CLIMBER, BOOK I

1. *(p. 251)* 19 October 1980.
2. *(p. 251)* 27 July 1981.
3. *(p. 252)* 17 September 1981.
4. *(p. 252)* 31 December 1981.
5. *(p. 252)* 31 December 1981.
6. *(p. 253)* 3 January 1982.
7. *(p. 253)* 3 January 1982.
8. *(p. 254)* 3 January 1982.
9. *(p. 254)* 3 January 1982.
10. *(p. 254)* 28 March 1982.
11. *(p. 255)* 28 March 1982.
12. *(p. 255)* 28 March 1982.
13. *(p. 255)* 28 March 1982.
14. *(p. 256)* 28 March 1982.
15. *(p. 260)* 20 May 1982.
16. *(p. 261)* 20 May 1982.
17. *(p. 261)* 20 May 1982.
18. *(p. 263)* 20 May 1982.
19. *(p. 263)* 20 May 1982.
20. *(p. 264)* 20 May 1982.
21. *(p. 264)* 20 May 1982.
22. *(p. 265)* 20 May 1982.
23. *(p. 265)* 20 May 1982.
24. *(p. 266)* 20 May 1982.
25. *(p. 266)* 20 May 1982.
26. *(p. 267)* 20 May 1982.
27. *(p. 268)* 20 May 1982.
28. *(p. 268)* 20 May 1982.
29. *(p. 269)* 20 May 1982.
30. *(p. 270)* 20 May 1982.

31. *(p. 270)* 20 May 1982.
32. *(p. 271)* 20 May 1982.
33. *(p. 271)* 11 June 1982.
34. *(p. 272)* 11 June 1982.
35. *(p. 272)* 11 June 1982.
36. *(p. 272)* 11 June 1982.
37. *(p. 273)* 11 June 1982.
38. *(p. 273)* 11 June 1982.
39. *(p. 273)* 11 June 1982.
40. *(p. 274)* 11 June 1982.
41. *(p. 274)* 11 June 1982.
42. *(p. 275)* 11 June 1982.
43. *(p. 275)* 11 June 1982.
44. *(p. 276)* 11 June 1982.
45. *(p. 276)* 11 June 1982.
46. *(p. 277)* 11 June 1982.
47. *(p. 277)* 11 June 1982.
48. *(p. 278)* 11 June 1982.

THE WORLD-EXPERIENCE-TREE-CLIMBER

BOOK 2

49. A gold heart

I didn't want anyone to meet me at the airport in North Carolina, so nobody was there. I got into a taxi and asked the driver to take me to my hotel. He said, "The hotel is so near. You should wait for the yellow bus. It will take you there for free."

I waited five minutes, but the bus didn't come. So again I asked the taxi driver to take me to my hotel. He said, "I will have to charge you five dollars, but the bus will take you free." He was so honest!

I said, "I will give you five dollars," and I got into the car.

Just then the yellow bus came. The taxi driver said, "Why don't you get out and take the bus?"

I said, "No, please take me to the hotel."

The hotel was not even five hundred metres away. The taxi made just two or three turns, and then we were there.

I gave him a ten-dollar bill, and he gave me five dollars in return. I took the five dollars and got out of the cab.

As I was talking to a lady at the door of the hotel, the taxi driver started shouting at me: "You gave me two ten-dollar bills by mistake!" They were new bills, so they had stuck together. He was kind enough to return the extra ten-dollar bill. Then I gave him the five-dollar bill as a token of my appreciation.

This is how this taxi driver showed his gold heart.

50. Let me see your ticket!

When I went to see Connors play Nastase in the U.S. Open at the National Tennis Center, Databir and Ashrita had gotten me a very expensive ticket. The usher showed me to my seat, which was in the front row.

After some time the man sitting beside me said to me, "I am so and so. Would you please show me your ticket?"

I gave him my ticket. He began looking at it and scratching his head. It was definitely the correct ticket for that seat. He asked, "How could they put you here?" According to him, his party had the whole box.

Then, after five minutes, he again asked for my ticket. That time I said, "Please don't bother me anymore. You saw the usher put me here."

His friends also were annoyed with him. After that he didn't bother me anymore.

51. *Assistance from Databir's mother*

At the U.S. Open there was a man standing almost on top of me, blocking my view. All of a sudden Databir came up, shouting, "Hey, Mom! Hey, Mom!"

I said to myself, "What is Databir's mother doing here? Does she like tennis so much that she would come all the way from Connecticut?"

But Databir's mother wasn't there at all. Databir was just trying to get the man to move. By drawing his attention, Databir was able to move the man aside. Then the man went away.

52. *An Indian without arrows*

When I went to my first World's Fair in 1964, I overheard a mother telling her child that I was an Indian.

Then the child asked the mother why I did not have any arrows.

53. A significant question

Long live Vijali! She is the founder of three Centres – St. Thomas, St. John and St. Croix. Altogether we have about fourteen or fifteen disciples there, and they all came to see me when I went to the Virgin Islands. About seventy or eighty seekers also came to see me.

Previously I had had a few very discouraging experiences in St. Thomas, but this time it was most encouraging. For seekers to meditate for thirty-five minutes in silence is a great achievement! I also played the esraj, and afterwards many, many soulful questions were asked.

After I had answered a few questions, a girl who was five or six years old said, "I have a question."

Everybody was amused. They wanted to hear what kind of question she had.

Then she said, "How do you know all that stuff?"

Her question was shorter than the shortest, but it took me ten minutes to answer it. She was very moved.

Later, when I was about to leave in the car, she came up to me with folded hands to offer me some candy and asked, "Why do you have to go away today?" Afterwards I learned that her mother is a disciple.

54. The governor's welcome

The Governor of the Virgin Islands wrote me a very nice and gracious letter, starting with "Honourable Sri Chinmoy". In the letter he appreciated me deeply. He also sent an album with his autograph. He is a Puerto Rican, and I am sure that he knew of me.

His assistant – a tall, strong-looking man – read out the Governor's letter at the end of our public concert. The whole time he was reading, his entire body was shaking. Afterwards, he asked to have not one, but two or three photographs taken with me.

55. Free advertising

In November I went to Puerto Rico to participate in the Conference of the International Yoga Teachers' Association. There were quite a few swamis, spiritual Masters and seekers there.

While I was there, articles about me appeared in three Puerto Rican newspapers. *The San Juan Star* actually had two articles about me. They mentioned that I would be meditating and doing a few other things at the Conference on a particular day from eight o'clock to twelve. And they said anybody could come for free, since I never charge any fee. Unfortunately, the Conference officials were actually charging ten dollars.

56. The greatest of all Masters

The day before I was scheduled to appear, the Conference authorities informed me that they could give me only two hours, instead of four. Instead of getting annoyed, I was delighted! I said to myself, "Why two hours? Why not one hour? The less time the better!"

I arrived at the Conference at ten o'clock. An Indian swami who was speaking before me went on and on about spirituality, while an interpreter translated into Spanish. So instead of starting at ten o'clock, I started at eleven o'clock.

When I finally went to the stage, they read out a very long introduction about me. The lights were quite dim, so they asked me whether I needed better light. I said, "I don't want to meditate in the dark. Definitely I need better light."

I meditated for a short time, played the esraj and sang two or three songs. Then the Puerto Rican women disciples sang four or five songs, and Uttama did *hatha yoga* for ten minutes to bring down cosmic energy. While Uttama was drawing cosmic energy onto the stage, I was meditating very powerfully. Master and disciple were bringing down cosmic energy together.

Around ten minutes to twelve, we finished our roles. The Conference organiser, who had been sitting in the front row, came up to the stage and bowed down in front of me with folded hands for about two minutes. Then she got inspired to start praising me to the skies. She said I was absolutely the greatest of all the spiritual Masters, not only for this era, but also for future generations. Like this she went on for five minutes. The swami who had spoken before me and so many other swamis were there while she was saying this.

Luckily, the audience was polite. Otherwise, the disciples of some of the other Masters might have caused trouble when they heard me getting such appreciation.

57. Aeroplane celebrity

In the plane on the way home, the stewardess who was serving the first-class section came to the economy section where I was sitting. I had finished my food and was writing poems. She noticed that I had not used the syrup that came with my French toast. It has millions of calories, so I didn't want to take it. She asked if she could give my syrup to somebody else. I said yes. I was very happy to give it away.

About forty-five minutes later, while I was in deep meditation, the same stewardess came to me and asked, "Why do you keep writing 'God, God, God'?"

Do I write the word "God" in all my poems? Perhaps only in one of the poems I had written the word "God". But she had seen it everywhere!

Then she asked me, "Did you come to Puerto Rico to attend the Conference?"

I said, "Yes, I did."

She said, "Which presentation did you like best?"

I said to her, "I didn't attend all the functions."

She said, "I was there on Thursday and Friday, but I couldn't come Saturday because of my work."

I said, "I was only there on Saturday."

Then she asked me who had participated on Saturday. I didn't know the names of any of the other participants, so finally I had to say that I was one of the performers, not one of the observers.

She asked, "Can you tell me your name?"

As soon as she heard "Sri Chinmoy", she exclaimed, "Mira!" Then she sat down right in front of me, and for at least an hour and fifteen minutes she asked me questions. Sometimes she was on the seat and sometimes she was sitting on the floor.

She couldn't believe she was speaking to such a "great man" and that I was answering question after question. At least two times her colleagues asked her to come and help them, but she wouldn't go.

58. Airborne philosophy

The airline stewardess told me she was a staunch Catholic, but she asked me questions not only about Catholicism but also about Hinduism, Buddhism and other religions. She said, "You say the Buddha and the Christ are one. How is it that the Buddha was so strict and the Christ had so much more compassion?"

I said, "You were born into a Christian family. So why do you have to worry about the Buddha? The Buddha and the Christ are one. Let us say that you are both the Buddha and the Christ."

She couldn't believe my words. She said, "I am the Buddha and the Christ?" She looked to this side and that side as if to say, "How can I believe that?"

I said, "For me, let us say, you are the Buddha and the Christ. Now, suppose you have a younger sister who did something wrong, and you are displeased with her. If I happen to be there when you scold her, I will say that you are very strict.

"Then, let us say, a few moments later you see that same sister doing something good – something that gives you tremendous joy. At that time, you will show her such kindness and affection. Now, if somebody else happens to be there while you are showing her your affection, he will see only this side of you.

"So I saw your scolding face and somebody else saw your loving affection. But you are the same person. Perhaps you have read something about the Buddha when be was being strict with his disciples. But the same Buddha has shown such tolerance and compassion many, many times. Sometimes he shows his strictness and other times he shows love and affection to mankind."

This kind of philosophical discussion we enjoyed on the plane!

59. A lesson in renunciation

At one point the stewardess asked me the significance of the colour of my track suit. It happened to be the colour of renunciation.

She said, "See, I can't renounce. Your Hindu philosophy is renunciation."

I said, "I could have been wearing any colour, but you have asked me the significance of this particular colour."

She said, "But I can't renounce."

I said, "You don't have to renounce anything except things that are unnecessary in your life. If you need only one car and you have two, then get rid of the extra one. If you have four or five houses and you only need one, then keep just one."

She said, "I have a beautiful ring. It is certainly not necessary in my life. Do you think I have to renounce it?"

I said, "If you are attached to it, then renounce it. But if you are not attached to it, then you do not have to renounce it. Just tell me, do you feel a kind of vanity about it?"

She said, "I do feel some vanity."

I said, "When you wear it, do you feel extra joy? Do you feel that you look more beautiful?"

She said, "That I can't say, but I feel happiness when I wear it."

I said, "All right, because of this ring God will not delay your God-realisation. But if you are deeply attached to your ring, then just discard it."

I was talking loudly, and the people beside me and behind me were all listening in awe. One man had been smiling at the beginning of our conversation. But after a while he started leaning forward so that he could hear everything. He was showing such respect for our marathon conversation.

Finally, this girl gave me her card and said, "You are a great man." She lives only five or six blocks from our Centre.

She was very simple, very soulful, very pure. Who knows, someday she may become my disciple. Then, the rest of her life she will be able to say that on the plane she had such a soulful and powerful talk with me.

60. Visits from the soul of Japan

The soul of Japan has come to me several times since we arrived in Japan. The first time was at the airport. The second time was in a furniture store, where Kirit was buying me a chair.

The third time the soul of Japan came to me was early yesterday morning. Since then, almost every morning I have had a wonderful talk with the soul of Japan. Yesterday it was all about Japanese political matters. The soul was advising me about Japanese politics. I said, "I am the right person to understand politics!"

61. Nakamura's oneness-feeling

Nakamura, the great Japanese running coach, has a big heart. He is like a grandfather. Anything that a grandfather says is philosophy. Whatever he says seems good. He says that Buddha's philosophy is the same as Krishna's philosophy.

His students have such faith in him and such admiration for him! They take him as a real friend, even a real father. Other university teachers often don't have any kind of oneness-feeling for their students. They teach what they want to teach, and the students learn what they want to learn. But Nakamura exercises his power of love, and his teaching success comes from his concern. It is not just strict military discipline. So his students really believe in him and believe that what he says is absolutely right.

62. Trick photography

After Nakamura came to our hotel in Tokyo to leave the gifts he had brought for us, I was talking with him on the way to the subway.

He wanted someone to take pictures of us. The one photographer who was with us had no more film left in his camera, but I said, "Just take it anyway!" So he just clicked the button and pretended to take our picture.

Before that, that photographer had taken seven or eight pictures of us. In one picture I was autographing something. In another, Nakamura was putting his hand on my chest after I had put my hand on his heart chakra.

My interview with Nakamura came out in a Japanese newspaper. It was a very significant interview.

63. Rogue taxi drivers

Twice yesterday a taxi driver took advantage of me. In the first incident, the ride was supposed to cost 400 yen, but the man kept driving around until the meter said 1,600.

In the evening another taxi driver took me to the wrong street. I was showing the driver the map, but even then he brought me to the wrong place. He told me in Japanese, "I don't know." What a rogue! I was so furious! In Japanese he apologised.

In Queens some taxi drivers charge 100 dollars for a ten-dollar ride. Such corruption!

64. Hiroshima

I was so moved by our visit to Hiroshima. There I felt spiritual grandeur, peace and tranquility. Some of the bomb victims' spirits are still hovering around and trying to take revenge, but most of the souls that were there when the bomb dropped have gone back to the souls' world, so for them the story is over.

65. Visit with the train driver

On the way from Hiroshima to Nagasaki, I had a wonderful conversation with the driver of the train. I was appreciating him, and he was smiling like anything.

How I wish I had his job! He works for three days and then has one day rest. Then again for three days he works. Each day he works for only a few hours. But his job takes great patience. Even after fifteen minutes, most people would be tired of doing it.

66. The polite workers

The people in Okinawa are very polite. I was taking exercise this morning in the hall. The Okinawa chambermaids were politely waiting for me to finish before passing by. In America the hotel people would have pushed by. Even the lowest bellboy in Japan thinks and acts as if it were his hotel, and you are his honoured guest.

67. Extraordinary souls

Some of the Okinawans who participated in our concert were absolutely extraordinary souls – extremely developed. When they were singing, I was not seeing their faces or bodies – only the souls. The souls were dancing right on top of their heads. They were enjoying the songs.

68. A show of emotion

Tagore wrote that the Japanese don't show emotion, and before I came to Japan I believed him. But now I see that perhaps Tagore touched the Japanese mind, whereas I am touching the Japanese heart.

When we were leaving, three Japanese women disciples were crying and crying at the airport. Psychically it was their souls that were crying. So Tagore was wrong. If you touch the heart, even if it is a stone heart, it will show emotion.

69. City and village consciousness

Comparing the Okinawa consciousness to the ordinary Japanese consciousness is like comparing the village consciousness to the city consciousness. The city consciousness feels it is superior because it has the mind, whereas the village consciousness feels it is superior because it has the heart.

The village consciousness says, "You say we are uncivilised. But what has your civilisation taught you? To be indifferent!"

If one village person needs money or assistance, others will give it to him. In the city, a rich man will not come to your aid even if you are the poorest man!

70. The children's performance is best

After the concert this weekend, a lady who came up for prasad said, "Everything was good, but the children's performance was the best." She said that my esraj was second.

71. Begging for a painting

The manager of the Marine Midland Bank in Jamaica is begging me for a painting. He wants to hang it in his home. For him to ask for a painting is really something!

He told Ashrita that even if I don't give him one, he still sends me all his love.

His daughter is taking a course from one of the disciples.

72. Ready to die

On the way to the Taj Mahal I was reading a cute Taj Mahal story. I have read that kind of story before. Many wives are more than eager to die if their husbands are ready to build another Taj Mahal for them. The wives are ready to be immortalised, but the husbands are not ready with the money-power or heart-power.

73. A chance encounter at the Taj Mahal

I was inside the main gate, about a hundred metres from the Taj Mahal, taking nice pictures with my Indian camera. I didn't take my American camera, but instead I bought the most expensive Indian camera. It was most expensive in Indian terms, but for me it was most inexpensive – less than fifty dollars.

All of a sudden Ranjana called out to me. She was standing with a woman who was wearing Western dress, and she said, "Guru, look who is here!"

Then immediately a young Western woman came over to greet me, and told me that her sister Susan was my disciple. We have quite a few Susans on our path, so I asked, "Susan who?"

The answer came: "Susan Elliott."

I know my disciples' first names, but their surnames only God knows! "Who is Susan Elliott?" I asked myself.

Fortunately, the young woman added, "She is from Canada."

Something within me said perhaps it was Susan and Vince. In the meantime Ranjana came over to me with the other woman. It turned out I was right, and this woman was Susan's mother.

I told her mother, "Susan is very dear and close to me."

Her mother corrected me, "You mean Susan and Vince!"

I said, "Yes, both Susan and Vince are very dear to me."

She was thrilled and excited to have met me there, and I too was very happy.

Over the years the disciples have given me thousands of gifts – good or bad, beautiful or ugly. But I remembered that a few years ago Susan's mother had sent Susan a shawl from India, which she had asked Susan to give me. I was blessing myself for remembering this! So I thanked her for the gift she had sent through her daughter. She was very happy.

Then she introduced me to her husband. While she was introducing me, she was so happy, thrilled and excited, but the husband – I have to be very frank – was stiff and uneasy; he was a little scared.

Susan's younger sister, Amy, was so happy and excited because she was the one who had been able to recognise me. How? Susan had sent her my picture. If she had sent the transcendental picture, perhaps her sister would not have recognised me. But Susan had sent a picture of me with my dogs, and Amy immediately recognised me from that picture. So you see, my transcendental picture is not the only one to send people. If you send more ordinary pictures, then immediately people can recognise me.

Can you imagine? Susan's family happened to be there on the same day and at the same hour as we were. Credit goes to my dogs, to Susan for sending the picture and to her sister, Amy.

Afterwards, Ranjana took a group picture of us, and then we all shook hands. Then Susan's father wanted to take a picture. While he was taking the picture, his consciousness started changing. He started to relax. After he took the picture, he was a totally different man – smiling and beaming with joy.

74. The visa broker

While I was in Calcutta, I was getting such joy that Chittagong was only an hour and a half away by plane. I was so eager to go there, so I went to try to get a visa.

Many, many stories I have heard about how difficult it is to get a visa to Bangladesh if you are not a big shot. But my taxi driver, who was from Bangladesh, said, "Those days are gone. You can easily go there now."

At the visa office there was a big line. Somebody came up to me and asked, "Do you need my help?"

I said, "Who are you?"

He said, "I am a broker. Here it will take you three days to get a visa. But if you give me 200 rupees, I will be able to get it for you by three o'clock this afternoon."

While I was talking to him, a young man standing nearby heard me mention Chittagong. He came up to me and said he also comes from Chittagong, so we started talking in our Chittagong dialect.

He said, "You can trust this broker. He is trustworthy."

So I gave the man my passport. Then he brought me to a place that was darker than the darkest to have my picture taken. It was so dirty that I wanted to take the picture with my eyes closed.

The broker was a Muslim. He said that he had never told a lie. He said that he had a big family and that the only way he could support them was by doing this kind of work. So we invoked Allah and all the Hindu gods and goddesses. At that moment, Hindus and Muslims were all one family.

At three o'clock I went to the place where I was supposed to meet him. He said, "I am sorry. You mentioned in your passport that you are a teacher. When you say that, everything becomes very complicated. So I could not get your visa. Tomorrow I will get it."

I said, "Please give me my passport."

He said, "I can't give it to you now. It is in the office, which is closed."

I scrutinised him inwardly and outwardly. Then I said, "Now bring my passport! Otherwise, I am going to the police station. I will keep my word and give you 200 rupees, but I want my passport."

He said, "Please go two blocks to a Punjabi coffee shop. I will come there with the passport."

I waited inside the coffee shop until I saw the Muslim standing outside a block away. He signalled for me to come to where he was standing. It seemed that we were in secret collusion. Either he was in trouble or I was in trouble.

He said, "Please write down that you have received the passport from me."

I said, "I have not received it yet, so why should I write down that I have?"

He said, "How can I be sure that you will give me the money? If I give you your passport and you don't give me the money, what can I do?"

This time I said, "I am ready to give you the money, but if you don't give me the passport immediately, I am going to the police!" Then from his pocket he took out the passport. Before I took the passport, I threw 200 rupees at him.

75. Registering for the Asiatic Games

While I was in Delhi, they were having the Asiatic Veterans Athletics Competition for athletes over forty. I read in the newspaper that athletes who wanted to participate had to be invited. Otherwise, they had to register for two rupees, the equivalent of ten or twenty cents.

I was not feeling well, but I thought that by the time the competitions started in two days I would be all right. So I went to register. Unfortunately, registration was closed. I said, "Fine! It is a hopeless case."

India has no money; that is absolutely true. But when it is a matter of a stadium, the new stadium in Delhi can compete with any stadium in the West.

Always I carry with me my five-cents-worth *Galaxy of Luminaries,* the tinier-than-the-tiniest book that shows pictures of me with many big shots. I showed *Galaxy* to someone at the Asiatic Veterans Competition office. He said, "Oh, you are a great man!" Then he told one of the officials how great I am.

Immediately everything changed. Five minutes earlier registration was out of the question. Now they were telling me only that I needed three pictures.

I said, "Where am I going to get three pictures?"

Then the official said, "He does not need pictures."

I entered my name for the 100-, 200- and 400-metre dashes, as well as for the shot-put, discus and javelin.

The registration fee was twenty rupees if you joined one item and thirty rupees if you joined more than one. By mistake it came out in the newspaper that the registration was two rupees. So I paid thirty rupees, a little more than three dollars.

76. Attack by the hostile forces

I was all ready for the competition. I was feeling better by the next day, which was practice for the opening march-past. I took my place in line and practised with the others. Everything was excellent.

But the hostile forces are always ready to show me their capacities. After the march-past was over, the officials had to give instructions. Suddenly it started raining cats and dogs. I wasn't wearing a hat, but people would have thought it was bad manners if I had left. So I had to stand in the rain with my bald head.

If I get even two or three drops of rain on my head, I start to sneeze, and there I had to stand in a downpour. By the following day I had such a high fever that I was practically blind, so I didn't go for the competition.

77. Trying to get my T-shirt

Instead of competing at the stadium, I just stayed at the hotel all day, suffering from fever. The day after that I decided to go to the Veterans Games office to get my T-shirt.

I said, "I could not join in the competition, but can I get my T-shirt?"

The man in the office said, "Yes, but not now. Come back after an hour."

THE WORLD-EXPERIENCE-TREE-CLIMBER

An hour later again I went there to get this precious thing – a T-shirt! This time they said, "You don't get the T-shirt here. You get it somewhere else. Go there in two or three hours."

A third time I went for my T-shirt. This time the place was closed.

The following day I went there at 9:30. Outside the stadium the race-walking competition was going on. Four different groups started together, but each was covering a different distance.

When I went inside the office, I noticed that quite a few Sikhs were there. If you call them *Sardar-ji* – which means leader – immediately their hearts melt. But this time they all started telling lies.

One of them said, "Yes, you will get your T-shirt, but first let me introduce you to the manager. His name is Ghuli."

So Ghuli and I chatted. Then Ghuli told me, "Yes, we will give you the T-shirt, but come at twelve o'clock. Now I am very busy."

I asked Ghuli if I could speak to Milka Singh. Once upon a time I was his great admirer. He used to be called India's "Flying Sikh". In one Olympics he stood among the top finishers in a photo-finish race. He did not stand first, but for an Indian to even be in a photo-finish with three Americans was really something.

When I asked for Milka Singh, Ghuli said, "Who is Milka Singh?" He meant it was beneath his dignity to introduce me to him. Then he said, "You come at twelve o'clock. You don't have to see Milka Singh."

78. Massaging the walker

After they crossed the finish line, at least seven or eight of the race-walkers immediately vomited. One South Indian fellow was very short and thin. He walked thirty metres past the finish line, and then he lay down on the ground, panting and vomiting. People were calling for the ambulance, which was only a hundred metres away. But the driver was missing. Meanwhile, nobody was coming to his rescue.

So, with my back pain and fever, I went to help the man. With greatest difficulty I knelt down on the ground and started massaging his right foot. God knows if he had pain there! For four or five minutes I massaged him here, there and everywhere.

Two or three times he kicked me. I know what I go through when the boys massage me sometimes. I don't kick them physically, but inwardly perhaps I do.

Finally the ambulance came, and three men picked him up and took him away to the hospital. While they were putting him in the ambulance, he was mercilessly kicking them.

79. The judges' mix-up

After that, I continued watching the walking races. In one race, two Bengalis stood first and second. One finished at least three minutes behind the other. But the judges mixed it up, and declared the second-place winner first.

When they made the announcement, everybody started laughing. The judges got mad because they felt they could not make such a mistake. The one who stood second went to the judge and said, "I was far behind him."

The judge said, "I don't want to hear that."

So the one who was second went and embraced the one who really had stood first. He said, "What can we do?"

The other one said, "Let us go out for a cup of coffee."

The wives of the first and second finishers were roaring with laughter. Fortunately the couples were good friends. So all four of them went out for a cup of coffee.

80. Watching the other events

I couldn't believe the fellow who stood first in the long jump! I used to do it in four steps, but now I would die if I tried. All the competitors were old men like me, but I wouldn't dare to try it.

When I saw the javelin competition, I felt sorry that I didn't join. Perhaps I would have won. But they used a 16-pound shot for the shot-put. The man from Thailand who stood first was three times my size. He threw it so far!

81. Meeting Milka Singh

At twelve o'clock I went back for my famous T-shirt, but the manager, Ghuli, was not to be found in the office. He was in the playground, not paying any attention to the time. For an hour I wasted time, then I went to another office to get the immortal T-shirt. They said, "Ghuli is very busy right now."

I watched a few more races and went back again. Finally I got mad. My fever was escalating like anything. I said, "I am going to say nasty things in America about how corrupt Indians are."

Then I saw the first Sardar-ji, Jogendra, the man who had been kind to me and who had introduced me to Ghuli. He happened to be the Secretary of All-India Athletics for the Veterans. He saw me going away, so he asked me, "Where are you going?"

I said, "I am sick of Indians. They are all liars!"

He grabbed me and said, "We are not so bad."

I said, "Yes, you are all like that."

Then he took me into a room and said, "Now sit down and say anything you like against us."

I told him, "Do I need this T-shirt? I paid for it, and three or four times I have tried to get it." I went on like this and insulted everybody, while he listened to me. "Also, I wanted to meet Milka Singh, and the manager didn't want to be bothered with that."

In the same room there was a very old man, an Indian reporter and a very tall Sikh, who was sitting on a chair. All of a sudden the Sikh came over to me. He said, "You have come to the right person."

I said, "Everybody says that he is the right person, but nobody has been able to help me. They just send me here and there like a football. Now tell me who you are."

The tall man said, "I am Milka Singh."

I said, "You are Milka Singh? I was your great admirer." Then I started telling him about his athletic achievements.

He said, "You say Indians are bad. But others are even worse." Then we had a long chat. We talked for about an hour, and he told me many stories about his career.

82. Blamed for everything

Then Milka Singh said, "Next year the Veterans Games will take place in Puerto Rico. I will be going there with a delegation. I hope they do a better job and make better arrangements.

"They have elected me President, so I am blamed for everything here. I don't get any salary, but every day I get a heart attack. Is there anybody who does not curse me? The higher you go, the worse your punishment is. What can I do? People are turning me insane."

At this point the reporter wanted to interview me. I said, "Please forgive me. I am not interested now. I am speaking to this man."

Then I told Milka Singh, "You won't believe it, but I am going to inaugurate the Games in Puerto Rico with a silent meditation and a brief message."

I still had my *Galaxy of Luminaries*. I showed him Governor Colon's picture and Governor Ferre's picture. He said, "You are a great man. Can I have this book?"

I said, "I am autographing it for you." So I dedicated the booklet to him. I gave him my phone number in Puerto Rico and my private phone number in New York. I said, "When you are in Puerto Rico, you will be my guest, along with the members of your delegation."

83. Meeting the big shots

From where to where! Milka Singh started introducing me to everybody.

One of the people he introduced me to was the President of the Singapore Athletics Association. His name was Chandra. When Milka Singh told him, "He will meditate to inaugurate the Games in Puerto Rico," Chandra grabbed me and said, "You have to sit with my delegation today in our box." He wouldn't allow me to sit with the Indians. Then he also started telling people what a great man I was.

Then the President of the Athletics Association in Thailand started speaking to me in broken English. He said, "May I speak to you for a while?"

Suddenly I had become a big shot. I said to Milka Singh, "I have come here for a T-shirt – don't forget!"

Milka Singh said, "Definitely you will get a T-shirt, but I really want to honour you. Please don't curse us."

84. Cursed by everybody

Because of Milka Singh's position, not a single person had any gratitude for him. Even the ninety-one-year-old man who had been sitting in the office with him when I first came in was cursing him.

The old man said he had come in first in his event but that the judges had made a mistake and given the first prize to somebody else.

The old man was short, quite fat and odd-looking. His eyes were frightening.

85. The blind photographer

I went with my friend Chandra to watch the races with the Singapore delegation for about two hours. Chandra told me, "My daughter Gloria is running the 200 metres. She has a six-year-old son." He said she was the best.

Gloria came and sat down and talked to me. While she was talking, she was putting Vaseline over her whole body. I was laughing to myself, saying, "Why should someone need Vaseline? Is it a marathon?" And in India it is so warm!

Chandra was right. In the 200 metres she finished forty metres ahead of the second finisher, who was from Nepal. The Indian runners were far behind her. The Singapore athletes badly defeated the Indians.

Chandra was supposed to run 200 metres and the 400-metre hurdles, and I was supposed to take his picture. While I was looking for him through the camera lens, he finished the race. Then he came back and everybody was congratulating him because he stood first.

I asked him, "Did you run?"

He said, "Yes, I ran. What were you doing?"

I said, "I was holding the camera, but I could not see you."
Afterwards, they took our picture standing together.

86. False start to finish

In one 100-metre race, there was a false start, but all the runners continued running anyway. The starter fired the gun twice, the judges and even the audience were screaming for them to stop, but they completed the whole hundred metres! Then after five minutes they had to run it again.

87. Getting the famous T-shirt – at last

Finally I became tired. I said to myself, "They are supposed to be honouring me, but this is just another joke. All right, Milka Singh was kind to me, but still I have not got my T-shirt. If I go to him again, he will just ask me to sit."

I was not angry; in fact, I was pleased. And I knew that if I went to Milka Singh, he would still honour me. But my fever was very high. So I left my friends from Singapore and secretly started going away.

I was almost at the last exit when whom did I see? Jogendra! He was the one who had been so kind to me and introduced me to the manager, Ghuli. He asked me, "Are you going away?"

I said, "Yes, I am tired."

He said, "Let me take you to Ghuli. This time he will give you the T-shirt."

I said, "No, I do not wish to speak to Ghuli. I would like to see Milka Singh again, but he is busy."

He said, "Milka Singh? I don't deal with him. You have to see Ghuli."

I said, "I don't want to see Ghuli."

This Sardar-ji had been there in the room when Milka Singh said he would honour me. So he reminded me, "Milka Singh has not yet honoured you."

I said, "I have a high fever. I would like to go home."

But Jogendra just took my arm and brought me back to Milka Singh. Milka Singh sat me down. This time I did not say anything about the T-shirt. I only said, "I am sick."

Milka Singh told me, "You have to stay. In five minutes we shall honour you."

Just then Milka Singh's secretary came to me with a T-shirt and placed it on my lap, very gently, and smiled at me.

I thanked him profusely.

So the famous T-shirt story finally ended.

If I hadn't been so persistent in my T-shirt quest, I wouldn't have met Milka Singh.

88. *A public honour*

In about five minutes' time I heard an announcement over the loudspeaker, "Sri Chinmoy, a man of peace and a world-renowned athlete, is now going to present the prizes for the twenty-kilometre walk. He will be escorted by the President of the All-India Veterans Association."

At the centre of the stadium were three girls wearing beautiful saris – not cotton, but silk. They held golden dishes, and the medals were lying on the dishes. The first, second and third place finishers stood behind the girls.

There were also three musicians with bugles. They marched in from one side, and I was escorted to the centre of the stadium from the other side by the big shot.

The person who came in first stood on the top platform in the middle. The second and third place finishers were on either side. We faced the winners.

The man who escorted me would go to each girl to get the appropriate medal, and then give it to me. Then I would go and present the medal to the athlete.

The first one bowed halfway down. I put the medal on him like a garland and shook hands with him. Then I did this for the second and third place finishers. Then we all stood facing the audience.

I was on one end, and the President of the All-India Veterans Association was on the other end. The girls were standing near the President. Then the first place winner raised the hands of the second and third place winners, while the buglers played for two minutes.

When that was over I wanted to go, but Milka Singh said, "No, you have to wait. I want you to see the Prime Minister. She will come here in a few minutes. I will try my best to introduce you, but I can't promise. Anyway, you can't leave yet." So I remained there with the other big shots waiting to meet the Prime Minister.

In five minutes again they announced my name. This time they said, "Sri Chinmoy of the United States will present the prizes for the 400-metre hurdles. We are so happy to have him here. He will be escorted by the Commander of the Air Force." So the Air Force Commander escorted me into the stadium.

Again there were three girls, the buglers and the winners. This time the Commander gave me the medals, and I gave them to the winners. In the 400-metre hurdles, the first place finisher in his age-group was my friend from Singapore, Chandra.

89. Meeting the Prime Minister

In ten minutes Indira Gandhi did come. I was sitting in the last row, and she came and sat not even a metre away from me. I turned and looked at her. She was wearing a cotton sari that was simpler than the simplest. She looked very tired and exhausted. She said, "Oh, I am so tired."

In three or four minutes they announced over the loudspeaker: "Our beloved Prime Minister Indira Gandhi will now give the prizes for the discus." During the announcement I was looking at her with folded hands. When she got up and started walking, everybody folded his hands.

She went down to the same place I had just been and gave the prizes for the discus. She also presented the prizes to the gold medalists of the previous meet in Singapore. Then the ninety-one-year-old man came up to her to say something.

Milka Singh, who is so tall, was all the time bowing with folded hands – trying to come down to her height. At that time Ghuli, the manager, was nowhere to be seen; it was only Milka Singh who was with the Prime Minister.

Then the Prime Minister disappeared and the story ended. Like me, there were four other persons sitting together who were supposed to meet her. But none of us got to see her.

There is one thing I would like to say about her: she definitely has a soulful smile – more so than any other big shot I have seen.

THE WORLD-EXPERIENCE-TREE-CLIMBER

90. Speaking my mother tongue

When I was leaving the stadium, the editor of a Bengali sports magazine said to me, "Sri Chinmoy, are you Bengali?" My surname is Ghose, so he knew I was Bengali.

I said, "Yes."

He said, "Can you speak Bengali?"

So I started speaking to him in Bengali. He said, "But can you read Bengali?" Since the announcer said I was from the United States, he thought that I didn't really know Bengali.

"Yes," I said. "Certainly I can read Bengali."

To have me prove I could read Bengali, he gave me his magazine. So I started reading out a little. Then he said, "I wish to give this magazine to you. Please write a few words to me from America."

It was such a thick magazine, with many pictures. I only kept the cover and his address. It was too heavy to carry back to New York.

91. Priceless photographs

I had with me a silly Indian camera. The first person who escorted me to give the prizes took my camera and gave it to one of his friends.

Later, my friend from Thailand came up to me and said, "Let us have our picture taken together." A photographer who was there took our picture.

My friend said, "Can we have our pictures developed?"

I said, "I am ready to pay, but I don't want to go to the photographer."

So he went to get the photographer and brought him over to me. I asked, "How much do you want to print the pictures for us?"

The photographer said, "Ten rupees."

I said, "I will be leaving tomorrow morning. If I give you 200 rupees, will you bring my copies to the hotel by 9:30? Then I will leave some for my friend."

The photographer agreed. But the next morning, 9:30 came and went, and finally it was twelve o'clock and I had to leave. So I had to write a note for my friend, who was staying at another hotel, telling him that the photographer never came.

I said, "What am I going to do? He didn't care for 200 rupees."

92. The massage artist

In Bangkok I was looking for someone to massage my back. But in the Grace Hotel, where I was staying, they only had ladies who gave massage. I said, "Thank you very much, but no thank you."

I started calling other hotels. Finally, the Ambassador Hotel told me they had a man who gave massage, so I went there for a massage.

The man who gave massage had been to Australia to learn Russian massage, Chinese massage and general massage. In Indian currency, he charged 120 rupees.

When he first saw me, he said, "You are a Hindu! I can tell from your name. But I am a Muslim."

I said, "Who cares whether you are a Muslim or a Hindu? There is only one God."

He said, "I also feel that."

At first he did Chinese massage, using his elbow. How painful! Then he tried Russian massage. I was lying down, and suddenly he jumped on my back and began jogging on it. I let him go from the base of my spine to my shoulder blades. But when he got to my shoulders, my chest was hurting so much that I asked him to stop. I said, "Russian massage is the worst!"

Then he gave me a general massage. After that I asked him, "Can you come to my hotel at 8 o'clock tonight? I will give you more money."

He agreed, and took down my room number.

93. The real big shot

Just before 8 o'clock that night, the man who had given me the massage phoned me and said, "A very important big shot is coming at 8 o'clock to get a massage, so I cannot come to you."

I said, "I didn't tell you what a big shot I am."

He said, "Since you are a big shot, I will come at 9 o'clock."

I asked him, "How much is the other big shot going to give you?"

He said, "The normal price – 120 rupees."

I said, "Then I will give you 200 rupees."

He said, "Oh, you are the real big shot!"

So he came at 8 o'clock and again gave me the Chinese, Russian and general massage. What a massage! Several times he pressed my knee until I screamed. Then, like Pradhan and others, if he heard something crack, he would say that everything was cured.

He weighed about 130 or 140 pounds. When he was on my back, I said, "You are killing me! I don't need this."

At one point during the massage, I said to him, "I want to lose twenty pounds from my stomach."

So he started pinching me and tapping my stomach. Then he said, "Twenty pounds? Impossible! You can lose a maximum of four pounds."

Even after he came to my hotel, I did not show him my *Galaxy of Luminaries*. You don't have to show these people anything so long as you give them enough money. In India I was ready to give the photographer 200 rupees to bring the pictures to my hotel, but he didn't come. At least this one kept his promise.

Before the man left, just to prove I was a real big shot, I gave him not 200 but 240 rupees.

94. *San Francisco Customs*

When I came back from Bangkok through immigration in San Francisco, they put on their red lamp, which means that special government officials will investigate. They took me into another room. Other people also were in the room. Then three more officers came.

I showed them my little *Galaxy* pamphlet, but they just said, "We have to search you thoroughly."

I said, "First search me thoroughly. Then let me write down your badge number."

Immediately they covered their badges with their hands. I said, "If you have the right to search me, I have the right to know who you are. First you do your duty. Then you have to give me your names."

When I got angry, one fellow said, "Sometimes we find drugs inside innocent people's suitcases because others put them there."

Then I opened everything, but they didn't really search my bags. I said, "Now give me your names."

They said, "All right, if you don't mind, take off this belt."

I took off the cloth belt I wear to support my back.

Then the officer said, "Sorry, this is only a formality." He did not suspect me; he was only harassing me.

Finally I got really furious. Then another officer started carrying my bags to the place where the baggage for New York should go.

When they start to harass you right and left, you have to challenge them. But in the end I didn't get their names or badge numbers. So even if I send a letter of complaint to the San Francisco Customs, nobody will know who the officers were.

NOTES TO THE WORLD-EXPERIENCE-TREE-CLIMBER, BOOK 2

49. *(p. 283)* 21 July 1982.
50. *(p. 283)* 7 September 1982.
51. *(p. 284)* 7 September 1982.
52. *(p. 284)* 30 October 1982.
53. *(p. 285)* 22 November 1982.
54. *(p. 285)* 22 November 1982.
55. *(p. 286)* 22 November 1982.
56. *(p. 286)* 22 November 1982.
57. *(p. 287)* 22 November 1982.
58. *(p. 288)* 22 November 1982.
59. *(p. 289)* 22 November 1982.
60. *(p. 291)* 19 December 1982. Same text also published in *The world-experience-tree-climber*, 95.
61. *(p. 291)* 21 December 1982.
62. *(p. 292)* 21 December 1982.
63. *(p. 292)* 22 December 1982.
64. *(p. 293)* 24 December 1982.
65. *(p. 293)* 24 December 1982.
66. *(p. 293)* 4 January 1983.
67. *(p. 294)* 5 January 1983.
68. *(p. 294)* 7 January 1983.
69. *(p. 294)* 12 January 1983. Same text also published in *The world-experience-tree-climber*, 97.
70. *(p. 295)* 31 January 1983.
71. *(p. 295)* 19 February 1983.
72. *(p. 295)* 4 April 1983.
73. *(p. 295)* 4 April 1983.
74. *(p. 297)* 31 March 1983.
75. *(p. 299)* 31 March 1983.
76. *(p. 300)* 31 March 1983.

THE WORLD-EXPERIENCE-TREE-CLIMBER

77. *(p.300)* 31 March 1983.
78. *(p.302)* 31 March 1983.
79. *(p.302)* 31 March 1983.
80. *(p.303)* 31 March 1983.
81. *(p.303)* 31 March 1983.
82. *(p.304)* 31 March 1983.
83. *(p.305)* 31 March 1983.
84. *(p.306)* 31 March 1983.
85. *(p.306)* 31 March 1983.
86. *(p.307)* 31 March 1983.
87. *(p.307)* 31 March 1983.
88. *(p.308)* 31 March 1983.
89. *(p.310)* 31 March 1983.
90. *(p.311)* 31 March 1983.
91. *(p.311)* 31 March 1983.
92. *(p.312)* 31 March 1983.
93. *(p.313)* 31 March 1983.
94. *(p.314)* 31 March 1983.

THE WORLD-EXPERIENCE-TREE-CLIMBER

BOOK 3

95. Visits from the soul of Japan

The soul of Japan has come to me several times since we arrived. The first time was at the airport. The second time was in a furniture store, where Kirit was buying me a chair.

The third time the soul of Japan came to me was early yesterday morning. Since then, almost every morning I have had a wonderful talk with the soul of Japan. Yesterday it was all about Japanese political matters. The soul was advising me about Japanese politics. I said, "I am the right person to understand politics!"

96. Self-torture never ends

In Japan I announced that I was going to write 27,000 more poems. Just as God-realisation never ends, my self-torture also does not end. In Japan I completed 1,500 poems for *Ten Thousand Flower-Flames,* and by August I plan to have all 10,000 completed. Then that will be followed by *Twenty-Seven Thousand Aspiration-Plants.*

Not only in the evening of my life but actually on the last day of my life perhaps I will be writing poems. Will you read them? Get ready! In August I will start the new series, but I will go very slowly – at bullock-cart speed.

97. City and village consciousness

Comparing the Okinawa consciousness to the Japanese consciousness is like comparing the village consciousness to the city consciousness. The city consciousness feels it is superior because it has the mind, whereas the village consciousness feels it is superior because it has the heart.

The village consciousness says, "You say we are uncivilised. But what has your civilisation taught you? To be indifferent!"

If one village person needs money, others will give it to him. In the city, a rich man will not give you anything even if you are the poorest man.

98. The spiritual realtor

I was looking for a small apartment in Florida. When you go apartment hunting, if you like something, you can't get it. The reason: because you meditate. Three apartments I couldn't get because I belong to a "cult". In Florida they observe Sri Chinmoy Day, but in Fort Lauderdale I got this kind of treatment.

The realtor was working so hard and taking me to so many places. For one particular apartment, the price they were asking was too high. The realtor was furious and disgusted. He told the owner he would give up his commission if the man gave me the apartment at a lower price. But the owner did not believe him. They were having a fight on the telephone.

The realtor came from Rhode Island. In his office he had a magazine that had a short article about our triathlon. Outwardly he does not pray, but he was more than spiritual. He wanted to invite me to his house for dinner. Most of the time I salute realtors from a distance. They have given me so many unpleasant experiences. But with this man God wanted to show me that there can be good realtors on earth.

99. The bald head

I went to our new Florida Centre for a rest. Between book stores and sports stores – that was my rest!

One funny story Dristi was telling about a lady she met. They were talking about spiritual matters, and the lady asked Dristi the name of her guru.

Dristi said, "Sri Chinmoy."

The lady said, "My guru is also Sri Chinmoy."

Dristi is the head of our Centre, and she had never seen this lady before. But the lady said that every day for the past ten or eleven years she has been meditating on my picture. She said, "The bald head."

A little bit painfully and hesitantly, Dristi admitted, "Yes, he has a bald head."

The next day the lady brought a picture of the person she was meditating on to prove that Sri Chinmoy was her guru.

It was a picture of Ramana Maharshi. Bald-headed people are all brothers!

100. The Italian lady

Always on long plane trips I write poems. On my flight to Puerto Rico I was deeply absorbed in writing poems for *Silence Speaks*. A very old lady was sitting next to me. After two hours she had to get up. She said, "Sorry to bother you." So I smiled at her and got up.

When she came back, again she said, "Sorry to bother you." Then in very poor broken English she started talking to me. She said she was three or four years old when she came to this country. Now she lives in Douglaston.

I said, "Our best tennis players come from there." She didn't understand what tennis is. She said she has been in America for seventy-four years, yet still she can barely understand English.

She was born in Italy. I said, "I have been in Italy at least six times. I met with the Pope." She couldn't understand the word "Rome". Then when I said "Roma", she understood.

An American lady sitting next to us said, "He has met with the Pope." The old lady didn't believe it. The American lady said, "In this world there are some people who will believe anything you say, and there are some people who won't believe you even after you do something right in front of their eyes." This is her philosophy. I should have shown her my *Luminaries* booklet.

Then the plane descended. My carry-on bag was so heavy because it was filled with weights and books. Also I had bought some candies. Because my bag was so heavy, I wanted everybody else to leave the plane first. I stood up to let the old Italian lady go by, but she didn't want to go. She wanted to wait.

It was so difficult for me to take my bag. I couldn't carry it in one hand; I had to keep it on my shoulder. The old lady was laughing at me in a sarcastic manner, saying, "Great man, great man!" She had a cruel nature. There are people like that on earth. Seventy years in America and she doesn't have to learn English! My neighbour, Mr. Cino, was Italian, but he could speak and understand English much better than this old lady.

101. Trying to lose weight

While I was in Florida, I weighed myself on a doctor's scale: 155 pounds. Savyasachi, Alo and the realtor were the witnesses! Then I came to New York and stood on my own doctor's scale: it said 158. I don't know whether I cried or laughed, but I did something.

From 158 pounds my goal was to come down to 150. Yesterday I came down to my goal in one day by eating very little and then running a lot.

Now I want to go down to 145 pounds in two days. But the mathematics isn't working. You can lose eight or ten pounds in one or two days by starving and exercising, but then you can't keep losing the same amount every day. The body just rebels.

102. Birthday in the air

While I was on the plane to Puerto Rico, one man said to the stewardess, "Today is my friend's birthday."

The stewardess said, "Really?"

The man said, "Yes!"

Then four or five of the airline crew brought out a cake, although the man's name was not on the cake.

I didn't know they observed birthdays on aeroplanes.

103. The mystery of the coconut water

During my first two days in Puerto Rico I fasted and starved, drinking only coconut water. Always Shubhra gave it to me. She does not allow anybody else to serve me. Nobody dares to give me anything if Shubhra is there. Saraswati and Shubhra are sisters, so Saraswati doesn't mind.

In the morning I was thirsty. I was in the meditation room and Shubhra was not there. Alo said, "I will go get you something. There is coconut water in a glass in the refrigerator."

So she brought the coconut water and gave it to me to drink. I took a sip. It was soap! Alo was so furious. A glass of soapy water inside the refrigerator! Then she said she knows Shubhra quite often puts coconut water inside the refrigerator, and she thought this was coconut water.

Everybody was saying Gauri was the one who had put the soapy water in the refrigerator, since she is the one who washes the dishes. But Gauri was begging me to use my occult power to see who was the culprit.

I said, "I don't know who did it, but everybody is blaming you."

104. *The cellist*

We have a new disciple who plays the cello with the Puerto Rico Symphony. She also has about fifty students and teaches five or six hours daily. One by one her students come and play in front of her. When her good students come, she gives them five minutes. When the bad students come, after a minute she says, "Oh, you are playing very well. I am pleased with you." Then she sends them away immediately.

I wanted to practise the cello while I was in Puerto Rico, but this new disciple did not want to let me play on her cello. But after she refused, then for the whole day she felt totally miserable. So on her own she brought me her cello the next day. She said her cello cost 5,000 dollars. It was good, but mine is better. She herself was supposed to play that day, so she borrowed a cello from somebody else.

When I tried her cello she flattered me, saying that my intonation was good. That is why she allowed me to use it.

The day I was supposed to return the cello, I told her to come at twelve o'clock and take it back. She came exactly at twelve. I had brought her a trophy, and she said, "Can I not also have a plaque to put on this trophy that says you gave it to me?"

After I returned the cello, she told Alo that she felt some higher power was guiding her hand when she played it. When she played she felt that it sounded as if Pablo Casals were playing. So she was very happy that she had let me use it.

105. Small world

The world is so small! The university of Cologne, where I was today, is where my ashram coach Saumitra studied. From this university in Germany he went to the ashram in India. And now I have come from India to his place!

106. A long journey

I went into a store to buy something, and a German lady came up to me and said, "Are you Sri Chinmoy?"

I said, "Yes."

She said she had come all the way from Munich to attend tomorrow's concert.

107. Before the concert

Before the concert in Germany, the technicians were looking at me with such respect, admiration and awe. It was because they saw how my disciples were behaving.

One of the security guards came near me and asked, "Are you nervous?"

So in a joking way I deliberately started shaking and trembling.

Then he said, "Don't be nervous, don't be nervous!"

108. The beginning of something unique

An unprecedented thing took place in Cologne on the 27th. It is the very beginning of something unique. *Peace: God's Beauty in His Oneness-Home* has started radiating its divinity and immortality all over the world.

The Germans have spent thousands and thousands of dollars. But I tell you it is not their money-power that achieved this tremendous success. It is their heart-power, oneness-power and cooperation-power that has succeeded. Heart-power, oneness-power, money-power: all the powers should go together.

Over eight thousand people came. Needless to say, they did not come to see the musician in me. They came to me to see a God-lover and peace-distributor. The inner peace that I have and that I am is what they felt long before they even came to the concert. So peace-lovers are the ones who have come to our Peace Concert.

God's fondest child is peace. Whoever needs peace in life, in his entire being, is bound to be the most perfect instrument of God.

109. Japanese talkers

In my hotel in Zurich, there was a group of Japanese making a lot of noise in the room next to me. They had left their door open. At first I thought they were fighting. But no, they were just talking very loudly. Writers long ago said that the Japanese could control their emotions. But when they talk, they scream.

Three times I went out of my room to see what the commotion was all about. But I just smiled at them. They were so young. I thought somebody would come and scold them, but nobody did.

Then at five o'clock I saw them in the elevator. They were leaving the hotel. Even in the elevator they couldn't stop talking!

110. The amateur photographer

At a restaurant in Germany, Pramoda was feeling so happy that she took my picture. But the cover was still on the camera lens! Oh, Pramoda!

111. Delayed arrival

Before my brother received the copy of the programme for the German concert that we sent him, a lady in the Sri Aurobindo Ashram gave him a copy. Had she attended the concert, or did somebody send her a programme from Germany? Who knows – but this is how my brother got it!

112. Aspiration defeats realisation

Flying to Australia is really an arduous journey! I don't know how my Australian disciples come to New York every year, sometimes twice a year! Had I been their disciple, I would have told God I could wait for a few more incarnations before coming to Australia to see my guru. The plane journey sincerely kills me – perhaps because I am an old man. Twenty-four hours – no, twenty-seven hours – we were on the plane.

I really admire my Australian children. Is this not a sign of their aspiration? Their aspiration has defeated my realisation! Of course the heart is very close. My children have a heart to know how much joy they can give me, and I do hope I give them a little joy as well. In the heart there is no distance, no distance, no distance.

113. *An apprehensive soul*

This time, when I arrived in Australia the soul of Australia approached me with tremendous apprehension about whether it would be able to please me. Even when I was in the plane, my disciples were so excited that I was coming, but the soul was suffering from apprehension.

The first time I went there, I was new, and the soul greeted me with immense joy. I did not expect much, and the soul did not expect much from me. But over the years we have developed a good friendship. Since I have done so much for the soul of Australia through my Australian disciples, and the soul knows how much I have done, not only for the disciples, but also for the Australian consciousness, the soul of Australia wanted to give me something very powerful and striking. Sometimes when you consciously want to give something great, very striking, you may be full of apprehension whether you will be able to give or not. When you want to do something or give something very significant, then you become apprehensive.

So right from the airport I was seeing a kind of apprehension. The soul greeted me with utmost joy, love and gratitude, but there was also apprehension about what was going to happen and whether I was going to be pleased and satisfied. But when the concert was over there was tremendous relief, tremendous relief. During the first concert, when there were people waiting outside, I saw that the soul felt great relief that I was well received. Even if nobody had waited for the second show, the soul would not have minded because the first concert was more than enough. It is not only the number of people but also the sincere enthusiasm.

The soul of Australia wanted to show me the sincere concern for peace and the sincere aspiration of its people, and when the soul saw that it was able to show me those things, the soul was more than pleased.

114. Training from the telephone operator

I have an Indian accent, but some Australian accents are far more difficult to understand. I have such problems when they say "eight". I was trying to get a number from the telephone operator one day. He was saying "ite", "ite". I couldn't understand what this word "ite" was. The first time he said it, I thought it was "heart". But what did "heart" have to do with the number? I made him repeat the number four times. Then I realised, "Oh, it is 'eight'!"

The next day, when I asked Ghanta his age, he also said "ite" – but it didn't confuse me because I had already gotten training from the telephone operator.

115. Race experiences

One morning the disciples held a race for the public. Two runners were going ahead of me, and one of them was telling the other, "This guy is everything. Turn around." He wanted his friend to see me properly.

After the race somebody else came up to me and said, "Why do you not allow people to eat meat and fish?" Perhaps he had become very hungry from running.

116. Happiness does exist on earth

Since my childhood ended, in my entire incarnation I have had only two or three happy moments. Of course, when I achieved God-realisation was one. And the day I rode with the engineer of the steam train in Australia was another. When I was young it was my greatest desire to be the driver of a train. God did not see fit to fulfil this innocent desire of mine, but now my Australian children have fulfilled it!

The engineer was so kind, so nice; he received so much. Every two minutes he was putting coal in the furnace, and talking, talking, talking, all about his experiences with this train and other trains. He has been in India, and he talked about the *Darjeeling* train, which is much more peculiar and dangerous than this one. This train is mainly for children and for tourists, and quite a few of the workers on it work for free. His real job is running a nursery, and driving the train is a labour of love. If everyone took a salary, they wouldn't be able to keep the train running.

Every year there is a race – the train versus runners. The runners start and finish at the same place as the train. But they run on the road, while the train goes on its track. The route is very hilly and very scenic. One year Kishore joined the race, and he was one of those who beat the train. But the driver told me, "We get joy by losing to the runners. Otherwise, could anybody defeat us?" The train can safely go about twenty-two miles per hour. If it goes much faster, it will go off the rails.

At one point the engineer asked me to sit on his seat, but it was so narrow! My thigh was larger than the seat. The sound the train made gave me such joy. And the whistle was so loud! He would pull the handle just half an inch, and such a loud noise it made!

So my Australia has given me tremendous joy by fulfilling an innocent childhood desire of mine.

117. Australia's success

Each country gave me joy. Australia gave me tremendous joy, and Japan gave me tremendous joy. India also gave me tremendous joy, plus a tremendous headache!

Australia's success is most, most remarkable from both the outer point of view and the inner point of view. They wanted 1,000 people, but 3,000 came. The hall holds 2,000. But 200 more came in, and there were still 700 or 800 people outside. When the first concert was over, I took a little rest and then played again for the ones who couldn't come in the first time. It was the first time I ever had to play twice. The concert was extremely well received.

118. The lady from Shakpura

When I was in an Indian restaurant in Australia, an Indian lady asked me where I came from. I said I came from Bengal. She said, "I am also from Bengal."

I said, "I am from Chittagong." Then immediately she said she was from Shakpura, which is where I grew up.

I asked her some questions in case she was fooling me. Although I am much older than she, she was really from Shakpura. Her name was Anita.

The restaurant we were in was only three and a half miles from her present home. She had come to Australia with her son.

119. The conversationalist

On my way to India from Japan, seven or eight times during the plane ride a lady came up to me only to chat.

I go to that side and she comes to talk. I go to this side and again she comes to talk.

What did she see in me that drew her back again and again?

120. A dangerous weapon

My flute gave me the greatest joy and also the greatest suffering when I stopped at Delhi airport on the way to Madras.

The customs man gave me a very hard time. He opened all my things. When he opened my flute case, he was positive it was a gun. He lifted up the three parts and held it to the light as if he were trying to see through it. O God! Everywhere there is suspicion, suspicion!

I kept telling him, "It is not a gun! It is a flute!" But he would not allow me to touch it in order to show him. He was afraid I might do something dangerous. I said, "For God's sake, allow me to play." Then I put the three pieces together and for a second I blew through it.

"Oh, it is a flute!" he said. "Okay."

121. Another armed passenger

Right beside me was another man who was also coming from Japan, like me. He had a small Japanese umbrella. On the top it was tied with something plastic that looked like a snake.

The customs man said, "This is something dangerous."

The man said, "It is only an umbrella," but the customs officer would not believe him. Then the customs man spoke to another officer, who was a little bit superior. He was an inspector.

The inspector said, "They are dangerous things." He asked the man to follow him into a room off to the side. Meanwhile the accused man was shouting and insulting the inspector in Tamil. This happened in Delhi, which is Hindi-speaking.

It took them practically ten minutes to finish their examination of his umbrella. In the meantime, I was sitting in the lounge, waiting for the final boarding call.

When he came out, he said, "Look at these idiots!"

I said, "My flute became a gun and your umbrella became such a dangerous weapon."

122. News travels fast

I arrived in the ashram only to hear all about the trip I was about to take to France. Three or four old friends of mine work in Paris. They are my admirers. They came back to visit the ashram just before me, and told everybody about the concert I was going to give in France – even what kind of posters we had. So my ashram friends knew all about the concert even before I arrived.

One of my friends told another friend that everybody wants to become world famous. He said everybody pretends that he has conquered desire, but it is only pretense. He said to his friend, "I am sure Chinmoy also had that desire. But in his case, God has satisfied his desire."

Recently that man moved to Holland. Now he teaches physics at a university there.

123. Consoled in Bengali

At the airport in Madras, one of my bags had not arrived. I was talking to one of the workers about it. We were speaking English.

All of a sudden an American started consoling me in Bengali, saying, "It will come one day. Do not worry!"

How did he know that I was Bengali?

124. Overweight luggage

At the Delhi airport when I was returning to Japan, the man behind the counter told me, "Unfortunately, your luggage is sixteen pounds overweight," and he gave me a very amused smile.

I said, "Yes, you are smiling and I am crying."

Then he checked in my luggage and said, "You don't have to pay extra. I don't want you to cry."

125. One old man to another

At the check-in counter in the Delhi airport, I was carrying two very small handbags. One of them was smaller than the smallest.

There was a very long line. When I finally got to the head of the line, the man asked me where was the tag for my little grey bag.

"For such a tiny one you need a tag?" I asked him.

"Yes, you need it," he said. So he sent me back to get a tag.

When I came back to the line, I said to the man who was second in line, "Perhaps you saw me earlier. I was already at the head of the line."

"Yes, I saw you," he said. "And even if you had not been here before, I would have allowed you to enter the line because you are an old man."

I think he was about my age.

126. Special treatment for the elderly

A minute or two later another funny thing happened. While we were waiting on line for something else, they were strictly checking to see if people had more than one carry-on bag.

A young girl right ahead of me had two bags. They pulled her out of the line and told her to wait on the side. I also had two bags: the little grey bag on my shoulder and another one I was carrying. The official saw my two bags. He said, "Why have you brought two?" Then he looked at me and said, "Allowed, allowed! You are an old man."

So I was an old man twice in five minutes. One of the reasons they thought I was old was because I was limping. I was limping on account of my leg pain. So every disadvantage is a blessing in some way. If you are an old man, you can take two bags onto the plane.

In India several friends of mine at the ashram said to me, "For the first time, you look old. What has made you so old? We are so sorry for you. Your stay in America has made you old!"

I said, "I am old because I have so many responsibilities."

127. The smoker

In the small bus that takes everyone to the aeroplane, a seven or eight-year-old boy in the group was smoking.

There was a Punjabi on the bus, a Sikh. He had a beard and a turban, and he looked like a saint. He said to the boy, "Did you get your father's permission to smoke?"

The little boy said, "Does my father take my permission to smoke?"

So the elderly man kept quiet. The boy was so smart.

128. The best restaurant in Canberra

When I was in the Delhi airport before leaving India, a lady near me at the counter was very angry. She was screaming, "I have a first-class ticket! How is it that I have to sit in the economy section?"

The man behind the counter was telling her that they would refund the difference between the first-class fare and the economy fare. But she was so furious, she looked like she was about to strike him.

O God, then they announced that on this flight there were no assigned seats; you could sit anywhere you wanted to. When one man in the airport heard this, he said, "Now the real trouble starts!" But I was very happy because I thought I would be able to get a seat on the aisle.

I was a little bit late getting onto the plane, so most of the aisle seats were occupied. I was looking and looking for a place, but everywhere there were people. Then I saw the same lady who had been screaming about her first-class ticket. She was sitting by the window, and beside her were two empty seats. I wanted to be on the aisle, so I asked her permission to sit there.

She said, "I bought a first-class ticket, but at the check-in they told me I wouldn't be able to sit in first class."

Then she looked at me and asked, "Where do you come from?"

I said, "India!"

She said, "You don't look like an Indian."

Then I asked, "Where do you come from?"

She answered, "I come from Canberra. Do you know where that is?"

I said, "I was there only two weeks ago."

She said, "You were there? Where is Canberra?"

I answered, "It is Australia's capital. I gave a performance in the School of Music. Some of my friends performed and I also played there."

The strange thing is that I never carry any pamphlets saying who I am. I can't prove anything, and others simply remain silent and unbelieving. What can you tell them?

She asked, "Why did you go to Australia?"

I said, "I have some friends there. The other reason was to see kangaroos."

Then the story started. I said, "I have a few friends who run a vegetarian restaurant."

At first I forgot its name, and then I remembered it is called Oneness-Home. I told her the name of the restaurant and said, "The food is most delicious. My friend's wife told me that it is the best restaurant in Canberra."

The lady again started to get mad. She said, "My husband and I have a restaurant, and *he* is the best cook in Canberra." She was really excited, and she stood up, as if I had said something very upsetting.

So immediately I invoked the goddess of sleep, and then everything was over. I didn't look at her again and I didn't speak to her.

129. The seat mate

After fifteen minutes I was blessed by a hostile force. A little girl about seven or eight years old came and sat between the Australian lady and me.

Then the girl said to me, "My little sister Sona is sitting over there. Could you let my sister sit here?"

Her sister was not sitting in an aisle seat. For me to go and sit between two people for eight to ten hours was too much. O God! I said, "No, I am very sorry, but I need to be on the aisle. I am an old man."

She said, "She is my sister, my little sister."

Again I pretended I was going to sleep. Then she started leaning on me to talk to her sister across the aisle. And that was not enough. Every ten or fifteen minutes she would say to me, "Please let me go out."

From Delhi to Bangkok, at least twenty times she had to go out – not only to go to the bathroom but also to speak to Sona. She would come out of her seat and stand talking to her sister. She said she was not able to hear from her seat.

Throughout the flight, how she disturbed me! She kept standing in front of me, talking and talking to her sister. At one time she was telling her sister to eat with her hands. She said, "Nobody is watching you, so you don't have to be embarrassed." Sometimes, the two of them were arguing and screaming.

First I had the problem with the Australian lady, and then I had a problem with the two sisters. In this way my whole trip was ruined.

130. Thrown out of my seat

In Bangkok we had a fifteen-minute stopover. The man in the Delhi airport who said that there would be problems because we didn't get assigned seats was right. If you don't have assigned seats, you are out, out, out!

I was sitting in seat 27C. I left my seat for a few minutes at Bangkok. When I came back, a lady was sitting in it. She said, "This is my seat." Her boarding pass said seat 27C. In Bangkok they gave out seat numbers, but in Delhi they hadn't. So I was thrown out of my seat.

I found another seat. In three minutes a man came and said it was his seat. I went to speak to the steward. He said, "I know in Delhi they didn't give out seat numbers. You sit here."

I had to sit in a middle seat between two people, and I suffered for so many hours.

When I travel alone, the forces very nicely attack me.

The Australian lady also left her seat at Bangkok, and I never saw her again. God knows what happened to her. Perhaps she also had the same problem that I did with the seat numbers.

131. The children's groups

There were also two groups of children on the plane – one group of forty children and one of sixty. They were so bad, especially the boys. The two teachers who were bringing them from Bangkok kept begging them to behave.

NOTES TO THE WORLD-EXPERIENCE-TREE-CLIMBER, BOOK 3

95. *(p. 321)* 19 December 1982 (same as *The world-experience-tree-climber*, 60).
96. *(p. 321)* 7 January 1983.
97. *(p. 321)* 12 January 1983 (same as *The world-experience-tree-climber*, 69).
98. *(p. 322)* 26 January 1984.
99. *(p. 323)* 26 January 1984.
100. *(p. 323)* 26 January 1984.
101. *(p. 324)* 27 January 1984.
102. *(p. 325)* 15 February 1984.
103. *(p. 325)* 19 February 1984.
104. *(p. 326)* 19 February 1984.
105. *(p. 327)* 23 March 1984.
106. *(p. 327)* 23 March 1984.
107. *(p. 327)* 29 March 1984.
108. *(p. 327)* 29 March 1984.
109. *(p. 328)* 31 March 1984.
110. *(p. 329)* 30 March 1984.
111. *(p. 329)* 7 April 1984.
112. *(p. 329)* 10 September 1984.
113. *(p. 330)* 16 September 1984.
114. *(p. 331)* 11 September 1984.
115. *(p. 331)* 12 September 1984.
116. *(p. 332)* 16 September 1984.
117. *(p. 333)* 29 September 1984.
118. *(p. 333)* 5 October 1984.
119. *(p. 334)* 28 September 1984.
120. *(p. 334)* 29 September 1984.
121. *(p. 334)* 29 September 1984.
122. *(p. 335)* 28 September 1984.

123. *(p.336)* 28 September 1984.
124. *(p.336)* 29 September 1984.
125. *(p.336)* 30 September 1984.
126. *(p.337)* 30 September 1984.
127. *(p.337)* 29 September 1984.
128. *(p.338)* 29 September 1984.
129. *(p.340)* 29 September 1984.
130. *(p.341)* 28 September 1984.
131. *(p.341)* 28 September 1984.

THE WORLD-EXPERIENCE-TREE-CLIMBER

BOOK 4

132. You are music itself!

This morning, while walking around London, I went into an Indian store that sold magazines and candy. Magazines I didn't get, but I did buy a chocolate bar – I think it is called "Tiger" – for 19 pence.

As soon as I came out of the store, a tall man said to me, "Good morning! Last night I was at your concert and I heard your music. I also am a musician. I play music, but you *are* music itself!"

Since he was flattering me, I gave him a piece of the chocolate bar. He took it with such joy and appreciation.

133. Please bless me!

After the London Peace Concert, a certain spiritual teacher came up to me backstage. He was bowing down and saying, "Please bless me, please bless me!"

Was I going to place my hand on his head? No! I only bless my own disciples. But I gave him a flower. This particular teacher used to be a doctor before he became a spiritual Master. Now he has quite a few disciples. He has asked his disciples always to participate in our activities because he has such love and admiration for me. His disciples keep my picture on their shrine, along with the pictures of other spiritual Masters.

Last week his disciples in San Francisco invited our disciples to come and play my music for them in their Centre.

134. You carry two worlds

After the Toronto Concert, I met with one of the officials from the Consulate of India. Many years ago I worked with him in the Consulate in New York.

He said to me, "Your very name is a phenomenon. You carry two worlds inside you – Eastern and Western. It is such a rare thing. Your music has transported my wife and me almost into a trance. Please let us know when you are coming again so we can be with you and be blessed by you."

I thanked him and said, "I am so grateful to you. Your very presence is a blessing to me and to us all."

135. Part-time invalid

The morning after the San Francisco Peace Concert, I went to visit Narada's studio.

While I was waiting for the elevator to come, a very fat man came up and shook hands with me for no reason. Then he said, "You are the most handsome musician I've ever seen. Now tell me something. One moment you walk across the stage like an invalid. But the next moment you play the cello so powerfully and dramatically. Your playing is full of life. And then, when you walk back to play another instrument, you are an invalid again. How do you switch back and forth like that?"

At that time the elevator came and we went inside. Both of us were smiling at each other in the elevator as it went up.

136. The saviour

When I went to the Spanish Consulate to get my visa, the clerk was very unkind. For a long time she was avoiding and ignoring everyone. Then a little girl came to our rescue; she came as our saviour.

She was only two or three years old, and she was smiling and laughing and making lots of noise. She was very cute, and she made everybody smile. Even the undivine clerk started smiling, and then everything changed for the better; she started to do her job properly. Soon we got everything we needed. Otherwise how many hours we would have stayed there!

So that little girl changed our fate. God sent her to help us and save us.

137. Visa problems in France

The first time I went to France, Air France told me I didn't need a visa. But when I arrived at the airport in France, the authorities wouldn't allow me to enter the country. For at least forty-five minutes they delayed me!

I had to call the Indian Embassy in Washington. The Ambassador happened to be Bengali. We spoke in Bengali over the phone, and then he spoke to the authorities at the airport.

The people at the airport were so impressed that I was speaking to the Ambassador himself in Bengali. All of a sudden they became very affectionate. They began finding fault with my tie, saying I didn't know how to put it on properly. Then they fixed it for me.

So first they were harassing me, and then they were fixing my tie!

138. New thoughts in an old building

When we were going to meet the Mayor of Madrid, I took with me only the singers. Then we found out that they were expecting 200 people!

When the Mayor was escorting me to the reception after the meeting, he was saying that although the building was old, he has new, modern thoughts there. The building was built in the 16th century.

139. Hanging up on the Master

I have an amusing, inspiring and illumining story about Ketan the great.

Last night he phoned our Madrid hotel from America. The switchboard connected him with my room. When I said, "Hello," Ketan said, "Oh no! Oh no! Oh no! I wanted to speak to Bipin."

I said, "Give me some news."

He said, "Oh no, they have made the wrong connection!"

I said again, "Give me some news. What is happening in New York?"

But Ketan just hung up. I was begging him to give me some news, but he got upset and frightened and just hung up.

140. How is it possible?

Then an Indian phoned me at the hotel. I had spoken with an Indian girl on the plane, and now her father wanted to come to our concert. When he phoned up to find out when and where the concert was, they gave him my number.

I said, "I do not know any of the details."

He could not figure out how it was possible for me not to know the name of the place and the hour of the concert, since I was the one performing.

141. When greedy meets cheap

When Agraha and I were shopping in Madrid, we saw a Chinese instrument with two strings. The sound was good, but the price was not good.

They said, "12,030", or something like that. So I wanted to say, "10,000."

But Agraha, the great Spanish scholar, told them 9,000.

"Agraha!" I said.

They said, "Impossible!"

I asked Agraha why he didn't say 10,000. He said, "Since you like bargaining, I said 9,000 so you can go up." Then he offered 10,000, but the man still said, "Impossible."

Agraha said, "11,000", but the man would not come down. They were greedy and they thought that we might again go up.

They were greedy and we were cheap, so we didn't buy it.

142. Andre starts chanting

After Andre's accident, I went to see him in the Spanish hospital. He was unconscious, but I said, "Now your Guru is singing *The Supreme*," and I started singing.

Then he started chanting *"pranam"*. As soon as he started chanting, the two nurses who were there jumped up from their chairs to see. Before this, the nurses had been calling him, but he hadn't responded.

Andre went on chanting so loudly that the nurses were pushing each other's shoulders out of excitement. He was so happy, and four or five times he smiled.

143. Signing the guest book

When I first arrived at the Tafoukt Hotel in Essouira, Morocco, they wanted me to sign the guest book, but there were only a few pages left at the back. So they went out and brought a new book and asked me to be the first one to sign the new book.

144. Wrong number

One morning at the Tafoukt Hotel, at six o'clock the phone rang in my room. A man said, "You wanted me to call to wake you up."

I said, "This is room 517."

He said, "Oh no, I wanted 217."

Room 217 asked the desk to wake them up at six o'clock, but they called me by mistake.

145. The Guru of the group

I wanted to telephone New York from my hotel room in Morocco. The telephone operator said to me, "What is your name?"

I said, "Ghose."

Then she asked, "What is your room number?"

I told her. Then the lady said, "The person in that room is not Ghose. It is Chinmoy."

I said, "Yes, that is my first name."

She said, "Are you the Guru of the group?"

I said, "Yes, I am the Guru of the group."

Then she was satisfied and she placed the call for me.

146. A highly evolved soul

Once when we went to a circus in Venezuela, I saw that one of the young girl performers was an extremely evolved soul. I felt miserable that Saraswati was not there, because I wanted somebody to approach her. Later, I told Saraswati to go and give her gifts.

That girl was one of the two hundred most evolved female souls living on earth at this time. Such an evolved, receptive soul in the silliest possible circus!

Our circus is far better; only we don't have animals. But we don't need animals because we represent animals.

147. The power of a smile

The first day I went to the eating place at the university in Puerto la Cruz, I saw a group of cute little boys watching me from about fifteen metres away. They were afraid to come closer. Then they all gave me very soulful smiles and took one step nearer, but immediately they got frightened again.

So I gave them a smile. Then they took another step towards me. Like that, we kept smiling at one another and they kept coming forward until they were only one metre away.

148. The earphones

I have been on aeroplanes many, many times, but only two or three times have I watched the movie. On a flight from Florida to New York, I was sitting in my seat drawing when they announced that it was time for the movie.

They were going to show George Burns in *Oh God*. I hadn't liked the movie when we showed it at the Centre, but I said, "To kill time, let me see it."

So I paid two dollars for the earphones and turned the switch to channel 9. With my right hand I was holding the earphones to my ear, and with my left hand I was trying to draw. Of course, I couldn't draw very well with my left hand, since I am right-handed.

The stewardess saw me and said, "Why are you not using the headphones?"

So she showed me how to put the headphones on my head. Then she asked, "Where do you come from? India?"

I said, "Yes."

She said, "Oh, that's why!"

I said, "I have been here in the States for twenty years." I didn't have the heart to tell her how many times I have been on aeroplanes. But if you don't use things, you don't know the proper way.

149. *The jealous husband*

Sitting in front of me on the plane was an elderly couple; they were both over sixty.

Before the plane took off, another old man came up to the lady and said, "Hi!" She also said something to him.

Then the man said to the husband, "Harold, how are you?" But the husband didn't answer.

When the man went away, the husband got so mad! For ten minutes or more he was insulting and scolding his wife.

When the plane landed, the other old man again had to come very close to the lady, and the lady again said something to him.

Her husband was holding two small bags. He got so furious that he just dropped them on the seat.

I was dying to get off the plane before he struck his wife. I saw his anger and wanted to disappear immediately.

THE WORLD-EXPERIENCE-TREE-CLIMBER

150. Entering East Berlin

Today Kailash and I went to East Berlin. At the place where you cross over, every ten metres they ask to see your passport. Within fifty metres, at four different places you have to show your passport! Can you imagine!

I have to change Kailash's name to patience. He was so patient with those people. If I had known German, I would not have waited there. After being stopped the second time, I would have just gone back.

In some cases they opened the car trunks and lifted up the seats to see if you had brought something illegal. They are very, very strict.

Germans have to enter through one place and Swiss through another place. Indians go the same way as the Swiss, so Kailash and I went together.

151. A peculiar rhythm

At the concert last night the audience applauded after I played the synthesiser. Strangely enough, what I played was absolutely original.

Sometimes a very peculiar rhythm comes, and for a few seconds that peculiarity remains. It gives me so much joy. At that time I don't have to worry about the melody at all!

152. A small world

This world is so small. In 1966 a German lady became my disciple in Puerto Rico. She lived right across the street from our first Centre there. From my apartment I could see where she lived. In my book *Yoga and the Spiritual Life,* there are quite a few questions on the soul that were asked by her. She also translated our *Invocation* into German. I gave her the Indian name "Abhaya", which means fearless, dauntless.

One day Nadeshwar, our supreme boxing champion, was saying unkind things about the strength of women. Abhaya could not tolerate it, so she challenged him to a boxing match. She didn't know anything about boxing, but she was very mad.

Nadeshwar said, "Oh no, I can't fight with women."

After that, Nadeshwar kept quiet.

Abhaya moved to Miami a few years later and left us.

At the end of tonight's concert, who should come up to me but Abhaya! I didn't recognise her until she told me her name. She was quite devoted.

153. *The fake Bengali*

During the walk-past, one man asked me in Bengali if I can speak Bengali. So Projjwal thanked him and he went away.

If he had been a real Bengali, he would know that I am Bengali from the way I pronounce English. Also, I was singing in Bengali during the concert.

At the ashram we had some Gujarati boys and girls who spoke Bengali with perfect intonation and pronunciation. They spoke so fast that they could easily fool Bengalis.

But we Bengalis had such pride. We never learned Gujarati correctly. We knew quite a few words, so we would use Gujarati nouns and then complete the sentence with Hindi verbs. Our Gujarati friends could speak Bengali, but we thought it was beneath our dignity to learn Gujarati!

154. The taxi driver

Once, when I was in Holland, I had a taxi driver who was not only from Queens, but from Jamaica. He was giving me such a vivid description of Jamaica because he used to live here!

155. A new incarnation

This is a cock-and-bull story. When I was a child in Chittagong, my family usually had two servants – one young and one old.

After tonight's concert, one boy came up to meditate with me after the concert. While we were meditating together, his soul said, "Madalia, you cannot recognise me?"

Not only did he use the nickname from my childhood, Madal, but he said it with an endearing term. I said, "Who can call me by my Chittagong name with this kind of endearing term? In my house, even my sisters and brothers didn't call me that, and here this young German boy is addressing me this way!"

Then the soul said that he had been our servant in Chittagong and he gave his former name. Then vividly I could see and remember him. I had heard that he had died, and now I see that he has taken a new incarnation in Germany. I was looking into his eyes and his soul recognised me.

156. A lady from the ashram

There was another lady who came to see me after the concert. When I was in the ashram, I was close to her brothers and her sister. But she was only four or five years old at that time, and during my twenty years at the ashram I never had any occasion to speak to her.

Her sister had been the ashram athletics champion. She had even learned how to box. She used to study with me. One of her brothers had been a wrestler. Once he injured his neck while wrestling and for three weeks was in the hospital. Her youngest brother once climbed up a tall coconut tree when he was three or four years old. Then he got frightened and couldn't climb down. He was crying and screaming because he was afraid.

The lady's name is Purnima. She started talking to me in Bengali. Then she introduced her husband to me. But she had forgotten the Bengali word for husband, so she said it in Hindi and added, "I have forgotten the word."

Then I was able to tell her the word in Bengali.

157. Comment from a childhood friend

In the comments book for the Hamburg Concert, someone wrote a comment in Bengali. His name is Himangshu Shekar Vadra. He called me "Chinmoy-da" and said he was overwhelmed and deeply moved by the concert.

He and I knew each other so well. My brothers and sisters also knew him. We were brought up together; right from childhood we knew one another.

His brother used to run with me; he was our third best runner.

158. Sudhahota's long jump

At the San Francisco airport, I asked disciples with birthdays in July and August to come up and meditate with me.

Sudhahota jumped over the shoulders of five or six girls so that he could come up. He did his long jump to come and meditate with me!

159. Aeroplane problems

The airline this time was so bad. In the San Francisco airport they kept us waiting in the plane for an hour and a half. Then they said that something was wrong with a battery and told us we had to leave the plane.

After an hour and a half, they decided to give us another plane. Then they said, "All right, we have fixed the battery. In ten minutes we shall start."

But after ten minutes they said that now one engine was not working. So we had to go out again.

We were practically three hours late in leaving.

160. Getting out on the wrong floor

I was on my way to our hotel lobby for the Montreal Peace Concert. I got into the elevator on the twelfth floor and went down.

Kirit and Surashri had pressed the button for the elevator on the tenth floor. When the door opened, I saw them standing there. I thought that was the lobby so I went out of the elevator. They didn't say anything to me because they didn't know what I was doing.

161. The suspicious customs officer

While travelling from Canada to New York, our bus stopped at the Canadian border. As I was coming out of the washroom, two customs officers came up to me very suspiciously. One said, "What are you doing?"

Just a few minutes before that they had caught a man trying to smuggle a lady in under his car seat. So now they thought they were catching me.

But the other officer said, "He was on the bus."

At that hour of the night they hadn't expected so many people. Our crowded bus was disturbing their sleep.

162. The fastest train

Last year when I was in Australia, I rode on a train that went only seven or ten miles per hour. Yesterday, while travelling between Paris and Lyon, I rode on the world's fastest train. It goes 180 miles per hour!

When you are in the passenger compartment you feel that the train is going only forty or fifty miles an hour. But if you are up front with the engineer, you can see how fast it is going.

For more than an hour I was with the engineer. I was sitting in the same seat that the French President sat in four years ago when he inaugurated the train. It is right alongside the engineer.

So now I have gone from the slowest to the fastest. This train broke the world record and defeated the Japanese bullet train. The French say they are going to stay ahead of the Japanese. They are working very hard to maintain their supremacy.

When I was young I wanted to follow in my father's footsteps and be a train conductor. That was my earliest desire. But instead, God has given me a far more difficult job.

163. The tea ceremony

In Tokyo we went to see a tea ceremony. When I came in, the hostess bowed to me three times. But I didn't dare bend so many times, so I bowed only once!

THE WORLD-EXPERIENCE-TREE-CLIMBER

164. Bowing and bowing

In Japan they bow even when they open the elevator door for you. Yesterday after the Peace Concert, I bowed at least 200 times during the walk-past for seekers.

As each person passed in front of me, he would bow. So I also bowed. Then I would have to bow a second time to show that the meditation for that particular individual was over.

For me to bow so many times and then look up is very difficult for my neck. So yesterday I had very good neck exercises!

I thought that they would keep their hands at their sides, according to the Japanese tradition, but most of them walked by with folded hands.

165. Lovers of Japan

There are very few disciples of mine who do not like Japan. The Japanese love the beauty of the East in their inner life and they love the power of the West in their outer life.

When I come to Japan, at every moment I am inspired to compose songs. Yesterday I composed a song about Japan in the sports store. Today I composed a song on the bus. The last time I visited the Kamakura Buddha, I composed *Namo namo* in front of the statue. The first time we visited it, I composed *Jaya jaya*.

166. None left!

When Alo and I went walking in Beppu this morning, we went to a 24-hour eating place. They have pictures of all the different dishes, so you can just point to the picture of what you want to eat. But whatever you point to, that very thing they don't have!

167. The fever-tree

This morning I woke up with a 105-degree fever. With greatest difficulty I opened my eyes, but then I couldn't see anything.

So instead of running the race we were holding, I walked to the 24-hour eating place and ate coffee and eggs.

Then Vijali came in and I had a long talk with her about Trinidad and Tobago and other countries.

While walking back to the hotel, again everything seemed to be turning white. My fever and back pain were killing me, and I couldn't see anything!

It is very difficult to climb up the aspiration-tree, but the fever-tree one can climb up very easily. The aspiration-flame-tree is difficult to climb up, but the temperature-fire-tree is easy.

168. The lost gloves

This morning I went into a restaurant in Kyoto. After I went out and had gone two blocks, I realised that I had left my gloves there. But I said, "I am not going to go back."

Then I saw Kodanda running. I wanted to give him the job of going to the restaurant to get my gloves, although I was a little bit afraid that he would go to the wrong restaurant and fight with the people there. But to my great surprise and joy, he went running to the right restaurant and brought back my gloves. He received my most powerful and blessingful smile.

169. The Supreme's Light manifested

This time Japan has responded most powerfully to the Supreme's Light. Throughout the length and breadth of Japan the Light of the Supreme has been really manifested. There have been over forty articles about our activities in Japanese and English newspapers.

Kirit's soul has proved that it can be of true service to the manifestation of the Supreme. I am very, very proud of Kirit and very proud of Japan.

Kirit represents his country. He represents the life of humility. If you run up the steps two at a time, you might fall and break your leg. But if you go very humbly step by step, there is no chance for you to break your leg.

170. A few mistakes

The *Japan Times* had a very nice article about me, but it had a few mistakes. They showed a picture of me playing the cello, but they said I was playing the viola. They also said that I came to the West at the age of thirteen. When the facts are wrong but the writer means well, their loving concern touches my heart.

171. Vajra is the answer!

When Vajra went to Yannick Noah's restaurant in New York, Noah's wife came and greeted him with folded hands, saying, "Sri Chinmoy is here." She thought it was me, and she was showing him utmost respect and veneration.

A similar thing has happened many times during our parades. I am on the sidewalk running alongside the marchers, and Vajra is marching in the parade. So they think he is the Guru, the chief.

Yesterday, Sri Chinmoy himself paid a visit to Noah's restaurant. But since Noah's wife didn't feel the same kind of divinity in me, the treatment could not be the same.

So if you want to see my divinity more revealed and manifested, then Vajra is the answer!

NOTES TO THE WORLD-EXPERIENCE-TREE-CLIMBER, BOOK 4

132. *(p. 347)* 10 October 1984.
133. *(p. 347)* 9 November 1984.
134. *(p. 348)* 10 November 1984.
135. *(p. 348)* 18 November 1984.
136. *(p. 349)* 11 December 1984.
137. *(p. 349)* 11 December 1984.
138. *(p. 350)* 21 December 1984.
139. *(p. 350)* 22 December 1984.
140. *(p. 350)* 22 December 1984.
141. *(p. 351)* 22 December 1984.
142. *(p. 351)* 27 December 1984.
143. *(p. 352)* 3 January 1985.
144. *(p. 352)* 3 January 1985.
145. *(p. 352)* 8 January 1985.
146. *(p. 353)* 13 January 1985.
147. *(p. 353)* 13 January 1985.
148. *(p. 353)* 19 February 1985.
149. *(p. 354)* 19 February 1985.
150. *(p. 355)* 22 March 1985.
151. *(p. 355)* 23 March 1985.
152. *(p. 355)* 24 March 1985.
153. *(p. 356)* 23 March 1985.
155. *(p. 357)* 24 March 1985.
156. *(p. 357)* 24 March 1985.
157. *(p. 358)* 24 March 1985.
158. *(p. 358)* 8 July 1985.
159. *(p. 359)* 8 July 1985.
160. *(p. 359)* 14 September 1985.
161. *(p. 359)* 15 September 1985.
162. *(p. 360)* 21 October 1985.

163. *(p.360)* 15 December 1985.
164. *(p.361)* 15 December 1985.
165. *(p.361)* 17 December 1985.
166. *(p.361)* 22 December 1985.
167. *(p.362)* 24 December 1985.
168. *(p.362)* 7 January 1986.
169. *(p.363)* 13 January 1986.
170. *(p.363)* 13 January 1986.
171. *(p.363)* 20 January 1986.

THE WORLD-EXPERIENCE-TREE-CLIMBER

BOOK 5

172. The dog Tina

On the aeroplane from Bombay, a lady carried a dog onto the plane in an ordinary handbag. From time to time she would open the bag, and the dog would jump up. Then she would talk to the dog for a few seconds before closing the bag. The lady was calling the dog Tina, which is our Upasana's former name. So many people saw the dog on the plane! Can you imagine? I am sure it is not permitted to carry a dog in that way.

While waiting at customs, I happened to be behind this lady. She was very smart, very pushy and very restless. Just because I was behind her, I was able to make headway in the line. Otherwise, I would have had a much longer wait.

173. The Long Island seeker

When I first arrived in India, a bald-headed man came up to me near the Air India office in our hotel and said, "Sri Chinmoy? Sri Chinmoy?"

I said, "Yes."

He said, "I can't believe it!" His eyes were swimming with tears. So soulfully he was shedding tears and embracing me. His soul knew who I am. He created a real scene in the hotel. So many people were watching!

He told me that he used to come to our meetings three years ago and then he stopped. He knows Adhiratha and he was telling me how Adhiratha stands next to my chair when he is guarding on stage on Wednesday nights. He also knows Sumantra and Ayoddhri.

He said he had come to India to visit some spiritual places, so I gave him the names of a few places to see. He said that he wants to start coming to our meetings in New York when he returns. He is a construction worker from Long Island.

174. In search of a Guru

In another case, a boy named Brad had been my disciple for a few years in California, but then he had left the path. Brad was going to India to search for a Guru. He and another seeker were going to visit a few spiritual places. I don't think the other seeker was looking for a Guru.

I happened to be on the same plane that they were on, so Brad found his Guru again in me. In his case, he touched the soil of India only to go back to America.

175. Travelling by car and train

From Dhaka I went to Chittagong by car; it took six hours. I wanted to visit all the places that I had read about in history and geography books. I wanted to see those sacred places where Sri Ramachandra and others were supposed to have visited. Now they have become places of pilgrimage. But in the end I was only able to visit my family homes in Chittagong and Shakpura.

I came back from Chittagong by train. I was in an Indian first-class car, which is like an American third-class car, or worse. They played very loud music, which was almost like jazz.

176. Delayed by the "flood"

While in Calcutta, for four days I tried to get in touch with my family. But the line was always out of order. There is something called a "lightning call", which costs eight times more than a regular call. I said, "I am ready to pay." But even the lightning call was not successful.

So I flew to Madras without informing them. Every time I go home, my brothers and sisters arrange to have a car from the ashram meet me. An ashram driver comes to Madras and takes me to Pondicherry. I know the driver well. It is usually a three-hour drive. But this time, because I could not get in touch with them, I had to hire a car. It was the biggest mistake!

Somebody came and said, "I have a car." When I went to the car, that person disappeared and I saw somebody else there – a driver with two helpers.

As soon as I entered into the car, I thought, "This car is older than the oldest. But I can't get out now. My things are inside the trunk."

The driver tried to reassure me. He said. "Oh, no, no, this is a very good car."

We started out at 8:30. The car broke down three times over the next four hours. Around 12:30 we had gone only seventy miles and still had forty miles to cover. Then they had to change the tire!

They were saying that we were delayed because there was a flood and there were no bridges.

I said, "Where is the flood? I don't see water here."

They said, "No, two weeks ago there was a flood."

I said, "Two weeks ago there was a flood, and that is why you can't drive now?" What can you do with people like this!

177. Changing drivers

At 1:15 I was only five miles away from our house in Pondicherry. The driver said he could not go any farther because he didn't have a Pondicherry license.

So the two friends of the driver took another car and went to a nearby hospital and brought back a car and driver with a Pondicherry license. Usually drivers charge five rupees to go to our house from there; 10 rupees maximum. But this driver said, "At this hour you have to pay 75 rupees."

He was shamelessly overcharging, but 75 rupees is only a little more than five dollars. I was so happy that I would finally arrive at my destination that I gladly agreed to pay him.

178. Paying the Madras driver

The ashram charges only 200 or 225 rupees to take me from Madras to Pondicherry. I had told the driver at the airport that I would give him 450 rupees for the ride. That is about double what the ashram charges.

But even then, that man didn't trust me. "In case anything happens, could you give me some money in advance?" he asked. What was going to happen? But to prove my innocence, I gave him 100 rupees.

But then look what happened! After so many hours, still he could not take me all the way to Pondicherry. I gave him his full 450 rupees, but I was so disgusted.

179. You are saving me

The man who asked for 75 rupees said, "You should not give him the whole amount since he is unable to take you the whole way."

Meanwhile, the three who had brought me from Madras wanted a share of this man's 75 rupees. They said, "You have to give us something because we found you a passenger."

The two drivers had a serious argument because the second driver didn't want to give them anything. He said, "I am saving you because you can't drive into Pondicherry."

I said, "No, you are not saving them. You are saving me." Then I begged him to take the 75 rupees and just drive me home.

When we arrived, I gave him 80 rupees.

180. A big favour

The first time I went back to India, I took a taxi from Madras to our house in Pondicherry. A young couple was going to the Pondicherry area also, so I said, "You don't have to pay. You come with me. I will sit with the driver and you can sit in the back." They were so moved by my generosity and very grateful to me.

In those days I carried my money in a little bag with no strap. When we finally arrived at my house, I was filled with such joy that I just opened the car door and practically ran to my house. O God, I didn't realise that I had left my bag on the seat next to the driver.

The driver drove away and had gone about half a block when the wife noticed that I had left my bag there. She was very short, so God knows how she saw my bag. Her husband was tall, but he didn't see it. So the wife told the driver and he brought the car back. Then the husband came out of the car and gave me the bag. The driver had known that the bag was there, but he didn't want to say anything.

So I did them a favour by saving them 300 or 400 rupees for a taxi ride, but they did me a much bigger favour. I had so much money in my bag, as well as my passport. It is because there are good people like this on earth that we still exist. Some divine forces always protect me in time of need; still the divine forces are not sleeping!

181. The Elephanta Caves

During my visit to India, we went to some sacred caves called Elephanta, where they keep Lord Shiva's statue. To get to the caves, we took a boat from Bombay, and then a little ferry to the island. You have to go up hundreds of steps to get to the sacred area, but there are strong young men there who will carry you up in a chair if you are too weak to go up the stairs yourself. In my case, I climbed up the stairs, but I paid to be carried down by four men. It was a frightening experience, because the chair slants downward when they are carrying you, and they go quite fast.

A lady at the caves begged me to take her picture. Then afterwards, she wanted me to give her five rupees for allowing me to take her picture.

182. A banquet in London

The London disciples arranged a banquet like the one the Governor of Agadir had given us. Ten or twelve people were sitting around each table and we were being served.

They gave me a cake with 200 candles for my 200-pound lift and started singing, *I can lift up 200 pounds*. They were singing the song so cheerfully and confidently that I began to suspect them.

I said, "You people are really great. I just wrote the song in New York and already you have learned it. When did you get in touch with Tanima?"

They said, "We didn't get in touch with Tanima. We just changed the words to one of your old songs!"

183. A cake with candles

We were at the Springfield Diner celebrating the birthday of one of the disciples. I went to the counter and asked them to bring a cake to the table and to put candles on the cake. The lady looked puzzled, so again I said, "I would like candles on the cake."

Finally the waitress brought the cake to the table, along with half a cantaloup. She was about to put the cantaloup on top of the cake when everybody started laughing. They asked her what she was doing.

She said, "You asked me to put cantaloup on the cake."

I said, "No, I asked you to put candles on the cake."

So this is how she understood my English!

184. Invitation to tennis

This morning in Berlin, I came back from my walk at around a quarter to eight. It had been very cold outside and I had not taken my jacket, so I was shivering.

When I came into the hotel, a middle-aged Englishman came up to me and said, "Do you play tennis?"

I said, "Yes, I do."

Then he asked, "Could you come and play with me? Nobody is at the courts."

Unfortunately I had not brought my tennis racquet on that trip, so I had to excuse myself.

185. Good Indian hearts

Today in Berlin when I sat down to eat something in the Maharajah restaurant, I put my bag on the floor at my feet. But when I left, I forgot to take the bag with me – and it had my passport and wallet inside.

I discovered that it was missing four hours later when I was about to enter into the hotel. I went back to the restaurant and everything was still there – passport, money, everything. I wanted to give them gifts to show my appreciation, but they wouldn't take anything.

I have the bad habit on occasion of calling Indians "rogues". You have no idea how many times Indians have deceived me! So because I am an Indian, I am entitled to speak ill of them. But here I found good Indian hearts. They had been wondering why I had not come back sooner for the bag, and they were so happy to see me.

These people had no greed – only sympathy, kindness and oneness. I was so deeply moved.

186. Gift of a painting

The lady who owned the meeting place that we used in Berlin came up to me after one meeting. She told me that I am a great man and that she was so grateful that I had come to her place.

She said, "You are an artist and I am an artist. You are a greater artist, but I would like to give you this painting of mine. I am giving it to the artist in you and not to the spiritual Master."

I said, "It is very beautiful."

She was so thrilled.

187. Nordic heart-power

We had a nice trip to Finland and Sweden, where I gave Peace Concerts. In both places we also inaugurated Peace Miles. Helsinki had a beautiful course, and Uppsala also was very good.

Just ten or twelve disciples worked on the Peace Miles, but they got 500 or 600 people to run. In their case it was not manpower or money-power but heart-power that succeeded.

188. The jumping boy

Always I have experiences with children on planes! When I was flying to California for our Peace Concert, one little boy was bothering me like anything on the plane. He was absolutely jumping and jumping, and two times he fell on me. I was so afraid he would get hurt.

His mother tried to take off his shoes, but he didn't want to take them off. Then so many times he kicked me!

What can you do?

189. Two artists

On the plane coming back from San Francisco, there was a very mischievous child sitting next to me. His mother was sitting on his other side.

He started playing with clay and throwing it around. Some of the clay landed on my pants.

I said to his mother, "He will be an artist."

The mother said, "How do you know?"

I said, "I am an artist."

Then I went to sleep. Otherwise, I would have had to enter into conversation.

190. *A different consciousness*

At our hotel in Viña del Mar, Chile, I was on the seventh floor waiting for the elevator. Also waiting for the elevator was a man who was absolutely ferocious and very drunk. Then a lady came up to him who also had a very bad consciousness. It was not just that they were drunk, but if you entered into their consciousness, you saw they were like animals. They had a beast-like consciousness; at any moment they might strangle you. So I pretended that I had forgotten something and went away.

A minute or so later I came back. This time a very civilised, elderly American couple was waiting for the elevator. They were talking about the wife's shoes. No matter what she wears, nothing fits her. The husband said that he was willing to go to the shoe store with her, but the next day was Sunday.

So this change happened in a matter of one minute. It is better not to get on an elevator with people like that first couple. And if somebody very undivine comes into the elevator when you are in it, just get out. If the person has time to come in, you also have time to get out.

191. *The best was Valdivia!*

Of all the places we visited in South America, the best was Valdivia! I got such joy there, although the people there were very poor.

In Viña del Mar the hotel people were very nice, but in Valdivia I got a very good feeling from the people in the town itself.

192. Almost robbed

In Lima, Peru, I left my bag in the car with Savyasachi. I had all my money in the bag, as well as my passport. Because the car door was a little open, the bag was almost stolen.

One person came up to Savyasachi's window and tried to distract him by showing him some keys and asking if they were his. Meanwhile, two other people opened the door on the other side and tried to take the bag. Fortunately, Savyasachi had tied the bag to the stick shift, so they couldn't take it.

Now we can laugh about it, but if they had taken it, we would have cried!

193. Nice reporters

Four reporters came to interview me in Lima. One of them was 100 per cent my disciple. She had a soul's connection with three or four disciples, and she was looking at me as if she had known me for a long time. Then she took the chair right near me.

She asked me a question in Spanish and I answered her in English. She was so surprised that I had understood her Spanish.

Then Agraha asked her something. Afterwards, he said he couldn't believe how kind she was.

All the reporters were so nice. Usually you talk for ten minutes and the reporters write down two words. But these reporters were writing continuously.

194. The diplomatic answer

I told the reporters two reasons why I like Peru. One of them was the fact that the U.N. Secretary-General came from there. That was my diplomatic answer.

Peru has both an Indian and a Western touch. India does not have that.

195. The celebrity

Yesterday when I entered into the elevator, I saw one of the hotel workers there. He raised his arms, with his fists clenched. He had seen my weightlifting pictures.

So I am a celebrity!

196. Defying the manager

On the flight back to Miami, we had such a nice captain on the aeroplane. He defied the airline manager and let me keep my cello on the plane. Good people will dare to fight against bad people. We invited him to come and eat at Annam Brahma.

We have been to so many places on this trip in Argentina, Chile and Peru, and we never had any problem with the cello. Only coming back to Miami, the manager had to give us trouble!

197. Showing off on the calf-raise machine

Last night after the Stuttgart Peace Concert, a famous German bodybuilder came up to talk to me. His name is Jusup Wilkosz. Many times I had seen videos of him competing with Frank Zane and others, but I had never met him. He was Mr. Universe in 1980. He also got third place in the Mr. Olympia contest behind Lee Haney and somebody else.

This morning I went to visit his gym. I have never seen a gymnasium as beautiful or as well-kept. Other gymnasiums are usually so dirty, but his was very clean – like a temple.

He had every kind of modern apparatus, including a calf-raise machine. The maximum weight it takes is 860 pounds, but they usually use between 400 and 600 pounds. They never try even 700 pounds.

I wanted to show off. So without warming up, I said, "Let me do 400 pounds." Then I did 600 pounds and finally I did 860 pounds.

Wilkosz couldn't believe that I did it. He knew that I had done a 2,000-pound calf raise, but when he saw me do the maximum of 860 pounds on his machine, he couldn't believe his eyes.

Nowadays, with my left leg I can do 1,200 pounds and with my right leg I can do 800 or 1,000 pounds. In spite of that I can't walk properly. When I told him that, he advised me not to eat meat. He eats meat once a week, but he was advising me not to eat meat at all.

198. Listening to a "great" musician

While Databir was driving me to an Indian store the other day, he was playing a musical tape. For about two minutes I listened to the music and inwardly I was so moved. I said to myself, "How I wish I could play like that!"

Then I asked Databir, "Do you know the name of the person who is playing?" I was being sincere. There was no mischief behind my question.

Databir said, "Guru, it's your synthesizer tape."

I had never dreamed that I was the one playing. It was far beyond my remotest imagination. I didn't even recognise the instrument!

For another ten minutes I soulfully and devotedly listened to the tape with genuine admiration and rapt attention.

199. *I am not your boss!*

About five years ago I was giving a concert in Canada. About 500 or 700 people were in the audience. As I came off the stage, somebody came from behind me and fell at my feet. Immediately I recognised Chander, who had been one of my sectional bosses when I worked at the Indian Consulate in New York.

I said, "O God, you are my boss!"

He said, "Inwardly I am not your boss!" He had felt something in me and had seen me in another consciousness.

200. *The area code criminal*

When we were in the Holiday Inn in St. Louis I wanted to call Queens, but I couldn't remember if the area code was 718 or 708.

The operator said, "You live there and you can't remember your area code?"

I said, "Is it a crime if you can't remember your number?"

She asked me where I wanted to call and I said, "Queens." She couldn't understand my pronunciation, so I said, "It is the feminine of king."

So I was teaching her vocabulary and she was teaching me pronunciation.

NOTES TO THE WORLD-EXPERIENCE-TREE-CLIMBER, BOOK 5

172. *(p.369)* 27 February 1986.
173. *(p.369)* 27 February 1986.
174. *(p.370)* 27 February 1986.
175. *(p.370)* 1 March 1986.
176. *(p.370)* 1 March 1986.
177. *(p.371)* 1 March 1986.
178. *(p.372)* 1 March 1986.
179. *(p.372)* 1 March 1986.
180. *(p.373)* 1 March 1986.
181. *(p.374)* 1 March 1986.
182. *(p.374)* 16 March 1986.
183. *(p.375)* 26 April 1986.
184. *(p.375)* 7 June 1986.
185. *(p.376)* 7 June 1986.
186. *(p.376)* 27 June 1986.
187. *(p.377)* 20 July 1986.
188. *(p.377)* 2 October 1986.
189. *(p.377)* 2 October 1986.
190. *(p.378)* 27 December 1986.
191. *(p.378)* 7 January 1987.
192. *(p.379)* 7 January 1987.
193. *(p.379)* 9 January 1987.
194. *(p.380)* 9 January 1987.
195. *(p.380)* 12 January 1987.
196. *(p.380)* 15 January 1987.
197. *(p.380)* 26 May 1987.
198. *(p.381)* 12 June 1987.
199. *(p.382)* 24 June 1987.
200. *(p.382)* 27 June 1987.

THE WORLD-EXPERIENCE-TREE-CLIMBER

BOOK 6

201. A crook

While I was shopping in Washington, D.C., I went into a restaurant and asked the man at the counter for a glass of orange juice. He said his cash register was broken and he could not make change.

The orange juice cost 59 cents and all I had was a dollar bill. So I said, "That is all right. Please give me the orange juice and just keep the change."

The man said, "No, I can't do that." Then he looked at me and said, "But you are a nice man, so I'll do it." Then he gave me a doughnut and said, "Here, you eat this. Then it comes to almost a dollar."

I said, "No, I don't want a doughnut." But he insisted that I take it.

While I was there another man came in – a nice-looking gentleman, tall and stout, wearing glasses. He also only had a dollar bill. But the man at the counter wouldn't give him anything. He pointed to me and said, "I only did it for him because he's a nice man."

As the stout gentleman was leaving, the man said to me, "I think he's a crook!"

202. The nice man

The story never ends. I was shopping and shopping and shopping – in other words, just getting lost. People told me to go to 14th Street and F. But did I know where F or G was? When you ask people, usually they give wrong information!

Finally I got back to the hotel and was about to enter the elevator when I saw the same tall and stout gentleman with glasses. I couldn't believe my eyes.

He looked at me and said, "So, you are a nice man and I am not a nice man!" What could I do? I just smiled at him.

203. The boxer

I went into a restaurant for a salad and onion rings. An elderly couple happened to be beside me. As I was about to leave, the lady said to me, "Are you a boxer? You look like a boxer."

I said, "No, I am not a boxer, but I do lift weights."

The lady said, "I thought you were very strong."

Her husband didn't say anything, but he was very amused that his wife was such a talker.

204. The useless receipt

The hotel where I stayed in Washington is so bad! No matter when you go, the hotel is always under construction and the rooms are so undivine. The people are also very undivine.

When I checked into the hotel, I paid the bill and got a receipt. Normally I do not keep receipts, but this time I did.

When I was ready to check out, they said to me, "You have not paid for your room."

I said, "I gave you three twenty-dollar bills and you gave me four dollars change. I have the receipt."

They said, "This receipt is no good. It wasn't stamped."

I said, "But how could I get the receipt if I didn't pay?"

For ten minutes this went on. The girl who had originally taken the money from me was not there. Finally, the assistant manager came and said, "There is no indication on the receipt that you have paid."

Meanwhile, Lord Chidananda was on the street waiting for me with the car.

Then out of the blue a young girl behind the counter said, "I think he did pay." She had been there at the time and she remembered me.

205. The *Sri Chinmoy*

When I went to get radiation treatment for my knee, the technician said to me, "Are you *the* Sri Chinmoy from the Sri Chinmoy Marathon Team?"

I said, "Yes."

He couldn't believe it. He was showing me such love and such respect.

He asked, "Can I take your picture?"

I told him to take it and gave him a nice smile.

When I went back the following day, the technician asked, "Can I have a picture taken with you?"

His name was John. I gave him a T-shirt and he was so happy. He has run two marathons and now wants to run our marathon.

206. *The Frenchman*

As soon as I sat down on the plane for my trip to India, a Frenchman was so kind to me. My handbag was a little big, so he took it from me and put it under the seat in front of him to give me more legroom. Then he asked me if I needed a blanket and a pillow. Who will do this kind of thing?

He asked me if I am interested in Indian culture. Being an Indian, I had to say that I am. O God, then he asked me what kind of Indian dancing I prefer. I am the right person!

He said he was learning to play the piano and was just a beginner. Then he asked me if I am also interested in piano.

I said, "I am also a beginner, although I have made a tape." I promised to send him my piano tape.

Then he gave me his card and asked for my card. Luckily, I was carrying some Centre envelopes with me, so I gave him an envelope that had my return address.

207. Meeting Ramesh Krishnan

When I was waiting in line at immigration at the Madras airport on my way back to New York, India's foremost tennis player, Ramesh Krishnan, was just behind me.

I congratulated him on winning the Davis Cup, and invited him to come to our Tennis Ground in New York. I made a spontaneous request, and he gave an immediate acceptance.

By the time we passed through immigration, he was way ahead of me. So he came back to where I was and asked for my card. In the future I have to carry a card!

Luckily, I still had a Centre envelope. But I also wanted to give him my phone number. I had brought six or seven ballpoint pens with me; but now that I needed one, none was available. I searched and searched and finally found one. So I gave him Annam Brahma's phone number.

Then some officials came and took him through customs. He was a great man so he got special treatment. Poor me, I had to wait on line.

On the flight from Madras to Bombay, God alone knows where he sat. But on the flight from Bombay to London, we both happened to be on the upper deck in Clipper Class. He was sitting very near me and we could see each other clearly.

He knows how to sleep! He slept through two or three meals. While he was sleeping, like a rogue I was observing how strong his wrist and arm were.

208. Bus ride to Niagara Falls

During the children's bus ride to Niagara Falls, Joanna did an excellent, excellent job as leader and Ragu composed a super-excellent song. I also composed a song for each and every individual on the bus.

Sanatan and Rupantar were driving. Ketan and Sagar were supposed to be their helpers and keep them awake, but they were lying down on the floor of the bus sleeping. Ketan had brought a big teddy bear, but instead of holding the teddy bear, he was holding Ragu.

209. Turning night into day

In Milan the audience showed me utmost devotion. After each instrument they clapped and clapped. After the girls sang, they also clapped. It was sincere appreciation.

Afterwards, four hundred seekers came onto the stage to pick up a flower petal. With such devotion they picked it up, and with such sincere and loving devotion they passed by me. Many were folding their hands, and some knelt down and gave me sweets or flowers.

I had quite a good experience in Milan. But the performance was absolutely useless because the acoustics were so bad. It was not Dhanu's fault at all. Everything that could possibly go wrong did go wrong. Also, it was raining cats and dogs outside. But the seekers' sincere oneness with my aspiration-heart saved me! Their aspiration and devotion turned that night of frustration into a day of satisfaction.

210. *Playing on the Vatican organ*

I was supposed to play the organ at St. Peter's Basilica, but at the last minute Kulai cancelled the appointment because he thought that I would not get there on time. Fortunately, they were able to reschedule the appointment.

People were already gathering for the mass when I started to play, so there was no time for me to meditate or anything. I was fighting against the clock.

While I was playing, sunlight was shining on a framed picture of a dove. It was very beautiful.

The priest who was observing me was stiffness incarnate. He was watching to see if I was going to break the organ. After five minutes he placed his hand on my shoulder, indicating that it was time for me to stop so they could begin the mass. The mass lasted for an hour and a half.

The man in charge said I could play for as long as I wanted when the mass ended. He was so kind to me. I played for fifteen minutes. Afterwards, he thanked me and said, "Bravo, bravo!"

211. *A very great man*

I was on the podium to give the opening meditation at the World Veterans' Games in Melbourne. Behind me were six or seven most distinguished persons and speakers. A lady came up and stood between them and me. She said that she had to stand there because I was a very great man.

212. Two immortal Australian runners

John Landy was very, very nice to us at the World Veterans' Games. They say he was looking and looking at me while I was in a meditative consciousness.

Then, after he gave his speech, I went over to shake hands with him. He was the second man to break the four-minute mile. I said that I had always admired him.

He said he was very grateful to me for bringing a moment of peace to his country, and he thanked me deeply.

Earlier, I had met Herb Elliott. He holds twenty-seven records. He also was very, very nice.

So two immortal Australian runners I have met!

213. The missing Kishore

One of the organisers of the Games was angry at Kishore because he could not find him the whole day.

Kishore was also one of the organisers, but he was with his Guru all day. That is why the other organisers couldn't find him.

214. Meeting the President of the Veterans' Games

The President of the World Veterans' Games, Don Farquharson, is a Canadian. At the Melbourne airport, he came up to me full of kindness and appreciation and said, "Do you recognise me? I saw you at the Games in Puerto Rico." He talked to me about this and that for quite a while; he was so happy to see me.

When I was at the stadium, again the President came up to me. At that time I was in a meditative consciousness.

He said, "Sorry to disturb your meditation. I have come to introduce my son to you. My son and his new wife are enjoying their honeymoon here. I want them to meet you and see your meditation."

So he introduced them both to me. Then he said, "Can we have a picture taken with you?"

I said, "Of course."

Then he, his daughter-in-law and his son all stood next to me for a picture.

215. A "10" for the Guru!

A member of the Melbourne football team came to our ten-kilometre race. While I was walking, he came up to me and said, "This is for you." Then he gave me a jersey with the number "10" on it. That is his number on the Melbourne football team.

216. The ex-joker

Shivaram's younger brother used to work with me at the Indian Consulate in New York. With Shivaram I was always serious; we talked all about spirituality. But with his brother there was no spirituality – only jokes and mundane things. We were two jokers.

I couldn't believe he was the same person when I saw him yesterday at the Los Angeles airport. How much respect he showed me! He prostrated himself right at my feet.

All credit goes to Shivaram. He has changed his brother's attitude completely.

THE WORLD-EXPERIENCE-TREE-CLIMBER

217. Night and day

When I went to New Zealand, I received VIP treatment. An officer came onto the plane and escorted me through customs.

But in Victoria, Canada, I had such a deplorable experience. The lady working in customs said that fifteen years ago she had heard a talk I gave at the university in Seattle when she had been a student there. "I know everything about you," she said.

But unfortunately our Peace Mile she didn't understand. Our Peace Concert she didn't understand. She was harassing me like anything!

When it is a matter of service, I have rendered much, much more service to Canada than to New Zealand. So many times I have given talks and concerts there! So this is what happens: New Zealand was so kind to me and Canada was so bad. It was like night and day!

Not only I but also my Canadian students have done so much for the heart and soul of Canada. My Canadian students have really awakened and illumined the consciousness of Canada. Nobody will believe how much they have helped Canada spiritually.

218. What a privilege

During our stopover in Japan, an American and I were waiting on the same floor for the elevator. He pressed the down button and I also pressed it and moved away. After a little while the elevator stopped and somebody came out. Then I started to go in.

The American said, "No, this elevator is going up."

So he prevented me from making that mistake. Then we went down together.

In the lobby he bought a newspaper and I went into the shops. A few minutes later he and I were again in the elevator together, this time going up. Several others got out on the third, fourth and fifth floors, so that finally we were only two together going up to the seventh floor.

Then out of the blue he said, "What a privilege it is to be with you!"

I did not know him at all. Perhaps he had seen the disciples looking at me devotedly, or perhaps someone had spoken to him about me.

My life is filled with stories like this – good and bad. This one was very good.

219. Saved by Tanima

In the Samudra Beach Hotel in Indonesia, Tanima and I got into the elevator together. As we went inside, all of a sudden the lights went out and the doors started to close.

Tanima understood what was happening and she forced the doors open before they could close. So we were able to escape. Otherwise, we would have been stuck in the elevator, and the electricity was off for half an hour or more.

So Tanima saved me!

220. Visiting souls

The souls of many disciples who have not come on the Christmas Trip with us have visited us while we were here. I have seen Madhuri's soul quite a few times and also the souls of a few German girls. But Hiranmoyi's soul has come the most!

Again, some disciples whose bodies are here have left their souls in America or Europe or Africa. They have brought their body here, but the soul is not functioning!

THE WORLD-EXPERIENCE-TREE-CLIMBER

221. The horse and carriage ride

In Bukittinggi I took a horse and carriage to the market.

If you go one way, it takes only two minutes. But the driver was such a rogue; he took me all the way in the other direction so that it would take a long time. Still, he was very nice and I gave him 2,000 rupees, so he was very satisfied.

After I did my shopping and was ready to go back, I saw that he was still there. There were ten or twelve other carriages in the market as well, but I went to him because he had been nice.

We came back to the hotel in three minutes. When I gave him 1,000 rupees, he was grumbling and fumbling because the previous time, when he had brought me the long way, I had given him 2,000 rupees. Later, everybody told me the price should have been only 1,000 rupees.

222. The full carriage

I saw Malati, Jamuna and Kiran in a carriage. How could three persons sit in one carriage? The horse was still alive? When I sit all by myself, I find it so uncomfortable!

I saw them get in the carriage and I saw them get out again a few moments later. For such a short distance they took a horse and carriage!

223. Interview with a Muslim

The sales manager of the Ambarrukmo Palace Hotel was begging me for an interview. I said that I would give him one at two o'clock the following day. I asked him, "In your office?"

He said, "No, I don't want anybody else to be there."

So we went somewhere else for the interview.

A Muslim wanted to have an interview with a Hindu – very good!

224. *The portrait*

When we came out of the Garuda Hotel, I went shopping while Savyasachi and Alo ate. In the first shop I visited, two boys were begging me to let them draw my portrait for 3,000 rupees. I said, "No, I don't want it."

Then I felt sorry for the younger one and said, "All right!"

They asked me to sit down on a little bench that was not even a foot long. They were very amused. When I sat down, the older one started to draw very seriously, but the younger one began to laugh. Then I said in English, "Don't laugh!" and he kept quiet.

They said it would take only five minutes. But after ten minutes they said it would take five minutes more. When I looked at what the older one had done so far, I was simply amazed that he had captured the right side of my face a little. I thought, "I will be able to show my disciples. It is so nice."

Then somebody came in smoking a cigarette. It was their boss. The boss snatched the picture away and began to finish it. In two minutes the boss redid what the boy had done and ruined the picture completely. The boy was doing it so nicely, but the boss was a hostile force. It didn't resemble me at all anymore, but I took it anyway.

When you sit to have your portrait drawn, people laugh at you as though you are doing something silly. Two French girls came and watched me. They were laughing and laughing.

225. Visiting Borobudur

All of you have visited Borobudur with me. People who go on the Christmas Trip may spend lots of money but they also get many inner experiences.

Those who have seen Borobudur have really seen something. It is so beautiful and it has such spiritual grandeur! I also like Kamakura.

Borobudur is the Buddha in the process of blossoming. Kamakura is the Buddha who has already blossomed. Borobudur has simplicity in purity and purity in simplicity. Kamakura has silence in power and power in silence. Both are totally different.

226. The half-blind driver

I have been to the main town of Yogyakarta three times. The first time I went, the man driving my horse and carriage was blind in one eye. The disciple who got the carriage for me chose him out of compassion.

Once or twice we almost met with an accident because the man could barely see. At one point he went against a red light. It was an experience!

227. The tennis audience

When I play tennis at the Ambarrukmo Palace Hotel, about fifteen or twenty children always stand outside the fence behind me and watch. And they always take my side.

When Mahiyan makes a good shot, they don't say anything. But when I do well, they are so happy.

Those children are more attentive than some of my disciples. Some of the disciples lie down or chat while I am playing, but the children watch attentively.

228. A fellow Hindu

Today we have been allowed to use the tennis court at the Bali Beach Hotel. Why? Because the ballboy is a Hindu!

At first when we asked if we could play, he said, "No can play. Last night, many, many rain!"

He told us that his name is Jana. He was very proud that he was a Hindu.

I said, "I am also a Hindu."

Then he was so moved. So he went to the higher authorities and got us permission to play on the court, even though it was still a little bit wet.

229. Heaven on earth

Of all the places I have visited in the last fifteen or sixteen years, Bali is undoubtedly the best. It has everything: sincerity, simplicity, purity, humility and peace. Is there any divine quality missing here?

Even outwardly it is so beautiful. You can see how beautiful the little cottages and villages are. They have such simplicity!

Bali has maintained most of its pristine purity. You don't even have to meditate here; nature will meditate on your behalf. Early in the morning if you walk around the villages, their divine qualities will enter into you and you will become a different person. Here in Bali, nature herself will accelerate your inner progress!

This place is Heaven on earth. If a businessman wants to make money here, he may have a problem. But in terms of consciousness, Bali is by far the best – both inwardly and outwardly. In many aspects it is even better than India. I am an Indian, but sincerity has to speak!

230. Mango lassi

Today we went to a smaller than the smallest restaurant. I asked for *mango lassi,* but instead the girl brought me a mango juice.

I said that it couldn't be a *lassi,* but she said it was. After ten minutes another girl came. She smiled and said that they had made a mistake.

Then they brought me a mango lassi. So I got two drinks. Because they made a mistake, they didn't want to charge me for both. But I became generous and said, "No, no! I will pay."

231. *The bamboo chair*

As soon as I sat down on the bamboo chair at that restaurant, I liked the chair so much. It was very large and comfortable, and I was taking lots of exercises on it.

I said jokingly to myself, "Since I am a multi-millionaire, I am going to buy the chair."

Savyasachi went to ask about buying the chair, but the boss was not there and the workers said they couldn't sell the chair. So we waited and waited for the boss. After about half an hour he came in, and Savyasachi offered him 20,000 rupees for the chair.

The boss looked at the workers and the workers looked at the boss. They didn't understand why we wanted this particular chair and they weren't sure what to do.

The boss said this chair was old, but we could buy a new one at another place. I said, "No, I want to buy this one."

Again they hesitated. The boss looked at us and the two girls looked at us, but nobody said anything.

Then Savyasachi took the 20,000 rupees and touched the hands of the two girls and the boss together. Finally they agreed.

What a crazy thing to buy a chair in a restaurant! But I had gotten such good vibrations from the chair while I was taking exercise on it that I said, "I am not going to leave this chair here."

232. The Jakarta reporter

Many reporters came to our press conference. Most of them were so nice. But the man from Jakarta was bad. Such nasty questions he asked!

First he asked why I was not going to Russia, China and North Korea. What kind of question is that!

I said that the time has not come for me to go to those places.

Then, when I was meditating before doing my lifts, he said, "Is there any special reason why you are looking towards the East?"

I said, "Here I don't know where East or West is."

Most of the reporters were so nice, but always there is someone to challenge and annoy us.

233. Three spiritual figures

The day before yesterday the manager of the Bali Beach Hotel said that he had seen three holy men in his lifetime.

He saw the Dalai Lama from a distance when he came to Indonesia. He also saw the Pope from a distance.

Then he said that I was the third spiritual figure he had seen. Only with me he could talk and take pictures!

THE WORLD-EXPERIENCE-TREE-CLIMBER

234. Everybody recognises me!

Since the television programme and the newspaper articles about me have come out, so many people recognise me.

Yesterday five young girls jumped up when they saw me. One pretended to play the flute and another pretended to lift a weight over her head. Then they sang "Bali, Bali," imitating our singers.

At another place three young men all pretended to lift weights overhead when they saw me.

235. Genuine receptivity

About a thousand people came to our Belgium Peace Concert. They were so receptive!

After the performance, about three hundred seekers passed by me. Many showed most sincere devotion. About a hundred of them prostrated themselves at my feet, according to Indian tradition. They were not showing off; they did it with utmost sincerity.

For years and years we have been offering Peace Concerts here, there and everywhere. God knows how much light the seekers have actually received. But here some seekers definitely and whole-heartedly received peace, love and joy from me. So I was very happy and grateful.

236. The organ Mozart played

When I was in Haarlem, Holland, for a television interview, I also played an organ that Mozart had played on when he was sixteen years old or so. The keys were so difficult to press! That organ was harder than the hardest to play!

237. You are very close to God!

After my television interview, a man from the Dutch radio station also wanted to interview me.

We were sitting face to face, and he was asking me many spiritual questions. At one point he stood up and came over to me and said, "There are some people who are very, very close to God, and I can see you are one of those."

238. Three important meetings

For the first time, I met with the President and Prime Minister of a country and the head of their spiritual community, all in a matter of two hours. This happened in Iceland.

First I met with the Prime Minister for about ten minutes or so. He had agreed to meet with me because some Members of Parliament had requested it. But he did not know anything about me. He asked so many questions!

The room where we met was simplicity incarnate. Even the mayors' offices that I have been to are all decorated very gorgeously. But this room was simpler than the simplest.

239. Heart-to-heart talk

Next I met with the President of Iceland. Her office was just next to the Prime Minister's. In the beginning she allowed the newspaper photographers and television people to take pictures, but then she asked everyone to leave. She knew all about me, and she wanted to have a very private talk, with no tape recorders or photographers. So we had a very soulful heart-to-heart talk for about half an hour.

We spoke about peace and both of us understood one another. Towards the end she was telling me that she wants to lead a spiritual life like us, but right now it is simply impossible for her.

She is very simple, very kind-hearted, very intelligent and quite dynamic. She is also mature, tolerant and self-giving. I was extremely pleased with the interview.

240. Such affection from the bishop!

The Bishop of the Lutheran Church of Reykjavik was so nice from the beginning to the end. He showed me such affection. We had an interview for over an hour.

At first he said he wanted a private interview and that nobody could accompany me. But then he changed his mind and invited all the disciples to come in.

He was begging everyone to drink tea or coffee and to eat the bread and cheese that he had provided. It was like a family gathering.

He could not understand why I do not drink tea or coffee, so I had to give a long explanation. Then, when he heard that I am a vegetarian, he had a volley of questions.

He knew all about prayer but had no idea what meditation is. He could not imagine how anybody could meditate without thought. So we had a long discussion about prayer and meditation.

I told him that when I was in India I used to meditate for six or seven hours at a time. He believed what I told him, but he said that it was impossible for him to keep his own mind quiet for more than a few minutes.

At the end we meditated for a minute or two and prayed with our heads down. Then he stood up and said, "You know, I am eighty-six years old." Then he placed his hands on my shoulders and pressed down on them with utmost affection! He was so sweet, so kind and so full of affection, love and wisdom!

241. The Jefferson Memorial

When I went to Washington, D.C., I spent a long time inside the Jefferson Memorial. The design I liked so much, but the statue of Jefferson really disappointed me.

They showed him as a military man – with a heroic spirit. But his so-called outer heroism was nothing in comparison with his inner vision and wisdom-light. These were his main qualities. America loves dynamism, and the outer dynamism of a soldier this statue has. But the inner wisdom of a statesman or true world leader the statue does not show.

On the wall were some significant statements by Jefferson. Unfortunately, he came long before the world, especially America, was prepared for his beautiful and powerful wisdom-light. Always prophets come at least one minute before the world is able to appreciate them. When they are here, they are not accepted. They have such wisdom, but they are not taken seriously. Only afterwards does the world accept and appreciate them.

242. I also need blessings

On our way to Hawaii, many disciples came to see us off and I gave out prasad. As soon as I passed the first security check, a lady came up to me and said, "I also need blessings from you."

Then Alo told her who I was. The lady said, "I know, I know. That's why I need blessings from him!"

243. The lucky ones

Then a man recognised me and said, "Sri, Sri, Sri Chinmoy! Your disciples are so lucky!" He had a little mustache and was drinking coffee on the way to the plane.

I wanted to say that I was the lucky one, but it didn't come out. So I just said "Thank you."

NOTES TO THE WORLD-EXPERIENCE-TREE-CLIMBER, BOOK 6

201. *(p.387)* 18 July 1987.
202. *(p.387)* 18 July 1987.
203. *(p.388)* 18 July 1987.
204. *(p.388)* 19 July 1987.
205. *(p.389)* 20 July 1987.
206. *(p.389)* 30 July 1987.
207. *(p.390)* 30 July 1987.
208. *(p.391)* 5 August 1987.
209. *(p.391)* 10 October 1987.
210. *(p.392)* 16 October 1987.
211. *(p.392)* 4 December 1987.
212. *(p.393)* 4 December 1987.
213. *(p.393)* 4 December 1987.
214. *(p.393)* 4 December 1987.
215. *(p.394)* 4 December 1987.
216. *(p.394)* 4 December 1987.
217. *(p.395)* 6 December 1987.
218. *(p.395)* December 1987.
219. *(p.396)* December 1987.
220. *(p.396)* December 1987.
221. *(p.397)* January 1988.
222. *(p.397)* January 1988.
223. *(p.397)* January 1988.
224. *(p.398)* January 1988.
225. *(p.399)* January 1988.
226. *(p.399)* January 1988.
227. *(p.399)* January 1988.
228. *(p.400)* 12 January 1988.
229. *(p.400)* 12 January 1988.
230. *(p.401)* 12 January 1988.

THE WORLD-EXPERIENCE-TREE-CLIMBER

231. *(p. 401)* 12 January 1988.
232. *(p. 402)* 13 January 1988.
233. *(p. 402)* 20 January 1988.
234. *(p. 403)* 20 January 1988.
235. *(p. 403)* 19 March 1988.
236. *(p. 403)* 19 March 1988.
237. *(p. 404)* 19 March 1988.
238. *(p. 404)* 19 March 1988.
239. *(p. 404)* 19 March 1988.
240. *(p. 405)* 19 March 1988.
241. *(p. 406)* 9 July 1988.
242. *(p. 406)* 14 September 1988.
243. *(p. 407)* 14 September 1988.

THE WORLD-EXPERIENCE-TREE-CLIMBER

BOOK 7

244. Simultaneous translation

At the television studio in Germany, they put a little transmitter inside my ear so that I could get a simultaneous English translation of what the interviewer was saying.

It was very confusing because I could hear the interviewer talking in German, and at the same moment I was hearing the English translation.

So in one ear I was hearing German and in the other ear I was trying to listen to English. The English and German were coming together – one word from this side and one word from that side.

It was very difficult to understand!

245. Carl Lewis' mental trainer

At the start of the television interview, they showed a video of the 100-metre dash in the Olympics, when Ben Johnson defeated Carl Lewis. But Carl Lewis was eventually declared the winner because Ben Johnson was disqualified. The announcer said Carl Lewis wins races because he prays and meditates. He said he was now going to introduce the man behind Carl Lewis' prayer and meditation. It was a very significant introduction.

Then they opened the side door where I had been waiting and I came out. On the television screen there was the title, "Carl Lewis' mental trainer", but I didn't see it. The disciples told me about it afterwards.

246. Lost in translation

I had so many problems with the English translator. At one point the interviewer asked how I help Carl Lewis with his prayer and meditation, but the translator said, "Now tell us something about how you help Ben Johnson with his prayer and meditation."

At another point when I said "pray and meditate", the translator said "*play* and meditate" in German. Kailash told me afterwards.

247. Hotel problems

Early in the morning I wanted to change some money at the hotel. There was only one person ahead of me in line, but it took me twenty minutes to get my money changed because that person and the man behind the desk were talking and talking.

At seven o'clock in the morning Ekantar did me a favour. Before I came down to the lobby, he paid my bill. Then immediately they turned off my telephone so that I could not make any more outside calls.

When I told the operator that I wanted to make a phone call, she said, "No, no, your room bill has already been paid. You can't make any more phone calls."

I said, "But I am still here in the room. I will come down and pay again."

After a long fight, they finally agreed.

248. The Athens airport

When I arrived at the Athens airport, I showed them my Greek visa, which was on page four of my passport. But they had to examine all the other pages as well. Then they asked me why I went to so many places.

Next they said, "How much money do you have? You have to show us."

My bag with most of my money was with Projjwal, so I simply emptied both of my pockets. Inside was all German currency.

They said, "Why do you have German money?"

I said, "Look at my ticket. I am coming from Munich."

They said, "No, you have to have American dollars!"

Then they called up another officer. Such a waste of time! For about half an hour they were harassing me.

249. Greek friends

When I was in Athens I saw Yiannis Kouros and his family. His wife Teresa is so sweet and polite. Their daughter Veronica acted as if she had known me all her life. They have put so many pictures of me in her room!

At the concert in Athens, Yiannis introduced me and gave a long talk about our philosophy. Then he and his family came with us to eat after the concert.

I brought little toys for Veronica. Luckily, I had bought two frogs – one for somebody whom I know was a frog in her last animal incarnation, and the other for Veronica. When the frog was turned on, it started jumping. She was so delighted. She was sitting on her chair, but then she jumped up to get her jumping frog!

250. The meditation club

In Athens I was invited to visit a meditation club that follows all the spiritual Masters, including Ramakrishna and Satya Sai Baba. They liked my meditation book and have translated an abridged version.

They sang *bhajans* and asked me quite a few questions. At one point they were singing "Ganesha" in various ways, but I couldn't understand what they were saying.

I asked, "What were you singing?"

They said, "You don't know? This is about your God Ganesha."

Then I told them a few stories about Ganesha and they were very happy. Finally they sang one of my Bengali songs, *Usha bala elo*. Suhriday and Nikunja had taught them.

251. Sulochana's surprise

The funniest thing happened with my dearest Sulochana in Athens.

I was standing in one place and Sulochana was about twenty metres away. She started coming towards me very fast, but she didn't see me. When she was three or four metres away, I said, "Sulochana!"

Then she saw me standing there and was so surprised!

Like a magnet I was pulling her towards me, but she didn't see me at all.

252. Concorde confusion

I was coming home on the Concorde. The man who gave me my ticket said it was leaving from Gate 10 at seven o'clock.

Before seven o'clock they made the announcement: "British Airways bound for New York is now boarding at Gate 10." So I went there and gave the lady at the gate my ticket. As usual, she tore off a portion and gave the other portion to me. Then I entered into the plane.

When I got inside, the man checking tickets said, "Wrong plane!"

I said, "How could it be the wrong plane? The man at the ticket counter told me to come to Gate 10, and the lady at the door took my ticket."

He said, "No, you are supposed to go on the Concorde, and this is a regular plane."

I went back to the lady at the gate and said, "Why did you send me into this plane?"

Then she started barking at me, saying, "Who asked you to go there?"

I said, "I gave you the ticket. What do I know about it? If it was not the right plane, you should have told me!"

Then an officer came and scolded her because it was her fault. He told me the correct gate to go to.

My plane was supposed to have left at seven o'clock, but it had been delayed. After that I had to wait several more hours for my flight. The Concorde is supposed to save time, so this is how I saved time!

253. Charlie and David

When I was finally on the plane, a man fatter than the fattest came up to me and said, "Can I see your ticket?"

I said, "Yes."

He said, "I have to see whether you are Charlie or David."

"C" and "D" he wouldn't say, only Charlie and David! My ticket happened to be 11C – Charlie. That was the aisle seat.

He asked, "Do you mind if I change with you? My seat is David."

I answered, "No, it is fine."

Unfortunately, the Concorde seats are very, very narrow, and he couldn't fit into the seat. His thighs went very nicely into the space where I was sitting, although I was trying desperately to squeeze myself against the window. How much I suffered!

He was very, very nice, but so fat! Although the Concorde is very expensive – even more than first class – the seats are very small. The Concorde is only for those who are in a tremendous hurry. But if the flight is delayed, it is really useless.

254. The false vegetarian meal

On my flight to Puerto Rico, an elderly man from Canada was sitting beside me. He said he had ordered a vegetarian meal, but the stewardess said that they had no record of this.

He said, "No, I confirmed it. It was registered on the computer." He was mad, mad, mad. So they had a fight.

Finally, after fifteen minutes the stewardess said, "We made a mistake. Your name was found. Unfortunately, we don't have even one vegetarian dish."

Then the head steward came and said, "We found your vegetarian meal."

But when they gave him his food, it was not vegetarian. There was no difference between his food and everybody else's. He was old but very smart, so he knew that it was the same meal.

Then he said to me, "My wife fell down in Miami Beach. Now she is in the hospital paralysed. I have only one son, but I do not know where he is. This is my fate!"

I deeply sympathised with him.

255. The shade

While flying back from Puerto Rico, I was sitting near the window. When they started showing the movie, the stewardess came and pulled down the window shade.

The lady sitting next to me on the aisle did not want to watch the movie. She was interested in *Time* magazine, so she lifted up the shade so that she could see better. Her reading light was on, but she wanted daylight as well.

Twice the stewardess came and pulled the shade down. But each time the lady reached over me and pulled the shade back up.

I watched this happen twice. Then I didn't want to see it anymore, so I went to sleep.

256. First-class experience

Coming back from Seattle, I was flying first class. But even that didn't save me!

First of all, after I sat down in my proper seat, they wanted me to move because they had given the same seat number to another passenger. They said, "You have to move because your seat number was issued in New York."

Finally, when I insisted, they took the other person's ticket and changed it.

Then, in two cases they had separated husband and wife. A man was seated next to me, but his wife was three rows behind. She came over to me and said, "Would you change seats with me?"

I went to her seat right away. Then, when the plane was about to start, another man came up to me and said, "Please, this is my wife here. Could I sit with her?"

So I changed seats again. This was my first-class experience!

257. *Two philosophers*

During the flight, the stewardess came over to me and asked, "Do you want cereal or sausage?"

I said, "Cereal." Then I started meditating and entered into a high consciousness.

They put some yogurt in front of me, but also ham. When I saw the ham, I said, "Great!"

I thought I would just eat the yogurt and cereal. I started to pour some milk on my cereal, but the milk immediately jumped up and spilled on my trousers. The cereal dish was covered with plastic, but I did not notice it.

A bearded man sitting near me saw what happened and said, "Are you a philosopher? I think you are a philosopher." Then he added, "I am, too!"

258. *No smoking!*

The manager of the Ambassador Hotel in Bangkok wanted to talk to me. He had been smoking a cigarette, but as soon as he saw me, he took it out of his mouth and cupped it in his palm because he wanted to show me respect.

This is similar to what happened in India when a friend of mine saw me. But in my friend's case, he put his burning cigarette in his pocket!

259. The ancient Abbot of Wat Po

The Abbot of Wat Po was so nice. He said that wherever I go, I will carry the Buddha's light.

Afterwards, a Thai newspaper reporter asked the old man if he could give a message about me, and the Abbot said the same thing again – that wherever I go, I will carry the Buddha's light.

260. Unfamiliar territory

The Royal Garden Village Hotel in Hua Hin is still unfamiliar to me. I go to this side and immediately I get lost; I go to that side and I again get lost. Then I ask the guard how to get where I want to go, and he always points in the other direction!

261. The living statues

There are two statues outside our meeting room in the Royal Garden Village Hotel that are not like regular statues at all. They actually have a living presence. They are very beautiful and soulful, and are sincerely aspiring.

I have blessed these two statues very nicely, and Nayana has put two garlands around them.

Already they have human souls. They are absolutely like living beings! They should have a human incarnation.

262. I need sleep

At six-thirty in the morning I was playing the cello in my hotel room in Hua Hin. All of a sudden I heard a pounding on my door: bang, bang, bang! A lady was screaming. I thought she was saying, "Police, police!" but she was actually saying, "Sleep, sleep!"

I looked through the viewing hole in the door and saw that she had only a white towel around her. So I didn't open the door. She was saying, "I need sleep, I need sleep!"

I said, "Sorry, sorry, sorry!"

I was playing the cello, not the saxophone, but she couldn't sleep.

Five or six years ago when I was playing the cello in my hotel room, a man came to my door and said, "You play well, but my daughter is sick, so I am asking you to stop."

263. The uncivilised Indian

At the Holiday Inn in Kuching, Borneo, there was an Indian restaurant. When I went there, they did not want to let me in because I was uncivilised – wearing shorts.

I said, "I am an Indian. You won't allow me in?"

The girl said, "Let me go and speak to the boss."

The boss said, "All right, as long as you aren't wearing sandals." Fortunately, I was wearing my running shoes.

Then I showed the girl what I wanted on the menu. Half an hour later the food still had not come. When I asked the girl what was going on, she said, "You have not ordered." She had forgotten!

I got mad at her and the boss scolded her. Then she came to me for consolation. I said that I forget things every day and told her that I was not angry.

The poor girl had been working there for only two weeks. She was so happy that I had forgiven her.

264. Borneo joy

We can see the Sarawak River from our windows in the hotel. It gives me such joy.

The people here are so nice! Where can you find such sympathetic souls?

I am so happy to be here in Borneo. My ancestors are blessing me from Heaven!

265. Surprising a gym owner

Today I went to a gym near the Holiday Inn. The gym owner recognised me the moment I walked in; he had seen my picture in *Muscle Mag*.

At first he didn't believe that I was really Sri Chinmoy. Then Savyasachi gave him our brochure, and he said that he had recognised me the moment I had walked in.

Like a child, he was showing me all his different equipment. I told him, "I have come here with some students."

He said, "Please bring them here. For them, everything is free."

I told him that I would lift him. He was so thrilled. He said he would keep the picture of the lift in his office.

266. The honorary chief

The oldest living head hunter (long ago retired) came to see me in Borneo. He was eighty-five years old.

Then the chief of the tribe came to see me. The chief liked me so much that he gave me his grandfather's ring. He put it on my finger and said, "I am making you an honorary chief of the Iban tribe."

I gave the old man a shirt and the young Iban chief an ocarina. They were both very happy.

I also gave each of them six pictures that I had taken myself when they were dancing. Long live my camera!

Both the old man and the chief had tremendous receptivity.

267. The Sultan's affection

When I met the Sultan in Kuala Lumpur, immediately I got a very good vibration from him. In a previous incarnation I had known his soul quite well. At that time the Sultan had a very, very close connection with me, but our relationship was totally different.

The Sultan also felt something in me. He was so kind and affectionate from beginning to end. He showed me the same kind of affection that Dan Lurie, the physical fitness proponent, shows me.

In the newspaper he had seen the picture of my lifting Samy Vellu. So when he saw me, he immediately said, "Do you want to lift me?" Of course I did! The whole time I was lifting him, he was in a trance; he was so happy.

268. Number One

When the singers were singing, the Sultan's soul was deeply moved — especially when they were singing the song I had composed about him — *Number One*. His soul was getting such joy from *Number One!*

269. *The missing bus driver*

After visiting the Sultan, we had to go to the airport to catch a plane. Unfortunately, our bus driver was nowhere to be found.

The Sultan immediately began ordering his people, "Get their driver!"

Then the police went into the town and found the driver having a cup of coffee with his friends.

270. *An inner connection*

The soul of Frank Zane, the bodybuilder, has a very close connection with the soul of that bus driver. While we were driving from the Sultan's palace to the airport, Frank Zane's soul was telling his soul who I am, and the bus driver's soul was listening with such admiration.

Now the bus driver outwardly has developed such admiration for me. It is because Frank Zane's soul is acting inside his soul.

271. *The Indian gentleman*

Alo and I entered an Indian restaurant in Kuala Lumpur. Some disciples also happened to be there. I was the only Indian in the whole place, but I was pretending to be a gentleman — using a plate, fork and spoon.

But the disciples – Americans, Canadians and Japanese – were all eating from a banana leaf, using their fingers, in the traditional Indian way.

272. The Emperor's visit

For so many years I have not had any connection with the Emperor of Japan. Even when I was first lifting weights in Japan and praying for him, his soul did not come to me.

But last night, at one-thirty in the morning, for the first time his soul came to me.

Now I see in the newspaper that the Emperor has died.

273. You have made him greater!

When the hotel telephone operator in Kuala Lumpur heard that I had gone to visit Datuk Samy Vellu, she said, "He is very great, but you have made him greater!"

274. Divine disobedience

So many times this telephone operator tried and tried to get through to India for me. Finally I told her, "Please cancel my call."

She said, "Yes."

After fifteen minutes the phone rang. I said, "I have cancelled it."

She said, "No, Sri Chinmoy, you told me to cancel it, but I didn't listen to you. Now I have got through."

My brother was on the line, and I was very happy.

275. Talking to the big shot

The telephone operator was also the receptionist. I asked her, "Why didn't you come to see me lifting?"

She said, "Here I can talk to you. There I cannot come near you because you are a big shot."

276. The elephant ride

In India if you see an elephant in the street, you get frightened to death. But the elephants in Chiang Mai in the elephant park are all tame. This is the first time I have ridden an elephant.

I feel sorry when the trainers strike them. The elephants are mild, with so much strength. We use the term "inner strength". Is this mildness not their inner strength?

When I saw Lucy riding on the neck of an elephant, my ego came forward. So when I took a second ride, I also did not use the seat.

277. Children are children

The abbots of the temples we visited in Chiang Mai had such depth. I also liked the little children who are practising spiritual life there. Such strict discipline they have to observe! They have genuine aspiration.

Still, children are children, and these were no exception. Everywhere children have to learn how to behave. Definitely I talk to the Lord Buddha when I visit temples, but these children were not aware of it. Perhaps they show more respect to the Buddhist monks when they come there.

278. Giving marks to the statues

Last night at the temple we visited, I was meditating on the statues of the monks praying and giving them marks for their meditation – the way I sometimes give marks to my disciples. One was so nice that he got 100 out of 100. Another got 79 and one got 61.

279. I remember you!

When I was in the Bangkok airport en route to India, I saw a very fat, middle-aged man standing on one side watching everything. He was the supervisor. As soon as he saw me, he said, "I remember you, I remember you, I remember you!"

I said, "From where?"

He said, "I have seen your picture in the newspaper, and I have also seen you on television. I am sure it is you."

I said, "Yes, yes."

Then he said, "What are you doing nowadays?"

I told him, "Just yesterday I set a new record; I lifted a man weighing 317 pounds."

He said, "So much weight? No good for your heart! No good for your lungs! Don't do this anymore!" With such concern he was advising me.

Then I smiled and thanked him and went away.

280. A vegetarian's strength

After we went through security and immigration, there was a long line of passengers boarding the plane. I said, "Let me just relax and be the last person."

After everybody else had entered the plane, I was about to give my boarding pass to the lady when, O God, I see that fat man running towards me. He was the one who tells them when to close the gate after everybody has boarded the plane.

When he saw me, he said, "Can you give me a picture?" Luckily, I had a picture of my lifting the man who weighed 317 pounds, so I gave it to him.

I was the last person to enter the plane, but he was delaying me. He said, "Now tell me, are you a vegetarian? I have been a vegetarian for five years."

I said, "I have been a vegetarian for forty-five years."

Then the lady collecting the boarding passes said to me, "Can you lift him?"

The fat man told her, "Easily, easily. I am not 317 pounds."

Then she asked the fat man if he could lift me.

He said, "Not yet! I have to be a vegetarian for another forty years. Then easily I will be able to lift him."

281. Blessed by children

On the plane from Bangkok to India, I was being blessed by children, as usual!

Just in front and to my right there was a woman with a little child. At first the child was fast asleep on her shoulder. But the mother wanted to show her fondness, so she was lifting up the child and massaging his shoulders very hard. Then, of course, the child woke up and started crying.

Then another child began crying right near me. He was with his mother two seats away. I was on the aisle and next to me was a middle-aged man. The child and his mother were next to the man.

282. I don't want to know

At the beginning of the flight they gave us two forms to fill in. The middle-aged gentleman beside me didn't have a ballpoint, so he asked the lady whose child was crying if he could borrow her pen.

Immediately the lady said, "No!" But that was not enough. Then she stood up and started insulting him.

Then I said to the man, "You can use my ballpoint."

The man said to me, "This lady and I used to be married, but now we are separated. Do you know why we are separated?"

I said, "I don't know anything, and I don't want to know."

But he didn't listen to me. He just continued, "That child is not mine, but she claims it is."

I said to myself, "Oh, I have to hear this kind of thing!"

Then the lady started screaming at him – using such foul language. O my God!

I put away my ballpoint and pretended I had to go to the bathroom. For more than ten minutes I stood near the bathroom door. Finally I went back to my seat, but the fight was still going on! So again I left, all the time praying to God that this story would end. When I came back the second time, it had stopped.

I was so lucky not to get involved. Such a foul tongue the lady had!

283. The culprits

How the tourists ruin the consciousness of Hawaii! If you enter into the heart of the island, you will see it is flooded with serenity, beauty, purity – every divine quality. But when you walk along the beach and see the tourists, it becomes something else. There is an immediate transformation. So we tourists are the culprits.

284. You have made my day!

The other day in Hawaii I was in a shop. A girl said, "Please tell me your name."

When I told her, she said, "O Guru, O Guru, you don't recognise me? I am Sambhava's sister-in-law – Lynn's sister. Thirteen years ago I came to New York and saw you. Then two years ago I came for your birthday. I can't believe you are here. You have made my day!"

285. A Brahmin in Bali

I went into a shop in Bali. A young man who was working in the shop said to me, "Are you a Hindu? I am a Hindu."

I asked him, "What is your name?"

He said, "My name is Normand."

I said, "Normand is not a Hindu name."

He said, "You do not know? There are four castes, and I come from the Brahmin caste. So Brahmins can have the name Normand."

I said, "Although I am not a Brahmin, I know the Indian caste system well. I have read the scriptures and there is no such surname."

286. The shameless bargainer

The lady in one store in Bali was a perfect rogue. I wanted to buy something, but she quoted a price which was very high – 30,000 rupees. I said to her, "7,000."

She looked at me very nicely and said, "All right, 19,000 – no less."

I said, "I won't pay 19,000. I will give you 8,000."

Then she said, "17,000." I took one step backwards and she said, "15,000."

I said, "No, 8,000 is enough!" and I started walking away. After I took seven or eight steps, she called out, "14,000!"

I said, "I am not going to come to your price."

Finally she said, "All right, all right – 8,000!"

In my mind I had been willing to go up to 10,000, but she accepted 8,000. So from 30,000 I shamelessly brought her down to 8,000. If they ask for 30,000, who else would dare to say 8,000?

287. The early start

At the Kartika Plaza Beach Hotel, the day begins at three-thirty in the morning when the workers start whistling and singing. That hotel is famous for that.

288. The problem dogs

It is so difficult to drive in Bali. The dogs create such problems. If you want to save their lives, you have to give your own life! So many times they almost caused us accidents!

289. Extra marigolds

A man selling flowers said that three marigolds cost 100 rupees. So I gave him 100 rupees and put three marigolds in the bag. Then I put two more in. I kept adding marigolds until I had eight. The man didn't mind, so I got eight for the price of three!

290. *Sympathy is not yet born*

When I was walking along the beach in Bali, I could not walk properly because of my knee pain. Not only young girls but also elderly people were giggling and laughing at me. I asked myself, "Where has sympathy gone?"

291. *The painful massage*

Yesterday's doctor tortured me like anything when he was giving me a massage. At one point he was biting my left toe with his teeth. He was biting down so powerfully that I had to scream so he would stop. And today I have such pain there – as though I had been stung by a bee.

He said that for one month he has been drinking only water. He said it is what God told him to do when he went to the mountains. He does not charge for his services, but you can leave a love offering on the shrine.

292. *Now you are better!*

Today's massage was not as brutal as the one I got yesterday. The doctor was saying, "Wherever it is hot, it is good. Wherever it is cold, it is bad."

Then the funniest thing happened. He said, "Now you are better," but I couldn't walk!

NOTES TO THE WORLD-EXPERIENCE-TREE-CLIMBER, BOOK 7

244. *(p. 413)* 8 October 1988.
245. *(p. 413)* 8 October 1988.
246. *(p. 414)* 8 October 1988.
247. *(p. 414)* 8 October 1988.
248. *(p. 415)* 8 October 1988.
249. *(p. 415)* 8 October 1988.
250. *(p. 416)* 8 October 1988.
251. *(p. 416)* 8 October 1988.
252. *(p. 417)* 8 October 1988.
253. *(p. 418)* 8 October 1988.
254. *(p. 418)* 13 October 1988.
255. *(p. 419)* 13 October 1988.
256. *(p. 419)* 30 October 1988.
257. *(p. 420)* 30 October 1988.
258. *(p. 420)* 18 December 1988.
259. *(p. 421)* 20 December 1988.
260. *(p. 421)* 21 December 1988.
261. *(p. 421)* 23 December 1988.
262. *(p. 422)* 27 December 1988.
263. *(p. 422)* 29 December 1988.
264. *(p. 423)* 29 December 1988.
265. *(p. 423)* 30 December 1988.
266. *(p. 424)* 6 January 1989.
267. *(p. 424)* 7 January 1988.
268. *(p. 425)* 7 January 1988.
269. *(p. 425)* 7 January 1988.
270. *(p. 425)* 7 January 1989.
271. *(p. 425)* 4 January 1989.
272. *(p. 426)* 7 January 1989.
273. *(p. 426)* 8 January 1989.

274. *(p.426)* 8 January 1989.
275. *(p.427)* 8 January 1989.
276. *(p.427)* 10 January 1989.
277. *(p.427)* 10 January 1989.
278. *(p.428)* 14 January 1989.
279. *(p.428)* 20 January 1989.
280. *(p.428)* 20 January 1989.
281. *(p.429)* 20 January 1989.
282. *(p.430)* 20 January 1989.
283. *(p.430)* 15 December 1990.
284. *(p.431)* 15 December 1990.
285. *(p.431)* 28 December 1990.
286. *(p.431)* 28 December 1990.
287. *(p.432)* 28 December 1990.
288. *(p.432)* 28 December 1990.
289. *(p.432)* 30 December 1990.
290. *(p.433)* 6 January 1991.
291. *(p.433)* 20 January 1991.
292. *(p.433)* 20 January 1991.

THE WORLD-EXPERIENCE-TREE-CLIMBER

BOOK 8

293. The knee specialist in the Bahamas

Today I went to a doctor that Edith recommended. This doctor is a great knee therapist. Snehashila went to the same one yesterday and she got tremendous results.

Her patients have to go for nine treatments and each one is an hour. I will go for four more days, two times a day, at 10:00 am and 4:00 pm. There is no heat, no sensation, when this doctor treats me. The same treatment is available in Munich, Germany, and it also started recently in Canada. A German doctor discovered it. For the last two years they have been doing it in Germany. America does not want to have this kind of treatment yet. But by next year or the following year America may have it.

I do not know how or why, but my German doctor-disciples did not think of trying this kind of treatment on my knee.

294. Morning blessings in the Bahamas

Around 7:15 this morning I was sitting outside. All of a sudden Vidura's soul came to me for blessings and love. I blessed his soul. Then I thought, "He is physically not here in the Bahamas, but his soul came to me for blessings. What is his wife, Devaki, doing?"

It did not take ten seconds! I saw Devaki passing by and I gave her a little smile. Just after Vidura's soul came to me, she passed by. How the souls work! Tomorrow is his birthday, but I blessed him at my place before we left New York. I had a birthday party for him. Today his soul came to me for more blessings.

295. Shopping for sandals

I went to buy sandals. I tried on one pair and then I told the young girl, "I need one size larger."

She did not understand me. She said, "Why can you not tell me the size? Then I can just get it for you."

I said, "I do not know the size, but I can see that I need only one size bigger."

This sales assistant was so rude and nasty, as if it were a crime that I did not know the size. With shoes, I can say that I wear seven and a half, but with sandals, what kind of size could I tell her? I looked at the sandals, but the size was not mentioned there.

This girl was so mad that I was not telling her the size. She was insisting and insisting. God knows why, all of a sudden I had to say to Alo, "She is so thin. Perhaps if she had been a little fatter, she would have been nicer to me." She was so thin and very nasty.

296. Fat equals nice

Then I went to the store next door to buy something else. At this store, the sales assistant was fatter than the fattest. And you cannot imagine how kind and how compassionate she was! She was speaking to me so kindly and compassionately. She made me feel that even if I did not buy anything, she would not mind. But I did buy quite a few things.

Then Alo wanted to buy some placemats. The young girl went outside the store to show Alo where to buy them. She was so kind to Alo.

So you see, my wish was fulfilled. In the first store I said, "Perhaps if this girl had been a little fatter, then she would have been nicer to me." Then, in the very next store, a fat girl was so kind and compassionate.

297. Shamelessly heavy

This time I am absolutely shamelessly heavy! Twenty-five or thirty years ago, once I weighed 178 pounds. In Puerto Rico, when Nadeshwar saw my stomach, he said, "Shame, shame!" I will never forget it! Strangely enough, those pictures show that I look even heavier than 178 pounds.

Now my fate has cursed me to repeat the story. Two days ago, I weighed myself and I cried. I wrote down in my notebook, "Shame, shame" and I put four or five exclamation marks after it. Now I am determined to lose twenty-five or thirty pounds. Each time I lose five pounds, I shall give prasad.

The day before yesterday, we came to the Bahamas. Yesterday my weight was 174 1/2 pounds, so 3 1/2 pounds I had already lost. Today I have lost a pound and a half more, so tonight I shall give prasad and share my happiness with you.

I arrived here at the ripe, heavy weight of 178. Today I am 173. Very often, when I weigh myself in my house, I go downstairs because the downstairs scale is one pound less. Upstairs I look at my weight on the scale and feel miserable. Then, when I come downstairs, the scale is one pound less and it gives me so much joy. Even a half a pound or a quarter of a pound less gives me boundless joy. I struggle and struggle only to see that I am a quarter pound less. That kind of torture I give to myself. When I really lose weight, I get tremendous joy. But to lose weight, one has to cultivate so much determination.

298. The kind weight-loss guru

I am telling you how kind my weight-loss guru, Savyasachi, is. I was at the doctor's getting treatment. To my widest surprise, Savyasachi came to me with a bottle. Inside it there was a kind of peanut. He put some peanuts on my palm. When I want to become a saint and lose weight, he gives me poison! But I was really hungry at that moment and he intuitively felt it. Then afterwards, when I went into the car, I begged him to give me more.

299. Nowhere frustration-thief

Here in the Bahamas, there is the hustle and bustle of life, but somehow everything flows very happily. Here the frustration is infinitely less than in America or elsewhere. Somehow, on this island, the frustration-thief finds it difficult to enter into us.

300. Bermuda reminiscences

I have so many memories from our visit to Bermuda many, many years ago. What pleased me most was a dance that two pairs of friends – Sanatan, Rupantar, Savyasachi and Ashrita – performed to my song *Nriter tale tale*. They dressed in such funny costumes and their dance was absolutely unique.

On that trip I also felt the devotional and aspiring aspect of the disciples when Alo took them on Christmas Eve to sing in the streets in the neighbourhood of our hotel. Their singing was so simple, sincere and pure. I did not go, but I was watching them. They were wearing white and holding candles. They looked absolutely like angels. These good experiences I will always treasure in Bermuda.

THE WORLD-EXPERIENCE-TREE-CLIMBER

Bermuda was also my humiliation. There it is very hilly. Everybody was riding little motorbikes. I thought I would also try. Savyasachi and another disciple were holding me on the motorbike because I could not keep my balance. Then God smashed my pride. Of all people, Maitreyi had to go by me so fast. And she is much older than I am.

I said, "Impossible! Enough, enough!"

In those days I had such pride in my physical. Was there anything that I could not do? Now there is nothing that I can do. Physical fitness always made me feel that I could do anything. But when I saw this disciple of mine driving away on the motorbike, I said, "Too much! Too much!" Then I said, "Stop! I do not want to ride any more."

Another painful experience was when I scolded very seriously the top girls' singing groups for the very first time because I was not pleased with their performances.

But again, if I have to speak frankly, the simple truth is that in those days the disciples had more love, more devotion and more surrender than they do nowadays. At every second they tried to please me. Now I try desperately to please them. The story has changed.

So in life there are always good memories and painful memories. The past that does not help us is worse than dust. But the past that helps us is better then gold. Most of the past is worse than the worst. Painful memories weaken the subtle nerves and then we become the losers. By remembering the deplorable past, we lose our divinity. It is all the time hurting like a very sharp sword.

So let us only try to remember the experiences that are golden.

301. The boat ride

Today I enjoyed our boat ride so much. When we take a boat ride, there is such joy. Water symbolises Infinity. When we look at the water, vastness automatically comes into our mind. The narrow mind disappears. We all have narrow minds, but as soon as we look at the vast expanse, our narrow minds disappear – at least for a few hours. Then again, when we come back to land, our narrow minds come back.

302. Morning greetings

The people are so nice here! Everywhere I go, people say, "Good morning, good morning!" When I am out walking, I want to enter into my own meditation, but at least twenty times people say, "Good morning!" If there are three ladies passing by, all the three ladies have to say, "Good morning!"

My answer is to smile. Again, how many times I have to smile! Sometimes I am walking so fast and I find it difficult to think of smiling at them. This happens on the path right in front of the hotel.

303. Conversation with a parrot

In the lobby of the hotel, there is a parrot. Today I was talking to the parrot and he was talking and talking and talking to me! He speaks very good English!

304. God's world

If this is not God's world, whose world is it? I am an Indian; I live in America; and, during my absence, my house is being taken care of by a German, Minati. So from where to where!

God has given us a family, a world-family. An infinite family He has given us everywhere. Here we come from America, Australia, Austria, Canada, France, New Zealand and so many other places. Infinity we have; only we need oneness.

305. The guard's deception

Savyasachi drove us to a village called Chichicastenango to do some shopping. As he was parking the car, he saw a middle-aged man nearby who had on a uniform. Savyasachi was under the impression that if he left the car there, this man would protect the car.

So we went to the market. At one place, I wanted to buy something. I bargained for about fifteen minutes, but it did not work. The man would not lower the price. So we went and ate. Then again I went back to that store. Alas, still my bargaining did not work. So I said, "I am not going to buy it." We were fighting not for American five cents difference, but for their five cents! It is next to nothing! I wanted to buy ten sheets of paper. Finally, the man said, "If you buy two more sheets, you can get your original price."

I said, "I am more than willing to buy twelve." So I bought the paper.

We came back to the car and it was unharmed. As usual, Savyasachi gave the man a generous tip for guarding the car. However, the man was not satisfied. He said that because he was guarding the car, he did not go out for his lunch. He spoke English quite well.

So Savyasachi gave him more money, plus peanuts. Then, as we were getting ready to drive away, we saw that just by the side was a bank and he was the bank guard! When we first arrived, he told us that he guards the place and we thought he was there to guard the cars for people who are going to the market. That is why we gave him the money. Then he asked for more money because he did not go out to eat. We gave him a second time, only to discover that he was actually guarding the bank!

306. The stomach sufferers

I saw Kanan in the market. He was alone. I asked him, "What is Hashi doing?"

Then I found out that Hashi was sick. Here many people have stomach problems. The sufferers suffer for at least a day or two. Somehow God saved me this morning. I was playing on my Australian instrument and I was feeling nauseous and sick in every possible way. But eventually it went away. I escaped. I was one of the lucky ones.

307. Shopping for President Gorbachev

I went with Alo, Saraswati and Savyasachi to the Hotel Atitlan, which is nearby. The garden there is simply beautiful, but the hotel shop was so expensive. All the prices were double what you would pay elsewhere and there was no bargaining. You just have to surrender, surrender.

I bought two T-shirts: one for President Gorbachev and one for me. These shirts show how many people there are in Guatemala. For President Gorbachev I bought extra large and, for me, large.

Recently, President Gorbachev endorsed pizza in one television advertisement. Some people criticised him mercilessly for it but, being his devoted friend, I strongly supported him. I have come to learn that his youngest granddaughter enjoys pizza. If ever she comes to New York, I would like to take her to a pizza parlour.

My favourite pizza is Sicilian. In Italy I have eaten pizza quite a few times, but American pizza is far better. The source of pizza is Italy. Why then does America far surpass Italy in pizza? Shikha, Sutikhna and Minati bring me pizza when I go to Italy and I cannot appreciate it.

308. The earthquake

What an experience we had at five minutes past four this morning! I was meditating with my eyes open. All of a sudden, I felt the whole building shaking. My room is on the top floor of the hotel. It was a really frightening experience. Because I was on the seventeenth floor, I was seeing the top of the building going this side and that side, like a tree. The top floor was not only shaking; it was bending sideways like a tree. At that time, when you are having the experience, the thought that they build the buildings to withstand earthquakes does not come. Only you have a rising fear.

So many people were awake in the hotel. Perhaps they felt that death was fast approaching. The whole experience lasted for a minute and a half. I think if it had continued for another two or three more minutes, perhaps some girls would have fainted.

309. *Visiting the Archbishop*

Perhaps you know that today I went to visit the Archbishop of Guatemala, Monsignor Próspero Penados del Barrio, at the Cathedral Metropolitana. He is a very kind, very compassionate and very loving personality.

I went with Agraha, Purnahuti [at that time known as Christian] and Aparajita. One of the nuns was waiting to open up the door for us, but she disappeared. Then a gentleman opened the door. Alas, I could not recognise that it was the Archbishop himself. Perhaps only Purnahuti knew he was the Archbishop. I do not think that Agraha and Aparajita knew. I was asking them if he was the one. In the meantime, he closed the door.

Purnahuti told us, "He is the one." Then the Archbishop came back and opened the door again. In the beginning, we were very respectful, but when he came back the second time, we showed him tremendous admiration and adoration.

310. *"Are you really a musician?"*

The Archbishop and I talked and talked. He looked at an album of our peace activities and there he saw a photograph of Muhammad Ali. It seems he is a great admirer of Muhammad Ali. Quite a few times, he asked me, "How long are you going to stay? How long are you going to stay?"

He asked me many questions on different subjects and I answered them. He cannot believe that I am a musician. Two or three times, he looked at me and asked, "Are you really a musician?"

I said, "Yes. I will give a concert here at the Cathedral in four days' time and I would like to invite you to come. I will sing and play musical instruments. My students will also perform." But he was fully convinced that my students are the musicians and singers, not me. He could not believe that a person like me would play music.

Then the Archbishop asked me, "How will people come to know about the concert?"

I said, "I only play. I am not involved in these things." I was looking at my assistants for the answer. A few minutes later, he asked the same question. He was sincerely concerned. He wanted many people to come to the concert.

311. The wooden carving of the crucifixion

In so many places I have seen paintings, sculptures and carvings of the crucifixion. When I look at some of them, I can feel the sufferings of the Christ, but somehow I can bear it. But when I saw one particular wooden carving of the crucifixion in the Cathedral, I was so overwhelmed. This carving shows the Christ's utter helplessness and, at the same time, his total surrender to his Father. It was the same type of carving that I had seen previously, but some portrayals are more heart-breaking than others. This was one of those carvings.

312. The hesitant interpreter

At one point, the Archbishop said to me that we had come at the right time. So much fighting was going on; there was no peace, no peace. He was deeply appreciating our arrival.

The building is so old. The rooms are very austere – austerity to the extreme. Perhaps modern churches are not so austere. I have no idea.

Purnahuti was our translator. Spanish is his mother tongue. Sometimes hesitation descended upon him. He ran short of his own vocabulary. I looked at him, and he was unable to translate.

Either nervousness was torturing him, or he has not been an interpreter before.

Sometimes I said quite a few things, at least eight or nine lines. Poor Purnahuti said only three lines to the Archbishop in Spanish. Agraha would only look at him. Agraha has super-excellent Spanish. He kept looking at Purnahuti as if to ask why he is not translating this or that. He was showing Purnahuti tremendous respect, but Purnahuti was missing quite a few things. I did not understand anything. Only I was seeing the length of time he was spending and he was not spending the same amount of time. Again, since I do not know anything about Spanish, I thought that perhaps it was all right. Twice I asked him if he had translated everything and he said he had translated it.

The funniest thing is that the Archbishop knows English well. Sometimes, when Purnahuti was not translating properly, the Archbishop would give a little smile because he had understood what I had said. He understood English, sometimes he said two or three lines to me in perfect English, but most of the time he deliberately did not want to speak it.

313. The Archbishop's hospitality

When we left, the Archbishop came out to the street, right up to our car, to say goodbye. He was very, very nice.

In the beginning, he was very friendly, but he wanted to maintain his dignity and height. But, after a minute or two, he came down to our level and talked and talked.

The pictures will show everything. You can see how happy he was, especially when he was holding our Peace Torch. At the end, he took out his appointment book and wrote in my concert on the 26th.

THE WORLD-EXPERIENCE-TREE-CLIMBER

314. A shopping tip

One tip for the shoppers: if you drive for an hour out of Guatemala City, there is a place where there are literally hundreds of shops, all cute, cuter, cutest. They are Indian-style shops. As soon as you see them, you will be reminded of Sri Lanka, Bali and other places. They are so beautiful. This lane and that lane have hundreds of shops on each one. And it is indoors, so the sun will not bother you. I do not know the name of the place, but I know that it takes an hour. You have to make sure you find the right place. Otherwise, you will see only a tourist street, but that is not the place. You have to go inside the compound and there you will see so many small, cute shops. They will definitely satisfy your curiosity, plus empty your pockets. The people there are very, very nice. I have a bad habit of bargaining, but it seemed to me that they enjoyed and I enjoyed our "discussions".

315. My driving experiences

Twenty-five years ago, the first time I took my driving test, I was successful. This time, I failed on my first attempt, I failed on my second attempt and, finally, the third time I passed. Now I have decided to drive in each country we visit. In the Bahamas I drove and here also I have to drive.

Sevananda always tells one story about my driving. He makes me laugh and laugh when he tells it. He says that it took place in Puerto Rico. Once, Ananta, Sevananda and I were coming back from El Yunque. At that time, I did not know how to drive even. But Ananta fell sick, so I had to drive. Sevananda says that I was driving with my eyes closed, in deep meditation.

Here, with my eyes open, I failed twice, but Sevananda has to say that I drove in El Yunque with my eyes closed. And it was such a difficult road, zigzagging and serpentine. That is Sevananda's story. He boosts my ego very nicely!

316. The Christ's blessings

Today is a very happy day. The Saviour came to bless us, so let us remember him always with gratitude. He also suffered, and his end was so painful. Again, when spiritual Masters come to earth, they may suffer, but they leave behind happiness, infinite happiness, for the world. This happiness always comes from our inspiration and aspiration.

Today is the Birthday of Jesus Christ the Saviour. He left the body at the age of thirty-three. Poor me, I am double his age. I am sixty-six. What I have accomplished and what I have not accomplished, God alone knows! Can you imagine? I am exactly double his age.

317. Breaking British tradition

The other day in the dining room at breakfast time, there was a British colony! Ongkar, Sanjaya, Kaivalya and Sanjaya's son were all there. You cannot imagine how heartily and how powerfully they were laughing. The way they were laughing, even the skies were trembling! Absolutely everything in the room was shaking. I was eating breakfast and I was in the seventh Heaven of delight to see them and hear them.

We say that the British are very conservative, very dignified and very civilised. Thirty or forty people were eating breakfast that morning, and the way these gentlemen were laughing, I said, "Oh, they are not keeping British tradition." I was so happy.

At times Kaivalya would bend forward and say something, and then they would all throw their arms up and roar with laughter. We did not want to hear what they were talking about; we only wanted to hear their roaring laughter.

318. My Peace Concert in the Cathedral

After my concert in the Cathedral last night, the soul of the church was very pleased and the heart of the church was very pleased. What more can I say?

Mother Teresa's soul did come. Then, when the disciples were singing the *Mother Teresa* song, Jesus Christ was dancing in front of me, saying, "She is my darling." He was pointing to Mother Teresa and saying, "She is my darling."

Mother Teresa had so many things to tell me and so many things to command me to do. The soul does not have to take a physical form when it visits us. But, in this case, the soul was wearing a white garment and Jesus Christ was also wearing white. The Christ is extremely, extremely fond of Mother Teresa.

About the Cathedral, I wish to say that the heart and soul I fully appreciate, but something was missing. They could have used candles, incense and so forth. The Cathedral in Cambridge, even though it is part of a university, has absolute sanctity, sanctity, sanctity.

Prabhakar said that during the concert, he saw one of the boys who worked there sleeping under the nativity scene. At least it was not one of our boys. If they had seen Pulak there sleeping, who knows what might have happened!

319. Religious culture in Guatemala and Mexico

Mexico has Indian culture to some degree. My brother Chitta has asked me to visit Indian temples when I go to Mexico. He said that many ancient religious temples are there.

Near Guatemala City we went to one convent. It is such a beautiful, huge place with many statues of the Christ, but they have turned it into a business. All spiritual places meet with the same fate. I saw hundreds of people eating there. We thought that no disciples would be there. First, we saw Madhuri; then we saw Diksha taking pictures.

320. My first goal

At long last, after strict dieting, today I have reached my first goal of 168 pounds. Ten full pounds I have lost. I do hope that by the end of the Trip I can lose much more!

321. Morning walkers

This morning, when I went out walking, I saw five or six disciples. All were running, except Chayanika and Vijali. They were walkers, like me. There was a very big restaurant right in front of them.

322. The eager cook

One of the hotel cooks came up to me and said, "Please tell me what you want. I will make you food. Do you like Spanish food?"

I said, "I do like Spanish food."

He went on, "Is there anything I can make for you?"

I replied, "Nothing right now, thank you."

Some people are of the opinion that the food is better here in Cancún, but I disagree wholeheartedly. I liked Israel and Lisette's preparation at Lake Atitlan infinitely more.

323. Chatting with a man from Sri Lanka

A Singhalese man came up to me. He lives in Canada and he wanted to chat with me. On that day all my guards were off-duty. They were enjoying a self-imposed holiday. They did not come to my rescue. Savyasachi was the worst culprit. He saw the man approaching me, but he did not do anything. Usually Savyasachi is quite good.

The man asked me, "Do you come from India?"

I answered, "Yes."

He continued, "Do you come from Bengal?"

I said, "Yes."

Then he started telling me about one great man who came from Bengal.

I said, "Yes, I know."

Then he told me that his name was Singha. I am pronouncing it the Bengali way, but he was pronouncing it the Singhalese way.

Then he went on with his questions. First he asked, "What religion are you?"

I said, "I come of a Hindu background, but I do not teach any religion. My love of God is my religion. For me, there is no other religion. I only pray to be a lover of God."

Then he wanted to know about my interest in politics. I said, "Some of the politicians are my friends and, by the way, do you come from Sri Lanka?"

He said, "Yes."

I said, "President Premadasa was so kind and compassionate to me."

He exclaimed, "Premadasa!"

I said, "Yes, President Premadasa."

Then he had to say, "All politicians are bad, but he was the worst possible crook!"

I was simply shocked. It was too much for me. I thought of changing the subject. I said, "My dearest friend is Ananda Guruge. He was Ambassador to the United States and in various ways he served his country. Do you know him?"

He said, "Yes, I know him." Then he said, "I shall come back and we shall discuss religion."

I said, "For me the only religion is love of God."

Then he said a few other things, but by that time I was only looking this side and that side for my guards to come and rescue me. I did not have the heart to ask the man his first name. As soon as I heard that, according to him, President Premadasa was the worst possible crook, I was desperately trying to find a way to end the conversation. President Premadasa was such a lion-hero in the battlefield of life. But how can you please everybody? It is impossible. I have such fond memories of Sri Lanka and all my meetings with the President.

In Kandy, in the Temple of the Tooth Relic, the main priest took me into a special room. He closed the door and said, "Nobody should see this." Then he put the crown on my head.

We Indians are so grateful to Sri Lanka. Sri Lanka saw spiritual genius in Swami Vivekananda. Sri Lanka embraced Swami Vivekananda's philosophy. That is why we have such love for Sri Lanka. Whoever appreciates our heroes, specially our spiritual heroes, will always be admired, adored and loved by India.

324. Trying to buy a gift

I have received letters from both of President Gorbachev's granddaughters. The youngest one is Anastasia. Her nickname is Nastia. Today, strangely enough, we went to a supermarket, and there I saw some bags with her name, "Anastasia". I wanted to buy one for her but I could not find out the price.

I waited and waited for the sales assistant to tell me the price. Finally, she said, "It is ten per cent off."

I said, "Ten per cent off what price?"

But she did not know the original price.

I said, "Say anything you like. I really want to have this particular bag."

Then she went to get the actual price, but, alas, she never came back. So I could not buy the bag.

325. Meditating and composing songs

Today I spontaneously set to music 201 Bengali songs during our four-hour meditation in the grounds of the Sheraton Hotel. Sometimes I was singing alone, and then the disciples were learning the song and singing with me. I was having a wonderful meditation. While we were singing, the sky made a solemn promise to meditate on our behalf. The disciples were not looking at the sky, but I saw that the sky was meditating on our behalf.

When we pray to God and meditate on God, everything helps us. When Lord Buddha realised God at the foot of the Bodhi tree, the tree itself was helping him. Today the vastness of the sky was helping us. The silence-swing of the sky was cradling us.

326. A visitor in the inner world

On January 7th, we had our first seven-hour meditation for this year. I do hope that we can have a seven-hour meditation on the 7th of every month.

During the meditation, when the disciples were singing *Nimne dharanir,* the great spiritual Master Gorakshanath came to me in the inner world and said, "When I was on earth I performed so many miracles."

Gorakshanath had tremendous occult and spiritual power. Because of him, for months there would be no rain. If I say there should be no rain, immediately there will be a downpour!

The higher you go, the less you perform miracles outwardly and the more you perform miracles inwardly. Again, sometimes a hero-warrior has to examine whether his swords are sharp or not, if they are blunt or if they are still working. He has to see if they are in good condition. Otherwise, they can be rusty and dusty. But, in the case of most spiritual Masters, all this takes place inwardly.

327. Passing along the good news

Perhaps some of you do not know that the day before yesterday the Mayor of Guatemala City, Óscar Berger, declared that Guatemala City has become another Peace-Blossom Capital.

How did I find out? I am staying here in Cancún, Mexico. I called Minati at my house in New York.

I asked her, "What news?"

Minati said, "Guru, I am sure you know already."

I said, "What is the good news?" Then she told me all about what the Mayor had done.

I was so surprised. I asked her, "How could you know? How did you get this news?"

She said, "Dipali told me."

And how did Dipali know? She found out from one girl in Houston. This girl phoned up Dipali and gave her the good news. So Minati is the right person to tell me!

Just one week ago, the Governor of the area where we were staying in Lake Atitlan declared that Lake Atitlan is now a Sri Chinmoy Peace Lake.

328. My elevator encounter

Now we have come back to Cancún for the second time. This place is so beautiful. I am happy we came back.

The other day I was in the elevator together with a stout, elderly man.

He asked, "Do you speak Spanish?"

I said, "No."

He went on, "Where do you come from?"

I replied, "India."

He asked, "May I ask you where?"

I told him, "I come from Chittagong." Then I asked him where he came from.

He said, "I come from Chicago."

He began joking with me that he did not know where Chittagong is.

I said, "It is not in Ill."

He said, "What do you mean – 'ill'?"

I said, "It is not in Illinois. The abbreviation I am telling you."

When I used to work at the Indian Consulate, how many times I used to write Chicago and then "Ill". I would put the passport inside the brown envelope and then write down the name of the Indians in Chicago, Ill.

What is the great similarity between Chicago and my disciples? Unpredictable weather! Chicago's outer weather is unpredictable, and the disciples' inner weather is also unpredictable.

NOTES TO THE WORLD-EXPERIENCE-TREE-CLIMBER, BOOK 8

293. *(p. 439)* 5 December 1997, The Bahamas.
294. *(p. 439)* 5 December 1997, The Bahamas.
295. *(p. 440)* 6 December 1997, The Bahamas.
296. *(p. 440)* 6 December 1997, The Bahamas.
297. *(p. 441)* 6 December 1997, The Bahamas.
298. *(p. 442)* 6 December 1997, The Bahamas.
299. *(p. 442)* 6 December 1997, The Bahamas.
300. *(p. 442)* 7 December 1997, The Bahamas.
301. *(p. 444)* 7 December 1997, The Bahamas.
302. *(p. 444)* 7 December 1997, The Bahamas.
303. *(p. 444)* 7 December 1997, The Bahamas.
304. *(p. 445)* 14 December 1997, Lake Atitlan, Guatemala.
305. *(p. 445)* 17 December 1997, Lake Atitlan, Guatemala.
306. *(p. 446)* 17 December 1997, Lake Atitlan, Guatemala.
307. *(p. 446)* 17 December 1997, Lake Atitlan, Guatemala.
308. *(p. 447)* 22 December 1997, Guatemala City.
309. *(p. 448)* 22 December 1997, Guatemala City.
310. *(p. 448)* 22 December 1997, Guatemala City.
311. *(p. 449)* 22 December 1997, Guatemala City.
312. *(p. 449)* 22 December 1997, Guatemala City.
313. *(p. 450)* 22 December 1997, Guatemala City.
314. *(p. 451)* 22 December 1997, Guatemala City.
315. *(p. 451)* 25 December 1997, Guatemala City.
316. *(p. 452)* 25 December 1997, Guatemala City.
317. *(p. 452)* 26 December 1997, Guatemala City.
318. *(p. 453)* 27 December 1997, Guatemala City.
319. *(p. 454)* 1 January 1998, Guatemala City.
320. *(p. 454)* 1 January 1998, Guatemala City.
321. *(p. 454)* 5 January 1998, Cancún, Mexico.
322. *(p. 454)* 6 January 1998, Cancún, Mexico.

323. *(p.455)* 8 January 1998, Cancún, Mexico.
324. *(p.457)* 8 January 1998, Cancún, Mexico.
325. *(p.457)* 9 January 1998, Cancún, Mexico.
326. *(p.458)* 9 January 1998, Cancún, Mexico.
327. *(p.458)* 12 January 1998, Cancún, Mexico.
328. *(p.459)* 13 January 1998, Cancún, Mexico.

PART IV

SRI CHINMOY VISITS INDIA

I – MY STOPOVER IN CALCUTTA

1. Going to College Street

India, my India, will always remain immortal, either positively or negatively. This was my very first experience on Indian soil this time. I landed at Calcutta airport, and there were many coolies who were welcoming the passengers and helping with the luggage. When I went outside the airport building, I looked for a taxi to take me to a particular place called College Street or Bankim Chatterjee Street. It is better known as College Street, which is its old name. There you can get thousands and thousands of old second-hand books. It is my most favourite place in Calcutta.

I had thought of going to Belur Math, the Ramakrishna Mission, and I was even planning to go to Mother Teresa's place. It falls practically on the way to College Street. But something within me was more interested in buying old books, Bengali books. College Street gives me immense joy.

2. Choosing a taxi

Now the taxi story starts. There were three or four taxi drivers waiting outside. I was examining the taxis to see what kind of condition they were in. One particular taxi had pictures of Mother Kali and Sri Ramakrishna. Both of them were garlanded. I said, "There cannot be a better taxi than this. I am carrying a picture of my Mother Kali all the time. Plus, this one also has a picture of Sri Ramakrishna."

I said to the driver in Bengali, "You have to take me to College Street and bring me back. How much will you charge?"

He said, "Oh, no problem."

"Meter?" I enquired.

He responded, "Babu, whatever the meter reads." When they say "Babu", it means gentleman or sir.

I said, "Perfect. Whatever the meter reads I will give you."

I entered into the taxi. I bowed to my Mother Kali and her dearest child Ramakrishna very devotedly. I was so happy. After we had covered about a hundred metres I realised that the driver had forgotten to turn on the meter, so I said to him, "Brother, now turn on the meter."

"Oh, I forgot to tell you that the meter doesn't work!"

Can you imagine! Just two minutes before he had told me that I would pay whatever the meter read. So I said to him, "How could you forget such a thing? You told me that you would charge whatever the meter read after I asked you for a flat rate."

So that is how the story started. Then I asked him his name. He said, "My name is Gauranga."

I said, "Oh, Lord Gauranga, Chaitanya Mahaprabhu." I was so pleased to hear his name. We began talking about Gauranga, and he had also read a little bit of Indian scripture. I said to myself, "All right, the first time he fooled me, but now let us see if Lord Gauranga will also fool me." We were talking and talking. He was telling me about his son. His son's name is Abhijit. He is studying at the Ramakrishna Mission High School, and he is very happy there.

But in the back of my mind, I was thinking, "His first deception I know. Now let us see what he is going to do."

3. Buying spiritual books

The taxi driver took me to quite a few stores on College Street, and he was telling me that Mother Teresa's place was not far; I could easily go there.

I said, "No, I have changed my mind. I am not going there. This place will give me more joy."

I went to a few more spiritual bookstores. There are so many spiritual bookstores on that street. As usual, we Bengalis do not know how to speak, we only know how to scream. Perhaps it is our national trait. The vendors were all screaming, encouraging people to buy their books. Everything is reduced, reduced to absolutely nothing, they say. But when you go to buy something, at that time you see that it has a high price.

I bought spiritual books from different stores. At one particular store, I saw a few books on Mother Kali and some that contained devotional songs. To my great joy, I found my favourite song that I sing, *Tumi nirmala karo* by Rajani Kanta Sen. I was so happy that one particular book had this as the first song.

The book stalls were all out on the street. I was standing there, reading the words to the song. The owner noticed what I was reading and said to me, "Babu, I am so happy you are reading that book. I myself am a good singer. Do you want to hear me?"

I said, "Certainly."

He said, "I can sing this song."

O my God, how sweetly he was singing the first song! I was so pleased with him. Then I said to him, "Do you now want to join me? I will sing the same song." Then both of us sang together standing there in the street.

Before that I had told him that I do not live in India; I live in America. The price of the book came to 80 or 85 rupees, which is under three American dollars because there are 30 rupees to a dollar.

After we had sung the song, he said, "I would like to charge 5 rupees less."

"Why?" I asked.

He said, "You live in America and there you study music, so 5 rupees less give me."

I said to him, "This is one of my most favourite songs, so I really want to give you 5 rupees more."

It was 85 rupees, so I gave him 5 rupees more, saying, "I am so happy to find that you can sing the song so well. Every day you are working so hard to support yourself."

That was my very first good experience. Then I bought quite a few more books, and I was very pleased. When I mentioned the titles of some books that I wanted, this fellow went running to other stores. He said, "I have three stores. Just wait here." Only he knew which ones had those particular books and so he went there and brought them back. As long as I got the books, I did not mind waiting.

4. Returning to the airport

We drove back to the airport, and again the meter did not run. Finally, I said to the driver, "Now for God's sake, tell me how much you want! Do not charge me too much. First, look at Mother Kali's picture, look at Sri Ramakrishna's picture."

He said, "Oh, I will never deceive you."

I said, "No, you will never deceive me! You started our trip with deception."

It was all in Bengali, so there was no problem.

He gave me the total: "Three hundred and fifty rupees."

I said, "Impossible! Three hundred and fifty rupees!"

He said, "Yes, yes, I charge 350 rupees."

Then I said, "I will give you 300 rupees and no more." So I gave him 300 rupees. I knew it could not be more than 150 rupees or maximum 200; 300 was absurd.

Then with folded hands he said, "What about my son?"

"What about your son?"

"My son needs your blessings."

I said, "I am blessing him."

He said, "No, with money. He is studying at school; he needs your money."

I said, "That is great." Then my stupid or compassionate heart had to come forward. My stupidity and my compassion are absolute synonyms; there is no difference. I said, "All right, I am giving you a hundred rupees for your son. I wish your son well. Let him become a good student."

In my pocket I had kept about 500 rupees. I saw that I had used most of the money to buy books, so I had only 90 rupees instead of a hundred-rupee note left. I counted the rupees and said, "I am sorry. I told you 100 but I can only give you 90."

He immediately objected, "Oh no, you said you would give me 100 rupees."

I said, "I have 90 rupees." I did not want to take out my main wallet from my money bag. I wanted to use only the money that I had kept inside my pocket to spend buying books. This was my fate. I said, "I have 90 rupees. What is the difference? I am giving 90 rupees instead of 100 rupees."

No, he wanted 100.

Then I became furious. I said, "Now look here, the time has come for me to call in the police. Enough!"

Immediately he brought my bags out of the car, took the money and disappeared. When I went inside the terminal, I asked a guard, "How much do they charge usually to go to College Street and come back?"

The guard said, "A hundred and twenty. But if you are kind, you can give them 140. Otherwise, it costs maximum 120."

I told him I had paid 390. Then in Bengali he used a foul tongue, saying what a bad fellow this taxi driver was. What made me sad was not the man's deception, but the fact that Mother Kali's picture and Sri Ramakrishna's picture were both in his taxi, framed and garlanded with fresh jasmine flowers. If he could behave like that, as a spiritual person, what could you expect from others? That taxi was my choice. There were three or four cars and I made the selection. Indeed, I found the right person!

5. The computer error

The time came to go to the ticket office to check my ticket. The agent said, "Your name is not there in the computer."

Inwardly I said, "Ashrita can never make a mistake! He is so smart. He will never fail me. How can Ashrita do this?"

The man went on, "Your name is not there. You cannot board the plane."

I replied, "Definitely my name is there. I was supposed to reconfirm from Pondicherry, not from here. It is not a matter of reconfirmation. I have got the ticket. I am supposed to go from Calcutta to Madras without any difficulty."

He said, "No, your name is not there. What can I do?"

I said, "Absurd!"

Then he took me to four different places, and they all said the same thing, that my name was not there.

I said, "Thank you. What is the matter? Now tell me what is there."

He said, "On the ticket it says Ghose, but there is no Ghose."

"How can it be that there is no Ghose?"

"We have Chose, but not Ghose," he said.

It was clearly an error.

I told the man, "That must be my name, only instead of 'G' it has been written with a 'C'. Is it my fault that it is spelt incorrectly?"

The man said, "It is not our fault. We can't go against the computer."

I was becoming exasperated. I said to him, "You cannot go against the computer? Look at my passport, and look at me. Is there any similarity?"

Then he said, "But your middle name is missing on the computer."

I said, "If my middle name is not there in the computer, what am I going to do? My middle name is Kumar, but if my first and last names are there, why do you need my middle name?"

Then he went on, "But here it is written Sri Chinmoy."

I said, "This is my name."

"Oh, so now your name is Sri Chinmoy," came the reply.

Finally, I got disgusted. I never carry anything with me, but this time I had one newspaper article from the last day in Myanmar. There were pictures of me with their highest Buddhist monk and the Minister of Religion. The whole front page was dedicated to me. I opened it and said, "Look at this. My name is Sri Chinmoy. I do not need Ghose."

He looked at the article and recognised my picture. What a rogue he was! My passport picture he did not value, but he valued the silly newspaper picture. Then he agreed, "Oh no, Ghose is not necessary."

After such a long time he allowed me to board. I was laughing to myself, "My passport picture has no value, but the silly newspaper picture has value because I am with some big shot. This always happens."

6. First-class treatment

From Bangkok to Calcutta my ticket was executive class, but from Calcutta to Madras it was economy class. When I went to the gate, the same man who had harassed me at the ticket counter put me in the first seat of first class – now that I was a big shot. He was afraid that I would make complaints to higher authorities!

II – AT THE SRI AUROBINDO ASHRAM (PONDICHERRY)

7. *Arriving home*

I arrived in Madras at eight o'clock in the evening of January 11th. It takes three and a half hours to reach the ashram by car. Around eleven o'clock I reached home. A friend of mine who works at the ashram car company drove, and my two brothers came. When I saw my brothers, I got a tremendous shock because age has descended upon them. But, strangely enough, in two days' time they looked much, much better than when I saw them at the airport. When we arrived home around eleven, my sister Lily was so happy to see me.

8. *Followed*

Now my sad story starts: how unfortunate I am! I was not getting any sleep that first night, so around three o'clock in the morning I decided to go out for a walk. If you walk for about 200 metres, you come to the seaside, the Bay of Bengal, and there you can walk for one mile flat. I had a very good, very powerful meditation, while I was walking and walking. Nobody was there. Around four o'clock an old friend of mine who was out jogging saw me and he was very delighted and excited.

Everything went well. I was only thirty metres away from my house when a lady approached me. She said she was from Florida, near Miami. She wanted to have an interview with me. I said, "No, no, no! No interview at this hour; I am going home. Some other day I will give you an interview. I will be here for four days."

Then the following day I went out at four o'clock in the morning to walk. Usually people go walking at six or six-thirty, but at four o'clock I left my house only to find that this particular lady was waiting for me! She lives near our house. She has been at the ashram for fourteen years, she said. She started following me. There is a Durga temple only two houses away from our house. When we reached the temple, I said to her, "Please do not follow me. I am in a meditative mood."

Was she going to listen? I walked for about a mile, sometimes slowly, sometimes a little faster, in my own way. I was on one side of the street and she had to walk on the other side of the street, across from me. I said, "O God, is it my fate? I do not care. I know how to meditate, so I do not have to worry."

Again I walked more than a mile, and I was coming back very slowly. Still she was following me. When I came to my house, only thirty metres away from the main street, again she said she wanted to have an interview. I said, "This is not the time. I shall see you on Sunday at 4:30 in the afternoon. Please do not bother me any more. I am giving you the time of the interview."

On the third day at a quarter to four, I went out. I was sure she would not be there. I had made it very clear that I did not want to be bothered and I had even given her an appointment time. But as soon as I reached the main street, she was there! I said, "O God, this is my fate with this crazy Florida woman!"

This Florida woman's friend had met me in Kathmandu. He came to see me three times, but Savyasachi saved me three times and did not allow him. Finally on the last day I agreed to see him for ten minutes. This is how the story started.

9. *The rainstorm*

While I was walking that third morning, it was drizzling at first. Then, after I had covered 400 metres, it began raining heavily. I said, "Since it is raining heavily, I hope she does not follow me."

O God, she followed me! But I was lucky because she was twenty or thirty metres behind me. I did not pay any attention to her. Then I had to take shelter under the shade of the ashram press. She also came and stood there.

Another time, I was standing under a big tree with many huge branches. A few seconds later, she arrived and stood under the same tree. I said, "God, You are so unkind to me!"

A third place I took shelter was at the end of one mile. It used to be Alo's place when she stayed in the ashram. It has an area where you can come out of the rain. When I went there, the crazy lady followed me. It was too much, too much!

When I was coming back, the rain would stop for two or three minutes and then again it would start raining heavily. It would not even drizzle first but all of a sudden it would rain heavily; then again it would stop. Still the lady was bothering me. Finally I said to her, "If you harass me, if you bother me in this way, I am going to cancel my appointment."

She said, "Oh no, I will not bother you." But she did not keep her promise.

10. The continuing ticket saga

The day after I arrived in Pondicherry, I said, "Let me go and reconfirm my reservation and see if there are any problems."

When I went there, it was the same story – Chose instead of Ghose. But the fellow who was the agent was a good friend of mine. He spoke to the Madras people in front of me. Madras and Calcutta both reconfirmed my booking, but in Bangkok they said my name was not listed. My friend was screaming at the people in Bangkok: "It is there under Chose. Change it, for God's sake, in the computer!"

They would not do it. This went on for two consecutive days. The first day I spent an hour and a half; the second day I spent about forty-five minutes. My friend was not deceiving me. He was screaming at them, "Why do you do this kind of thing?"

Then he told me, "The Calcutta people could have made the proper spelling change, but perhaps they wanted money from you."

Finally he got them to change Chose to Ghose.

11. At Sri Aurobindo's Samadhi

Very peacefully I came down the staircase after visiting Sri Aurobindo's room. As soon as I came down, one lady started screaming with joy: "Oh, Chinmoy, Chinmoy!"

I had completely forgotten her name. She said, "This is what greatness has done! Because you have become so great, you don't remember my name, but I do remember your name." Her name is Vishwabani. She deals with flowers. She said, "Now come here. I have flowers for you, and these flowers you have to offer to Sri Aurobindo at the Samadhi."

She gave me flowers, and she asked me the spiritual names of the flowers. I was only able to tell her "Protection" for one flower, and for another flower I was doubtful. It was either "Divine Love" or "Power", but the red hibiscus for Kali has different varieties and I was not sure. I said "Power". She said, "No, this is 'Divine Love', not 'Power'." Then she asked me the names of six or seven other flowers, but I had totally forgotten. Very seriously she told me the names.

How could I forget the spiritual names that Mother and Sri Aurobindo had given to the flowers? How many things I have forgotten!

Then she gave me some sandalwood incense. The incense sticks were at least four times as large as the ones in America. They were so thick! She told me, "Now, most devotedly go there and pray and meditate. The way you used to meditate in those days, go and meditate. Although you have become very great, I know, go and bow down most devotedly to Sri Aurobindo's Samadhi."

She is older than I am, so she commanded me. With such affection she was barking at me.

So I went to the Samadhi with the flowers. True devotion captured my entire being; it was absolutely overflowing. I meditated at the place where Mother's message is written. The first two or three lines on the marble I remembered: "To THEE who hast been the material envelope of our Master, to THEE our infinite gratitude...." I had forgotten the rest. In those days I knew it by heart. Every time I used to bow down, I would recite it, sometimes in French and sometimes in English. Most of the time I used to do it in English because I liked the English version better.

This time I tried to recite it, but I had completely forgotten the words. So I looked at the marble inscription and read it out very soulfully:

> "To THEE who hast been the material envelope of our Master, to THEE our infinite gratitude. Before THEE who hast done so much for us, who hast worked, struggled, suffered, hoped, endured so much, before THEE who hast willed all, attempted all, prepared, achieved all for us, before THEE we bow down and implore that we may never forget, even for a moment, all we owe to THEE."

12. Anton and Joseph, the rickshaw drivers

Coming back, after visiting Sri Aurobindo's Samadhi, I took a rickshaw. There was a flat rate of 20 rupees per hour. Perhaps for us visitors it was 20 rupees, while for others it would be 10 or 12 rupees per hour. We are all stupid foreigners to these drivers! My visit took about half an hour or forty minutes, and still I had twenty minutes left. My rickshaw driver's Christian name was Anton. Anton was supposed to wait for me at the ashram gate. He spoke absolutely perfect English, so there was no problem.

But when I came out to look for him, he was not to be found. Where had he gone? I was searching for him, but he was nowhere. An old friend of mine who was at the main ashram gate was screaming like anything: "Anton, Anton!" But Anton did not come. Instead, a driver named Joseph came and told me, "Anton said something was wrong with his rickshaw, so I have come to replace him." This driver was also a Christian.

I said, "Are you telling me the truth? Now I will be in your rickshaw, and Anton will appear."

Joseph said, "No, no, Anton will not appear."

I wanted to keep the rickshaw for another hour so that I could go to the market and see my friends. I told Joseph, "Now I would like another hour."

Joseph said, "Anton asked me to take his money."

I said, "As soon as I give it to you, Anton himself will come to take the money."

He said, "No, no, no! You don't have to give it to Anton; only give it to me."

Then we went to the market.

13. Caught by the Florida lady in the market

When we got to the market, I said to myself, "Before I buy a few saris or God knows what, the best thing is for me to buy a small bag so that I can keep my stuff inside it."

I found a big bag for 25 rupees, which is less than a dollar. I bought the bag. While they were wrapping it, out of the blue the Florida lady came! I am "Ghose", but my ghost was chasing me. She came and stood in front of me. This time I could not bring myself to say anything. I do not remember whether I laughed at her or smiled at her. In the end, I just went away and entered into the main market. Perhaps she could see that I was very angry and, for once, she did not follow me.

14. Nolini-Da's birthday

The 13th of January was the birthday of Nolini Kanta Gupta. He was my main boss. He passed away a few years ago. Among the disciples of Sri Aurobindo and the Mother, he was the seniormost and, according to Sri Aurobindo's brother, Barindra, he was Sri Aurobindo's mind-begotten son. According to Tagore, Nolini-da's contribution to Bengali literature is unique.

Early in the morning, at eight o'clock, Nolini-da's youngest son, Robi-da, came to our house with Indian sweets. He and I had been very good friends. He thought that by this time I would have forgotten his father's birthday, but I said to him, "Let us meditate together for a few minutes and offer prayers to the Mother and Sri Aurobindo to bless your father's soul. Today is his birthday."

He gave me a broad smile. By this time, he knew that I had remembered his father's birthday. We meditated together and then we had a very deep heart-to-heart talk.

15. Inside Nolini-Da's room

Two hours later, I went to Nolini-da's room. Manoj, who now works in his room, had been my class friend, but Manoj was not there. Nolini-da's bedroom and the adjacent room were both open and they were very beautifully decorated for Nolini-da's birthday. When I arrived, the lady who keeps the rooms clean saw me. I was standing in the doorway, hesitating, because my friend was not there.

I did not know the lady at all, but she said, "Come in, come in," as if she knew me.

I went inside and looked at Nolini-da's picture. The lady began asking me questions about when I worked there as Nolini-da's secretary. She was very, very kind to me. I had been told that you cannot take pictures in Nolini-da's bedroom; it is forbidden. Pictures can be taken only in the front room. But the lady saw my camera and said, "Normally it is forbidden to take pictures here, but for you nothing is forbidden. You can go inside and take as many pictures as you like. I was told you used to work here."

I showed her where I worked, on the floor right beside Nolini-da's bed. The bed that is in the room now is very large and beautiful. The previous one, the one that Nolini-da had used, was half the size. It was very small and narrow. Sometimes Nolini-da used to take rest in his bed while I was working and sometimes he used to sit there.

Then I showed the lady all the files that I used to take care of. Nolini-da had about two hundred files of his writings and ashram activities. I had to know them almost all by heart.

Then the lady said to me, "Please take my picture." At that moment a friend of hers came into the room and I took their picture together.

I was so happy to see the place where I had worked for years.

16. The imperfect birds

My cousin, Soma, is only a few months younger than I. She is my father's cousin's daughter. According to our Indian tradition, we have to touch the feet of our elders and show them tremendous respect. This time when I arrived, my cousin bent down, and her hands were only a foot away from my feet. But I stopped her, saying, "No, I will not allow you to touch my feet. I live in America. I am modern; you are also modern. Now we live in modern society."

Soma cooked a delicious meal and we chatted and chatted.

On the second day I was drawing birds. As she stood in front of me, her comment was, "Oh, they are nice, but they are not perfect."

I said, "You are right; they are not perfect. But, tell me, what do you mean by perfection?"

She answered, "Perfection will be found if you take five minutes for each bird. Here you don't take even five seconds. If you take five minutes, it will look nicer, and I will call it perfect."

I said, "I can take ten minutes, but I will still say that the one that took only five seconds gave me more joy. I am doing this only to get joy. I cannot explain to you fully what perfection is for me, but anything that gives me joy and satisfaction is perfection."

She said, "Indeed, this is your philosophy. But who is going to accept your philosophy?"

I said, "I am going to accept my philosophy. If nobody else does, what can I do?" And then I continued my drawing.

17. Two missing pages

Two days later I was again drawing. My cousin came up to me and asked, "Do you mind if I take two pages from your notebook and show them to the ashram's best artist?"

I said, "Why do you have to invite unnecessary criticism? I am happy with what I am doing. Now you will bring unnecessary criticism, and then I will feel sad. You will feel sad, too, that you are going to an artist who will not appreciate these little birds."

I am older than that artist by nine or ten years. I knew her grandfather. He was a doctor and he liked me very, very much. Once more I said to my cousin, "I sincerely do not want to be blessed by her criticism even though, according to you, she is now the greatest artist in the ashram."

But my cousin insisted, "No, no, I really want to show her."

Finally I gave my permission. "All right, if you really want to show her, then you have to be prepared to accept her criticism."

Then she looked at me and gave me a very broad smile. I said, "What?"

She said, "I already took two pages from your book the other day. I brought them to her and told her all about your drawings. As soon as she saw the birds, you can't imagine how happy, how delighted and how excited she was! She showed these two pages to her students, and she told them how fast you draw the birds. She was so thrilled. The birds gave her tremendous joy. She wants to keep those two pages."

18. The stretching exercises

Soma wanted to teach me stretching exercises to help my back pain. She herself takes regular stretching exercises. A Canadian had written a book called, *Oh, My Back Pain!* or something like that. She had read that book, and she showed me some stretching exercises that it recommended. They were really difficult. I deeply appreciated and admired her flexibility.

There was one particular exercise that she tried to show me, but she was unable to do it properly. "I am also getting old," she admitted.

My sister, Lily, happened to be with us. So Lily said to her, "Yes, I can see you are getting old." Soma is thirteen years younger than Lily. Anyway, Lily immediately did that particular exercise so easily and quickly. Lily put us to shame. I surrendered because I cannot bend that much.

Six or seven exercises Soma showed me. Alas, I could not do even one. She wanted me to learn those exercises so that I would have no more back pain.

19. My ninety-six-year-old aunt

This story has to do with my own aunt. She is my mother's younger sister and she is still alive. She is enjoying or suffering, God knows, ninety-six years of age. Previously, she lost her sight in one eye. Now she has lost her sight in the other eye, so she is completely blind.

From the day of my arrival, I sent her messages that I would come and see her without fail. She is ninety-six years old, and still she is all affection for me. Even when I was a little boy, when my mother was alive, this aunt was so indulgent to our whole family, giving us affection in boundless, boundless measure. God alone knows how many hundreds and thousands of times she blessed us, in season and out of season. We Indians feel that without the blessings of mothers and aunts one can never become great. She was very close to our family, and even now she is extremely close.

I promised I would go and see her, but the first day went by, then the second day and the third day. If I did not go on the fourth day, it would be time for my departure. Several times I was planning to go and see her, but friends of mine came to our house to see me. What could I do?

Finally, on the fourth day, I went to see my aunt. She was lying down when her daughter, who is twelve years older than I, announced my arrival. My aunt was so happy. She beckoned me, "Come, my son; come, my son." I went to the side of her cot and placed both my hands on her head, blessing and blessing her. She said, "I am so grateful to you. I know who you are. You are no longer the little kid that I used to scold. I used to scold you like anything. Again, you know how much love I have for you. I am so happy, so happy. Soon I will be going to the other world, and you are blessing me. I will be able to carry your blessings with me."

Then she started asking her usual question: when was she going to die? Every time I see her, that is her very first question. I was cutting jokes with her, saying, "There is no empty room in Heaven, so you have to wait here. There is simply no room for you there. It is like a hotel. Since there is no vacancy in Heaven, you have to stay here for another four years until you reach 100 years of age."

She said, "Is that a blessing or a curse?"

I said, "God alone knows whether it is a blessing for you or a curse for you, but I would like you to stay here. You belong to our immediate family. Four years more you should stay." My aunt was four and a half years younger than my mother. She had heard all about my mother's centenary celebration last year, and she was very happy and very proud of it.

She said, "In our family I was the youngest."

Then she said, "What am I going to do for another four years on earth?"

I said, "I told you last time and this time also I am telling you the same thing: think of all the good things you have done. Just remember them. You will be able to count them, even though you cannot see now. Only one by one remember them. Choose the things that you feel are absolutely the best things you have done in your entire life. Ninety-six years you have been on earth. Now please start by remembering one excellent thing you have done. You do not have to tell me what it is; I do not need to hear. Just think of that. The last time I came, five years ago, I told you to remember all the good things that you had done. Now I am saying that only the very best things that you have done in this life you should try to remember."

Then she started talking to me about my mother and about my father, asking where they are in Heaven. She said, "It seems that I am not to go now. Otherwise, my sister would have come to see me, and all my dearest ones would have come to visit me from the soul's world. Your mother has not come, your father has not come, your brother and your sisters are not coming. This is the proof that my time has not come."

I said, "True, true. Your time has not come. You just stay."

Then she said, "They say that you have occult power. Can you not cure my eyes, or at least give me a little eyesight?"

I said, "No, no, no, I do not have that kind of power. I am not another Jesus Christ. I want your eyes to be operated on."

She said, "No! I am ninety-six years old, and the doctors have said they will not be able to cure me. Don't tell me to go to them at this stage of my life. Doctors don't know how to cure me. Doctors are butchers, and you want me to be treated by butchers!"

I said, "I am sorry. You do not have to be treated. You just stay here. Except for your eyesight, I can see that you are all right. You are speaking quite normally. You are the same person and you have the same affection for me."

We went on talking, and I was blessing her. Now, you will not believe it, but this ninety-six-year-old lady had to remind me about something that happened in my life in 1952 or 1953. Suddenly she said, "Yes, you did it for your sister but you do not want to do it for me."

I said, "What do you mean?"

Then she reminded me of the incident. At that time, when I was quite a young boy, one evening my eldest sister, Arpita, said she was unable to see. Something was wrong with her. She was only seeing very faintly. I started bragging. I said, "Oh, I can cure you!"

What a cure! I massaged her eyes only to make her blind, totally blind. She absolutely could not see at all. Then this particular aunt scolded me mercilessly. But my sister was full of affectionate compassion. She was saying she would be all right.

On the fourth day she had to go to the hospital for an operation on her eyes. I was so miserable because I was the culprit. Previously, she was able to see a little; then, after I massaged her eyes, she could not see at all. I said, "I will cure her. I will not allow my sister to go to the hospital. At this time I am taking full responsibility to cure her."

This time there was no massage. This time there was something else, call it inner prayer or occult power. My sister got back all her eyesight and she was so happy. Believe me, my aunt is ninety-six years old. How could she remember this incident that took place more than forty years ago? And just before that we were talking all kinds of nonsense, saying that there are no vacancies in Heaven and that is why she is not allowed to go there.

I said to her, "Everything depends upon God's Will. At that time, it was God's Will for me to cure my sister, but now it is not God's Will for me to cure you. God's Will is for me to pray for you. Let His Will be done. If He wants to give you back your eyesight, He will do so. If He wants to take you to Heaven tomorrow, you should go, but happily. We shall always remember you, all the affection that you have poured on me and on each and every member of the family. You carry all our affection, all our love and all our good will."

In the evening of her life, everything is very happy and peaceful for my aunt. For those over ninety, these last years are the golden chance for them to have a new life, to act like a child again and to cry and pray to God.

On my previous visit several years ago when I went to see my aunt, her daughter, Pushpita, was cutting jokes with me. My sister was also present. Pushpita said, "Look how haughty and proud Chinmoy has become! He can't even bend to touch your feet. He doesn't want you to bless him. Previously how many times you blessed him, and now he is so proud and haughty, he does not even bend his head."

But my aunt took my side. "No, no, he did bend. I saw him. Again, why does he have to bend his head?"

Then the daughter began scolding her own mother. "All right, he is bad, it is true. But how is it that you did not stretch out your arms to bless him?"

My aunt said, "Oh no, I can't bless him. When I look at his eyes, I don't dare to bless him anymore." And again, how many times in my life this aunt, my mother's sister, has blessed me! But on that occasion she said, "I don't dare to bless him anymore."

How is it that when we see elderly ladies, at that time seriousness is not born? We only enjoy cutting jokes with them.

20. *The cycle-rickshaw rogue*

Now I will tell another rickshaw experience. This was a cycle rickshaw. As you know, cycle rickshaws are much easier to drive and they go much faster than the old-fashioned hand-drawn rickshaws. The hand-drawn rickshaws are made of wood and they are quite primitive, but the cycle rickshaws are made of metal and they go much faster.

The driver of the cycle rickshaw was such a clever fellow. He wanted to kill time, so he would cycle for about fifty or sixty metres, and then he would jump off and start dragging the rickshaw.

I said, "Why are you doing this? Can you not pedal with your legs?"

He said, "No, you are very heavy. I have to pull it by hand."

I said, "According to you I am very heavy. Perhaps it is true. But I know that this kind of rickshaw can take two persons. I am definitely not as fat as two persons. I do not have the weight of two human beings. I know the real reason why you are doing this."

He said, "Why?"

I said, "Because you want to kill time. If you do this, you will take more time and I will have to pay more."

The driver was wearing a wristwatch. I had asked him to take me around the circumference of Pondicherry. I know the route so well. It is only three miles. In an hour easily we could have come back. But the driver was playing a trick. He did not want to go all around, so he would pedal for fifty or sixty metres, and then he would start wasting time and walk slowly. So in an hour, I could not cover even one mile. Can you imagine? This is how he took time. Even while walking he was saying he was so tired, so exhausted.

Finally, I got disgusted and asked him to take me back to the starting point, our house.

21. The stolen rickshaw

On another day, I really wanted to go around the Pondicherry streets and do the full round, which is about three miles. So I approached another rickshaw driver.

This man said that the flat rate was 20 rupees per hour. Everything was settled. I got in and we covered one mile without any incident. Then somebody came up beside us and started screaming at the rickshaw driver. Why? It seems that this fellow had stolen his rickshaw. There were about ten rickshaws stationed near my place. Without telling the real driver, this elderly man had taken a rickshaw that was in very good condition. Now the real owner was screaming at him like anything. This happened 200 metres away from Alo's old place.

The owner wanted the old man to leave the rickshaw there and return to the starting point to get his own rickshaw so that we could continue our journey. Then I got mad. I said, "What do I know about this? He will take me back. Then you can punish him or do anything you want. But I am not going to leave this rickshaw. I am not going to come down."

When I screamed at the real owner, he got frightened. So he allowed the old man to take me back.

Then the old man surrendered the rickshaw to its rightful owner and said to me, "You wait here. I am going only 100 metres away to bring my rickshaw."

O God, I waited five minutes, ten minutes, fifteen minutes. After twenty minutes he came back. By that time I was disgusted, so I went back home. This was another rickshaw experience.

22. *My favourite Pondicherry tailor*

In Pondicherry I have a favourite tailor. I went to him again this time to have a pair of shorts made. I said, "My waistline is thirty-six inches, but how I wish it could be thirty-four!"

So he measured me. He said, "You are fooling me."

I said, "What?"

He said, "Your waistline is more than thirty-six."

I said, "No, no, no, this is all my sister's fault and my cousin's fault. They have been cooking and cooking for me. Please do not tell me I am over thirty-six."

He said, "No, you have come to a truthful person, you have come to a sincere person. I am telling you, people are fooling you if they say your waistline is thirty-six."

I said, "I do not want to hear that. I want to hear less."

Then he measured me and showed me the tape. O God, O God! It was all true. "Now, can you say you are thirty-six?" he asked.

I said, "For God's sake, make it thirty-six and put elastic on each side. I am wise, I am clever."

He said, "That I can do."

I said, "Now put whatever measurement you want. You do not have to tell me what it is, but put elastic."

So he has put elastic on both sides. I am wearing these shorts today. I do not know whether my real measurement is thirty-five or thirty-six or thirty-seven, because elastic is solving the problem.

III – MY JOURNEY FROM PONDICHERRY TO MAUI

23. The stuck car

It takes three and a half hours to drive to Madras airport from Pondicherry. My plane was supposed to leave at 7:30 in the morning, so I said that at 2:30 I would leave. Of course, my two brothers would accompany me. We were getting ready to leave when my friend who was supposed to drive us to Madras started screaming, "Chinmoy, Chinmoy, come and help me!"

I asked, "What kind of help?" I was upstairs packing my things, and I had to come down. "What is wrong?" I asked him.

Only ten metres away from our house was a big hole. His left wheel had entered into the hole and the car was stuck. He could not get it out, but he made a suggestion: "I will turn on the motor and then you have to lift up the car."

I said, "I do not have the strength. My back pain is killing me! I cannot."

"Then it is all a bluff," my friend said. "You never lifted all those cars and other things!"

I said, "I never did it this way. I did it with a machine, with a special apparatus so that I could take the weight on my shoulders. But this way I will not be able to lift the car. It is so huge!"

"Then you be at the wheel," he answered.

I said, "I have not driven for years. God alone knows what I will do! I cannot do that."

O God, his whole wheel was inside the ditch. Now somebody had to come along and witness our misfortune. The witness was the Florida lady! Suddenly she appeared there. Luckily she was not helping me. I was trying desperately, but I could not lift the car out of the hole. The Florida lady did not even try. What were we going to do?

My friend was screaming for assistance. Then three young men from the neighbourhood came. They were enjoying the commotion but they did not offer to help us. Such wonderful people! First my friend scolded and insulted them for behaving in such an unkind way. That did not work. Then he was very pitifully begging them to help us. When they saw his pitiful face, all of them came to our rescue. And when four of us tried to lift the car, easily it came out of the hole. So my driver-friend was very happy.

24. *Maintaining my poise*

I had to bring from my house my suitcase, my bag and my other things. Also, I had to say farewell to my sister because she was not going to come to the airport. My usual farewell is to meditate with her. We went inside to meditate, and then, can you imagine? The Florida lady, who was outside in the street, had to come inside our house! The door was open because I had gone back to collect my things, and suddenly the Florida lady was standing inside the house. It was too much!

My sister said, "Don't be mad. This is not the time. Prove that you have got poise; you have got poise; you have got poise. Don't be mad. For God's sake, don't ruin your day! And I have seen your disciples. They are no better than this crazy lady! I know all your life you have been crazy. That is why you are blessed with all crazy disciples. All your disciples are crazy and you are crazy, so now here is another crazy person. For God's sake, don't get mad! Don't ruin the meditation."

Then I entered into my sister's room. The Florida lady was inside our house, but luckily, not inside my sister's room. I meditated with my sister for five or six minutes. Very nicely I went into my highest consciousness to prove that I can meditate. My sister was extremely pleased.

25. Farewell to the Florida lady

When I went outside again, I was wondering what to do. In one of my encounters with the Florida lady she had begged me for money. Now I just took from my pocket whatever I had and gave it to her. It was two hundred-dollar bills. I said to her, "Thank you." Then she thanked me like anything.

I entered into the car and my two brothers followed me. Even at that moment, after receiving the money, the Florida lady had to come and knock at the window: "May I come with you?"

I did not have to answer. My driver-friend insulted her like anything in front of everybody. My sister perhaps did not appreciate it. She was standing outside the door of our house in tears. First she gives me advice, but when I am about to leave, she is always in tears, tears, tears. Just before I left, she told me what my Indian horoscope said and what a particular palmist said about me. She herself studied astrology and she believes in these predictions. I told her, "It is all rubbish! Do not trust him. Do not believe it, do not believe it!"

26. The delayed aeroplane

We arrived at Madras airport at 5:30 a.m. At 7:30 the plane was supposed to leave. Around 7:00 they announced that the plane would be delayed by three hours. A delay of three hours can easily become five hours. I knew that if I missed this flight, I would not get the connecting flight from Calcutta to Bangkok. So, as you can see, everything was going wrong.

But one of the workers, the deputy manager of the airline, liked me very much. He said, "Mr. Ghose, I will do my best to send you to Calcutta by another plane."

So we went to Dominea Airlines. He was from Air India, but he was begging the Dominea people to help. They said they would help. They were all sincere people. At 8:30 they had a flight to Calcutta and if I could catch it, I would be able to get my connecting flight. Five or six times he was begging them in front of me.

There was a young man from Dominea, a Muslim named Mohammed Isman. He was also saying I could take their flight, but he would only be able to offer me a seat after eight o'clock. Right then he could not.

Once I tried to give 400 rupees to the deputy manager. It was only because of him that I had hope. He said, "No, I can't accept that."

I said, "Nobody is watching."

He said, "Nobody is watching, but my heart is seeing it. I can't do that." He was such a nice man.

I said, "Then give me your card."

He said, "You can take my card, but I can't take any money from you."

27. Saved by Dominea Airlines

The young fellow from Dominea went to so many people and so many higher officials to get me on the flight. Finally he said, "Now it is five past eight. I have taken a risk. I have no idea whether people will come, but I don't want you to worry any more."

In India, there is a system that you have to identify your suitcase. First it will go to customs. Then when it goes to the other side, you have to go there and verify that it is yours. This young man said to me, "I know your bag. You don't have to worry. I will go and identify your bag on your behalf. You just enter into the plane. I will go and check your bag for you."

By that time it was 8:20. I entered into the plane. Whom did I see standing at the entrance but this young man. He said,

"Mr. Ghose, I identified your suitcase. You don't have to worry at all."

I asked him for his card. He said, "I am an ordinary person. I don't keep a card."

I said, "Then you write down your name and address." So he wrote it down. He was a very nice man.

I took the flight to Calcutta, and I did not have any problems in Calcutta with my ticket because it had been properly confirmed in Pondicherry.

28. The bomb threat

When we were leaving Narita airport, in Japan, there was a long delay. We spent three hours in the plane outside the gate. At first they said it was a mechanical problem. After some time, the pilot happened to pass near me. I was absolutely in the first row of executive class. The pilot was very upset. He said, "Nothing is wrong mechanically. Why can't they tell the truth?"

The truth was that there had been a bomb threat. The airline officials suspected one fellow from Thailand, who was holding a Thai passport. Before we boarded, they had been announcing, "All people who are holding Thai passports must come to the counter immediately." So something must have happened, and they suspected a passenger holding a Thai passport.

The result was that we had to deplane. They took us back to the Narita View Hotel, where we spent the night.

29. The stewardesses' appreciation

The following morning everything went well. The plane took off for Honolulu. I did not feel like writing poems. I had wanted to write 200 songs during these few days but I ended up doing 150. Anyhow, I took out a notebook and began to draw birds. One by one the stewardesses went by and saw the birds. One would say, "Cute!" Another would say, "Beautiful!"

One stewardess asked me, "Are you an artist?"

Quite hesitantly I said, "I am an artist."

They all came and watched the birds. They were appreciating my drawings like anything, standing there right in front of me. One particular stewardess was very soulful. On my right side there was an empty seat. She sat there and said, "You have to tell me: have you exhibited your drawings?"

I said, "At Kennedy airport once, my friends exhibited a few thousand, but I do not know the exact number. Then in Ottawa, Canada, they showed one million or two million. I have forgotten the exact number."

She just looked at me. Then she asked me more about my art. "Where are you going?"

I said, "I am going to Honolulu. There I have an apartment, but I do not know where my apartment is. My friends will come to meet me, and then I will go to Maui. I have been to Hawaii many times. I used to walk near the canal."

She said, "I also live by the canal. Now I will give you my address, and what you will do, you will give me only your name. I don't want an address from you. Only give me your name." So she gave me a postcard with her full address, on Ala Moana. I believe it is very near my apartment. She said, "If you could send me something of yours, I would be so grateful. I can see that you are a very important person."

I said, "I am very important? All right, I will send you something."

She said, "You don't have to write down your address or phone number. I don't need that. Just write down your name."

I wrote "Sri Chinmoy". Immediately she put the piece of paper over her heart. Can you imagine? When she stood up, she reminded me once again, "Please don't forget to send me something of yours."

Some of the stewardesses looked Chinese or Japanese. This one perhaps was Hawaiian. They were all saying "Cute!" and "Beautiful!" They would come at intervals of half an hour or forty minutes to see my progress. I was going on, going on, drawing on large sheets.

So this is how my artwork received appreciation on the plane. It seems that people appreciate my art. They like the little bird drawings like anything!

I did keep my promise. I asked Pratyaya to write a letter to her and send some of our peace-activity books.

30. Hawaiian customs

A lady at customs in Hawaii was very politely talking to me. Then a man came with a note for her, saying that she was needed somewhere else. So she said to the man, "Just sign here."

But the man started the whole procedure over again. She said she had done everything; he only had to sign. But for some reason he started harassing me. What is worse, people can never understand my tote-a-tune. I explained how it works: "It is a musical instrument. You can play it like this."

I was showing him, but the stupid man thought that something electronic was hidden inside it. That was too much!

31. The airport thief

In Honolulu, you have to take a bus to go to the baggage section, although it is not even 200 metres away. We were all coming out of the bus when a man started screaming: "Stop him, stop him! He has stolen my bag!" One of the passengers, as he was getting off the bus, had grabbed this man's bag and started running away very fast. So the poor victim was screaming, "Stop him, stop him! He has stolen my bag!" His wife started crying. She could not even walk properly, but her husband began chasing the thief. Everybody was saying, "What happened? Who has stolen the bag?" They were all panicking.

Can you imagine? This happened in the Hawaiian airport! Near where they were checking our baggage tickets, the thief was caught. Ten or twelve people grabbed him and accused him of stealing the bag. There were no police available.

He said, "I didn't know that I was carrying somebody else's bag."

"Then why are you running?" they asked.

He said, "I only wanted to go fast."

I was one of those watching. Luckily, ten people grabbed him; otherwise the elderly man alone would not have caught him. Now, look at this! The man could have thrown the bag aside, but he did not do that. Then, when he was eventually caught, he said that he did not know he was carrying someone else's bag. How could we believe him?

1–6. *(p. 467)* Stopover in Calcutta – Wednesday, 11 January 1995, five hours.

7–22. *(p. 475)* Sri Aurobindo Ashram (Pondicherry) – late evening Wednesday, 11 January 1995 to early morning Monday, 16 January 1995, four days and five nights.

23–31. *(p. 493)* Journey from Pondicherry to Maui – Route: Monday, 16 January 1995, drive to Madras. Then by plane to Calcutta, Bombay, Tokyo (overnight), Honolulu (overnight) and arrival in Maui early on Thursday, 19 January 1995.

PART V

MY EXPRESS VISIT TO INDIA

1. Author's preface

I go to my Mother India for affection, compassion and illumination, and I do get these divine realities in boundless measure in the inner world. But, unfortunately, the outer experiences that I get in India are extremely painful. Alas, my life-boat plies between the confusion-shore and the deception-shore!

2. The saga of my Gujarati neighbour

From New York to London everything went well. The stewardesses were extremely kind to me in every way. I can give them one hundred out of one hundred. The funniest thing is that they served pizza for vegetarians. They gave me three pieces and they wanted to give me more! Plus it was real pizza.

In London, I went to transfer for the flight to Bombay. Again, it was British Airways, and I got the upper deck once more, so I was very happy.

When I went to my seat, there was an Indian lady, middle-aged, on my right. It was executive class, so there was plenty of room between the seats. I put my small bag in front of me.

The lady said to me, "You cannot do that!"

I asked, "Why?"

"Because I am not feeling well, and I need plenty of room to stretch my legs."

The bag was right in front of me, and she wanted to put her legs there!

A few minutes later she called the stewardess. "I need a couple of pillows," she said. She already had one pillow, and so the stewardess brought her another. Then their fight started.

The lady, who was Gujarati, said, "I asked you for a couple of pillows, and you have only brought me one!"

"But you already have one pillow," the stewardess pointed out.

"I am not feeling well, so I need lots of pillows," said the lady.

3. *More complaints from the Gujarati lady*

A few minutes later, the Gujarati lady called the stewardess again. She said to the stewardess, "I need aspirin. I am not feeling well."

"Only aspirin?" the stewardess asked. The stewardess brought two aspirin, and gave her one of them.

The lady cried, "I need four at least!"

The stewardess told her, "I am not authorised to give you four. I can give you at most two. I gave you one, and I am giving you one more."

"No!" said the lady. "You have to give me as many as I want."

"No, I cannot do that," the stewardess said, and she left.

4. *Shaking the whole plane*

Can you imagine? The story never ends, and the plane had not yet even started! I was sitting on the aisle, and the Gujarati lady was sitting on the other side near the window. My left foot was in the aisle. It was aching, so I was shaking it a little.

The lady saw me, and she said, "You are not allowed to do that. I am sick, and you are shaking the whole plane." She was on my right side, and my foot was nowhere near her.

O God, O God, we were still on the ground and I was shaking the whole plane! There were only sixteen seats in our section. I stood up to see if there were any empty seats, but there were none, so I surrendered to my fate. Then I was obedient. I did not shake my foot anymore.

5. Saved by the head steward

In executive class the seats recline so far back; it is not like economy class where the seats go back two inches. An elderly man, bald-headed like me, was sitting right in front of the Gujarati lady. He pressed the button and went back, leaving a very small gap between his seat and this lady. She also could have reclined her seat in the same way; everybody can do it.

The man was near me, so I could easily see him. He fell asleep in five minutes, and he started snoring very loudly, perhaps deliberately – God knows! The lady began shaking his seat, and then afterwards she started shaking his shoulder, saying, "Stop snoring!" I was sure that he was ignoring her; otherwise, the way she was shaking his shoulder, he would have been furious. But he stayed fast asleep.

Again she called the stewardess. This time her complaint was, "He is snoring! He is making so much noise and not allowing me to sleep."

I buried my head in my palms and said, "O God, what am I going to do?" There was no seat empty.

Then a man came to me and said he was the head of the stewards. He asked, "How do you pronounce your name? Do you say Ghosé or Ghose?"

I said, "My name is Ghose, not Ghosé."

He pulled me by the left shoulder and whispered, "Are you comfortable?"

Very quietly I told him, "She is torturing me."

He said, "Let me go downstairs." Downstairs also there was executive class. He came back and said, "There are three seats empty. Where is your bag?"

He carried my small bag and took me downstairs. Then I got excellent treatment. Three seats were empty and nobody was there to bother me. Behind the seat of the person in front of you there is a television screen. You just pull it out and you can watch whatever is on the big screen. And the seats are so comfortable. So I was the happiest person, and I was far, far away from that crazy lady!

6. The Gujarati lady's parting blessing

At the end of the flight, when I was gathering up my things, I remembered that I had left a small bag upstairs. It had some candy bars and newspapers inside. When I approached my former seat, the Gujarati lady asked, "Where have you been?"

I just smiled at her. Then she said, "Shame on you, shame on you!"

That was her parting blessing.

7. Three minutes becomes twenty

When I reached Bombay, I wanted to go to a hotel nearby named Samraj. I was going to be in Bombay for three hours, and I wanted to stay in the hotel for two hours. At the airport I asked a hotel representative, "How much do you charge for two hours?"

The man said, "Eight hundred rupees."

I asked, "For half a day there is no special rate? I will be there only for two hours."

He told me, "No, this is our fixed rate."

I decided to go anyway. I asked, "How long does it take to get there from here?"

The man said, "It takes only three minutes."

"Then please take me," I told him.

He said, "Just wait, the coach is coming."

Five minutes went by, then ten minutes, fifteen minutes, twenty minutes. Finally, I said to the man, "Instead of the coach, let me take a taxi." I was ready to give him money, but he said, "We do not take money here. We only make arrangements for the hotel."

After twenty minutes had passed I got disgusted. I said, "I am going to another travel agency to make arrangements."

He cried, "No, no, no." At that moment, somebody came and said the coach was there. Instead of three minutes, it became twenty minutes!

8. *God, allow me to see my dearest sister*

When I arrived at the hotel, they asked me to pay in advance, so I gave them eight hundred rupees. Then they asked me, "At what time do you wish to leave?"

I answered, "I want to leave this place at three o'clock."

They said, "Oh yes, we shall call you at three o'clock."

I told them three, but I knew that if I left at 3:15, it would also be all right. The plane was due to leave at 4:30. It was only three minutes from there and I had my ticket. In the room I took out my timer. I said, "In case they do not call me, I will use this." So I set the timer.

Then I called my brother to find out how my sister was. He said, "She is still alive. You will be able to see her."

I said, "This is the greatest news I have got." This was the only message I wanted to hear; I was so happy that she was still alive.

Then I phoned up the nursing home. The nurse shouted, "Lily-di, Lily-di, Chinmoy-da is calling you!" Then she took the phone to my sister, and said, "Say something, say something! Say hello at least or call his name."

My sister was not able to do me that favour. She could not speak. I thought, "The boat is sinking. Before I touch the destination, before I reach Pondicherry, she cannot even say hello.

She is so sick." I was praying to God: "Since I have taken such trouble to come to see my dearest sister, God, allow me at least to see her."

9. The expensive phone calls

The two phone calls that I made to Pondicherry from Bombay were not even one minute long. The first time I only asked my brother how my sister was. Then I dialed the nursing home. At the nursing home, my sister did not even come to the phone. But the hotel charged me for four minutes per call. Then I placed a phone call to New York. The hotel operator dialed the wrong number. When I challenged them, they denied it, and before I came downstairs, they changed the number on my bill. I happened to see that on their copy the incorrect telephone number was still there.

So they told me lies. They said that because somebody answered the phone in New York, I had to pay two hundred rupees, even though it was a wrong number. Plus I had to pay more than six hundred rupees for the two calls I made to Pondicherry, which should have been forty or fifty rupees. So in the Bombay hotel, deception started.

10. Speeding to Pondicherry

The plane to Madras was delayed by an hour and a half. From Madras to Pondicherry it takes three and a half hours if you drive very fast. One of my close friends came to take me. He always comes. He is such a kind friend. He was waiting for me at the airport and he said, "At ten o'clock the nursing home closes. After that they do not allow visitors."

I said, "What are you going to do?"

He said, "I will drive as fast as possible, and Mother will protect us."

I said, "Yes, Mother will protect us."

On the way two or three times big lorry trucks unnecessarily blocked us. He used all his Indian mantras, but the trucks did not listen. Whenever he got the opportunity, he drove very fast. Where it says you cannot drive more than thirty-five miles per hour, he was going very fast.

I said, "Let us hope and hope that we can reach Pondicherry in time."

11. *The ten o'clock closing time*

At five minutes to ten, my friend and I arrived at the nursing home. I forgot that I had knee trouble. There were three staircases inside the building. One was short but the other two were long. I went practically running up the stairs. There were nurses and servants in the hallway and I said, "I have come to see my sister."

They said, "No, it is past ten o'clock."

"My watch says five minutes to ten," I said and I showed them my watch.

They replied, "No, ours says ten o'clock."

I said, "I am coming all the way from America to see my dying sister."

They said, "Come tomorrow at eight o'clock."

I looked around and saw a huge picture of the Mother. With such devotion I looked at her picture, and the Mother saved me. When they saw me with folded hands praying to the Mother, they said, "All right, we have changed our mind. You can be there, but only for two minutes."

I said, "Two minutes is too much. Just allow me to see her."

12. Swimming in a sea of tears

When they took me into my sister's room, my sister was eagerly waiting for me. As soon as she saw me, she started screaming with joy. There were tears in her eyes. She became hysterical. I placed my hand on her head and started blessing her. She immediately grabbed my hand, pulled it down and placed it on her heart. She pressed my hand against her chest. Both of us were swimming in a sea of tears. She told me that she did not want to live on earth any longer. Now that she had seen me once more, she wanted to go to the other world.

I said, "No, you have to stay on earth. Your soul wants you to stay."

We were together for perhaps three or four minutes. We created a scene! Then they sent a servant to knock at the door to remind me that it was closing time. He was knocking at the door very hard. I opened it and said to him, "There are four patients in this room. All of them are sick. What are you doing?"

He said, "But two minutes are up."

I said, "You could not have come here and whispered?"

When I was leaving, my sister was so happy and, at the same time, she was so miserable that I had to leave her.

The nurses told me again, "Tomorrow morning at eight o'clock you can return."

13. The kind and compassionate doctor

That night I did not have a wink of sleep. I did not have even one minute's rest. I was extremely tired, but I was so happy to remain awake so that I could go and see my sister and we could have a good talk. I had promised her that I would be there at eight o'clock. The next morning finally arrived. Exactly at eight,

I presented myself at the nursing home. I was so eager to see my sister.

One of the nurses said to me, "What are you doing here?"

I said, "I was told to come at eight o'clock."

The nurse said, "No, the visiting hours are between four and seven in the afternoon."

I said, "Last night they told me to come back at eight o'clock."

She would not allow me to see my sister. Then I said, "All right, let me see what I can do." I sat on a chair in the hallway for about ten minutes. "O God, is this to be my fate?" I thought.

All of a sudden, a lady wearing a sari appeared and said, "Ah, Chinmoy-da, what are you doing? Why are you here? I am Doctor Salila. What are you doing here? You did not go to see your sister today?"

I said, "I am not allowed. Last night I came at five minutes to ten. At first they did not allow me. Finally, with greatest difficulty, they allowed me. Then they told me to come at eight o'clock, but now I cannot go to see her."

The doctor said, "You go and tell them that I am the doctor. Any time you want to come, you can come, and as long as you want to stay, you can stay. I am giving you permission."

I said, "The nurses will not believe me."

Then Dr. Salila called one nurse and introduced me, "This is Chinmoy-da. Any time he wants to come, he can come here, and he can stay as long as he wants to."

She is one of the main doctors. There are two doctors: Dr. Datta, who is from Calcutta, and Dr. Salila. Both of them are extremely, extremely, extremely kind to me.

14. My experiences in the nursing home

I went to see my sister, and we chatted for about an hour. Then a nurse came and said, "Now we have to bathe her, so you go out for some time."

I said, "I am going to stay outside. Will you kindly inform me when I can come back in?"

The nurse said, "Definitely."

My sister was not the only patient in that room. There were three more patients. The lady right by her on the left side was constantly screaming so loudly: "Yeeah, yeeah."

I asked my sister, "What is wrong with her?"

My sister said, "Somehow she was responsible for her husband's death. She poisoned her husband or she did something, so now she is getting the karma back."

I asked, "How do you know?"

My sister told me, "We hear from people that she was responsible."

While the lady was sleeping, she was quiet. Otherwise, when she was awake at every moment she was screeching very loudly: "Yeeah, yeeah."

Another patient does not sleep at all. The doctor confided to me that this lady is mentally unbalanced. Unfortunately, I had to pass by her to see my sister. On one occasion, the lady said to me, "Is she your sister?"

I said, "Yes, she is my sister."

Then she said, "How is she? Is she still alive? Then no problem, my mother is in Heaven. My mother will take care of her."

Her mother will take care of my sister, and my sister is still alive? All kinds of rubbish things she was telling me. I had to pass by her to see my sister, and she would always say something crazy. This was my experience at the nursing home.

15. Our family friend

At the nursing home, I went to visit a lady who is our family friend. It was at her place that I met our great ashram sage, Anirvan, when I was very young. She is twenty years older than I am. Her younger son is extremely close to me.

As soon as I went there, she said, "Chinmoy, Chinmoy, Chinmoy, come and bless me. I need your blessingful presence."

I said, "Oh no, I cannot bless you. I am praying to the Mother and Sri Aurobindo to bless you."

Then she said, "Let me see how soft your hand is."

I knew she was playing a trick on me. Her son was there in the room, and he said, "You should allow my mother to touch your hand."

So I gave her my hand. She immediately grabbed it and put it on her head.

16. My bicycle teacher

I also went to see another old man who was there. He said to me, "Ah, who are you?"

I said, "Chinmoy-da. Do you remember me? I came to the ashram in 1944, and it was you who taught me how to ride a bicycle."

Then he said to me, "I taught you how to ride a bicycle. Now you are teaching the whole world how to run!"

So that incident he did remember, but when I first stood before him, he could not recognise me!

17. I am mistaken for my brother

The main doctor took me from one patient to another, introducing me. One fellow was the funniest. He is now an old man, but in his youth he was very, very strong. The doctor said to him, "This is Chinmoy-da."

"Who is it?" the old man asked.

"Hriday's youngest brother," the doctor replied. Then the old man said to me, "How are you, Hriday? And how is Chinmoy? Oh, I am sorry. Chinmoy is long dead!"

18. Shopping for Lily

Every day I went at least four or five times to see my sister. I would arrive at eight o'clock and spend an hour or so. I would return at 10:30, and again at 12:30 and six or seven o'clock. When I first arrived in Pondicherry, she could not get up from her bed, but when I went there the following morning, she was ready to walk. About fifteen metres she walked and sat on a chair to chat with me properly.

All of a sudden, as she was talking, she said that she did not like the garments that the nursing home had given her to wear. The petticoat was no good and she did not like their nightgowns. I said, "You do not have to worry. I will go and buy some for you."

Immediately I went to the market. I have never bought petticoats before. My sister said that they had to be light and they had to look nice. I went to six or seven stores, begging them to give me very light ones made of cotton or silk. With greatest difficulty, I got six petticoats and six nightgowns, but not from one store. Happily I brought them back to my sister.

But she liked only two nightgowns and one petticoat. Then she said, "Take the rest back to New York."

I said, "I do not take petticoats for the girls."

She said, "No, you have to take them. I do not like them."

Then I told her, "As soon as I go back to New York, I will find light ones, nice ones, and I will immediately send them to you."

19. *The callous nurses*

How callous some nurses can be! My sister wanted to eat at six o'clock, but they do not give food until seven. When I saw that she was so hungry, I tried to talk to the nurses, but they ignored me. I called them, saying, "Sister" or "Hello", but they just passed by me.

I said, "This is too much."

The following day I went to the doctor. The doctor was very kind and full of admiration for me. The doctor got furious: "What can you do with these people? We have some ashramites here but the rest of the nurses are from outside. They are paid nurses. The paid ones are so bad."

Recently, I sent from New York seven or eight kinds of vitamins for my sister, as well as eggnog, which the Mother took for three years. Three hours before the Mother passed on, the last thing she took was eggnog, according to one of her assistants.

This time I gave more vitamins and eggnog to the doctor, and he assured me that they would give them to my sister. Then I discovered that for two days they did not give anything to my sister. I asked her, and she said, "No, no, they have not given me anything."

When I told the doctor, the doctor got furious. He asked one of the nurses in front of me if she had given the vitamins and the nurse admitted she had not given them. The doctor said to me, "We can only get angry with them. If we fire them, we will have nobody."

One nurse said that they gave the vitamins inside some milk, but my sister did not take the milk. They said, "Is it our fault she did not drink it?"

I said, "Can you not tell my sister when you are giving the vitamins that they are from her brother?"

The main doctor told the nurses, "Definitely you have to say these things are from Chinmoy-da."

So they agreed they would tell my sister. Now they do mention it. Three different things they give, and each time my sister knows that it is coming from me.

The two main doctors are so nice. They have such love and admiration for me, but some nurses were so bad!

20. *Glimpses of the other world*

I was begging them to keep my sister in the nursing home. Lately for ten days Lily remains in the nursing home, and then for five days or so she goes home. Over the last few months, five or six times she has done this. I begged the doctors, only if she is much better should they allow her to go home. The problem is that as soon as she feels a little better, she fights with the doctors, and then she goes home. At home her condition gets worse. Then they bring her back to the nursing home.

Some days my sister and I would be talking together in a normal way. All of a sudden she would say, "Ah, it is so beautiful, I can see such a beautiful room with flowers, and Hriday and Ahana are there." She would say that my brother and sister, who are no longer alive, were already talking to her.

I would say, "No, they are not here. I do not want that place, I do not like that place."

One moment she is all right, and suddenly she will see my brother Hriday and sister Ahana and a beautiful house filled with flowers. She is having a glimpse of the other world. Otherwise, she is quite normal, but weak.

21. *A fight with the maid*

One day my sister had a fight with the maid, not the nurse. When I went to visit her, my sister made complaints that the maid had struck her. I asked the maid what had happened.

The maid said, "At two o'clock in the morning, she wanted to get out of her bed. I did not want her to get out. Where would she go at that hour? I was not allowing her to get up, so she struck me."

I said, "But my sister is telling me that you struck her."

The maid said, "In order to keep her in the bed, I slapped her three times." I was in between the maid and my sister; both had complaints against the other.

22. *The out-of-order phone*

During my entire visit our home phone was out of order. I had to go to a booth outside in the street to place calls. There you have to stand in a long queue. People were making phone calls to Calcutta, Bombay and other places. You can give them the number you want or you can dial it yourself, and it is absolutely as if you are dialing a local number. It is called ISD. Immediately you get a connection, but you have to wait your turn in the queue.

So many times we went to the telephone office to ask them to repair our phone. Then one day one of the men where I made ISD calls said, "Just give them twenty rupees."

I said, "Twenty rupees? Is that all? I am going there immediately."

I went to the office and gave them fifty rupees. They promised it would be fixed. On other days when I went there, they said in a vague way, "Yes, we shall do it."

After some time I tried to call home to see whether they had kept their promise, but the phone was not working. Again, I went to the office. Finally they sent a repair man the day I was leaving. I gave him another forty rupees as soon as he came. I said, "Now start working."

He started, and in ten minutes he fixed it. Then I called the manager in Madras. I said, "Our phone is always out of order."

The manager said, "What do you do?"

I said, "My brother goes to the office here and gives them some money. Then the phone works for two weeks and stops. Then again he goes to the office and gives them money."

The manager said, "That is the mistake your brother makes."

I said, "That is what we have to do. If my brother did not give them any money, God knows how many months they would take."

Everywhere in the Madras-Pondicherry area, the telephone workers disconnect the phones deliberately so that they can get some tip. How horrible they are!

23. *My eternal friendship with the rickshaw world*

Now comes the story of my eternal friendship with the rickshaw world. My brother said, "You have so much money. For God's sake, do not argue with the poor *rickshaw-wallahs*."

I said, "I promise I will not argue with them. I will tell them, 'Whatever you say'."

Unfortunately, when I would say to the rickshaw-wallahs, "Whatever you say, I will give," they would say, "No, you have to tell."

What could I do? I said, "Last time I gave you ten rupees per hour. This time I am ready to give you fifteen rupees per hour, and each time I hire you, it will be for two hours. So I will give you thirty rupees."

The rickshaw-wallahs were overjoyed: thirty rupees they would get. I told them, "Now, only do me a favour and do the right thing."

Usually four or five rickshaws would be right in front of my house. I would say, "I need only one," but each day at least four would be waiting. Then I had to choose among them. When I chose one, I got the "blessings" from the others. They would say nasty things to me, and they were ready to beat up the one that I chose. But how could I take four rickshaws?

24. Two narrowly avoided accidents

This time I was saved from two very serious accidents while I was riding in a rickshaw. Once a bicycle came and dashed against the rickshaw. I thought that we would fall down, but the cyclist fell down instead. I told the *rickshaw-wallah*, "Stop! Let us see whether he is hurt."

He said he would not stop because the cyclist was the one who had dashed against us, and he went on.

The second incident was absolutely the most dangerous. As usual, I was sitting in a relaxed way and my right knee was outside the rickshaw. A motorbike was coming directly towards us on the right side. I thought, "O my God, my right knee will be finished!"

The motorcycle stopped within one foot of the rickshaw. If the driver had come a little closer, my right knee would have been smashed. Luckily, nothing happened and I was saved.

25. Caught in the middle

Another day I took a rickshaw early in the morning. A man followed us screaming that he was the owner of that rickshaw. He was asking the *rickshaw-wallah* to give him twenty rupees. The driver said, "No, I have just started."

The owner said, "Yesterday you did not give me the money. You have to give me twenty rupees at least. Otherwise, I will not allow you to use the rickshaw."

Already I was one mile away from my house. I said, "I am supposed to give the money to the rickshaw-wallah. Instead, let me give the money to you."

But the rickshaw-wallah, the one who was pulling me, said, "No, if you give him the money, he will not give it to me."

There was a fight between the owner and the rickshaw-wallah. The owner did not want him to drive the rickshaw. Poor me! I was completely lost between the two. I was ready to give the money. The one who was driving was asking me not to give the owner money, but the owner wanted to have money from me. I said, "I really do not know what to do."

Finally the owner went away, hating this fellow, and we continued on to the nursing home. When I came out after two hours, I gave the driver his money. I had said that I would give thirty rupees, but then I would always give the drivers forty rupees to make them happy.

26. Deceived by the rickshaw-wallah

It would take ten minutes to bring me to the nursing home, and the *rickshaw-wallah* was supposed to wait for me. I booked the drivers for two hours. One day I took a rickshaw to the nursing home, and before I went upstairs, I said to the driver, "Please stay here."

The driver said, "Definitely I will wait."

I saw my sister, and we talked and talked for half an hour. Then the nurses said that they had to bathe her. I said, "Then let me go out, and afterwards I will come back."

The weather was so unbearably hot. It was the coldest season, they said, but for me it was so hot. When I went down, there was no rickshaw. I walked for about half a mile in the hot sun looking for a rickshaw, and eventually I found another one, so I got in. I said, "Now drive me to a place where I can get something to eat."

On this trip I did not eat at home. My cousins were so sad and upset. I said it was difficult for me to eat at home because my sister was not there. I used to take *idli* or *masala dosa* and tea at a particular restaurant. The driver was taking me there. After we had covered practically a mile and a half, the driver that first brought me saw us and started screaming, "I am your driver. I am coming back to get you."

I said, "Now, look here, already a mile and a half I have covered. What were you doing?"

The man said, "I was hungry. I went to eat."

I said, "You were not supposed to be there waiting for me?"

Instead of replying, the first driver began screaming at the second, asking him to leave so that I could go into the first rickshaw. I said, "I am not going into your rickshaw. You have fooled me."

There was a real fight between the two. Then the first one said, "Now you have to give me ten rupees, since I brought you to the nursing home."

I got so mad. I said, "I am going to give you five rupees. You brought me, but it was only a ten-minute ride, so I am giving you five rupees." I was so mad that I had to walk so far in that heat.

I gave him the five rupees. We did not go even twenty metres, before the first driver came again, saying, "It is false, false! It is no good, no good." He gave me back my five rupees.

I said, "All right," and I gave him another five rupees. I threw away the "false" coin that he had returned. Then the driver came down from his rickshaw and collected the first coin.

I said, "I knew it was not false. You wanted to have ten rupees. For God's sake, take your ten rupees!"

27. *The story continues*

I went to the restaurant to eat. I ordered rose milk, *masala dosa* and tea. The street was right in front of me, not even ten metres away. I saw that there were many drivers keeping their cycles and rickshaws at that place. The restaurant gave me very fast service. In three or four minutes they gave me the food, and another ten minutes I took to finish my meal. I ate very happily.

When I went back to the rickshaw, the fellow told me his sad story: he had gone out to eat. When he came back, somebody had taken away the cushion or seat of the rickshaw. People were saying that the place was illegal, so the police had come and taken it away.

I looked at the seat inside the rickshaw. Now it was a hard surface, and it was so uneven. I said, "I will not be able to sit there. I am giving you the money because the seat is gone. I will find another rickshaw."

He said, "No, if you do not go with me to prove that I was waiting for you, the police will not give me my seat back."

I said, "What am I going to do with this fellow? He is begging me. If I do not go with him to the police station, he will not get the pillow back."

The police station was out of my way. It was God knows where! We were driving and driving, and I was being tortured because of the hard seat. I have such a bad back. Sometimes I tried not to sit; I stayed two or three inches above the wood because it was hurting me. And in three places there were nails! Usually the pillow covers everything. This is how I was enjoying my journey.

I decided that since the police had taken the pillow away, whatever the police charged, I would give the money to the driver. He also had a bald head. I said, "Poor fellow."

We went to the police station and asked the police for the pillow. The police scolded and insulted him: "As if we have nothing else to do than to bring your pillow here!" Then I spoke to the police chief. He said, "No, we do not do this kind of thing."

Some people had told the driver that the police took it away, but it was not true. Then I was begging him, "Please, this time take me to my house."

For another fifteen minutes we drove on, and I could not sit because it was all wood and nails. He did not get his pillow. I think the other fellow, the first driver, followed us and removed the pillow to punish me because I did not wait for him. When we reached my home at long last, instead of thirty, I gave the driver fifty rupees. I said, "God knows when he will get his pillow."

28. Lord Krishna's favourite flower

One day when I was in a rickshaw going home, a lady said to me, "Chinmoy-da, stop, stop."

I could not recognise her. She asked, "How are you?"

I said, "I am fine."

She said, "No, you are not fine."

I asked, "Why?"

She told me, "Because I can see. Your eyes are red and something is wrong with you."

I said, "I have got a little fever, but there is nothing wrong."

She had a few flowers. She gave me one flower which was the most favourite flower of Lord Krishna when he used to meet with the *gopis*. She said, "Here, this is Krishna's most favourite flower. If you take it and put it on your head, then you will be all right."

I said, "Even now I cannot recognise you."

She said, "You cannot recognise me because you are so great. How will you remember? Do you remember Kanak?"

I said, "Yes."

She said, "I was very young. You were so fond of my uncle. Do you remember my uncle?"

I said, "Yes. I was so fond of Joganananda."

She told me, "I was one of his nieces. Now do you recognise me?"

I said, "Yes, where are Bokul and the others?"

She said, "They are all out of the ashram. They are not here. They got married, this and that, but I am still here. I remember you. You take this flower and you will be all right."

So I was very nice to her. In those days she was so thin, but now she has become extremely fat.

29. *My cousin's colleague*

I had gone another half a mile, when another girl called out: "Chinmoy-da, stop, stop!"

I said, "I am sorry, but I do not know you."

She said, "You do not know me, but I know you. I work with your cousin Soma at the ashram press. I have read some of your books. You were brought up here. You are such a great man. I have been begging her to bring me to your place, but she will not listen. She says she comes to your place and she does not see you. You are such a big shot, you do not speak to people."

I said, "Fine, fine. Whatever my cousin has said is true."

She said, "I want to speak to you."

I said, "I am sorry, but I am very busy with my sister."

She said, "All right, since I have seen you, I am very happy. Now I can feel that I have seen a really great man."

She never saw me at the ashram when I lived there. She came afterwards.

30. Nolini's assistant and his sisters

I gave my book of talks at the United Nations to one family. That family was very close to us. There are three sisters and one brother. When I left the ashram in 1964, Nolini made this young boy his assistant to take care of his mail and so on. I studied with him and we did sports together. His older sisters were extremely nice to me from the very beginning. Their names are Priti, Tapati and Arati. Arati is a professor at the ashram university. She is older than I am by two years, I think. Once when I was going to the nursing home, I saw her. She said, "Tomorrow I am going to take the book to show my students and tell them all about you."

31. The admirers

One day I was supposed to go and visit the Head of the Physical Education Department at nine o'clock. I was at the nursing home, and my sister was not doing well, so I decided to go the following day.

At eleven o'clock they called me to say that Pranab-da was waiting for me. I said, "I am so sorry. It is eleven o'clock. Please forgive me. I will come tomorrow."

Pranab-da came on the line and said, "No, you have to come today."

I said, "Why?"

He said, "You have so many foreign admirers. In their own countries they cannot approach you. When they came to know that you would visit me, they asked if they could be present. They have been waiting here since 8:30 to see you."

I said, "O my God, O my God!"

So I went to visit my friend. One foreign admirer was from Africa. God knows how he heard about me! One was from Manchester, and somebody else was from New Zealand. There were these three non-Indians, plus a few Indians. I was supposed to go there at nine o'clock, so from 8:30 they had been waiting with the hope of seeing me.

When I arrived, the visitor from Manchester approached me with folded hands. He begged me to have a photo taken with them. He said, "We know so much about you in England, but we can never come near you. Now that you are here, and people said you are accessible, we wanted to see you. Please allow us to have a picture taken with you."

Unfortunately, my friend Pranab-da is now confined to his chair. When the visitors saw that we could not all be in the picture together, they said, "Let us at least have a picture of you and Dada together."

They took two very nice pictures of Pranab-da and me sitting side by side.

32. My two brothers

I always ate out, but my brothers would never eat out. Chitta would cook something for Mantu, and they would eat at home. Our two cousins are so close to us, but Chitta will not take food prepared by them, and Mantu eats whatever Chitta cooks. Lily is seventy-two or seventy-three and Chitta is nearing his eighties. God knows what he cooks – potatoes and other things! Many, many years ago Chitta used to cook when he was working at our bank. Whatever food the ashram gives, they eat, plus Chitta's food, and they buy fruits, such as bananas and papayas.

My cousins brought prepared food for me. But I did not take it. I said, "It is very sentimental. My sister is not here. That is why I do not feel like eating at home. I am so happy to go out to eat." They were very sad. I said "When my sister is not here, it is too much for me."

I went to a restaurant once or twice a day to eat *masala dosa*, rose milk, *sambhar* and tea.

33. The sari store owner's false devotion

Early one morning, around seven o'clock, I went to a restaurant. They gave me three *idlis* and *sambhar*. They did not have rose milk, so I asked them to give me lemonade. The prices were cheaper at this restaurant and they were very nice.

After breakfast, I told the *rickshaw-wallah*, "Take me to the bazaar."

He said, "It is not open. At eight o'clock nothing is open. It opens at nine or nine-thirty."

I said, "Take me slowly, and I will just see nature's beauty. In the afternoon I will come back."

I saw one particular sari store. The owner had opened the door a little, and he was praying so devotedly with folded hands.

He was not paying any attention to people passing by. All the other stores were closed. I did not want to buy anything. I did not even have money; only a small amount I had taken with me. I said, "He is such a nice man. Let me see the name of the store, and I may come back." This was my stupidity.

O God, the man happened to see me and said, "Oh no, no, no, do not drive away! I was praying to God, and God has listened to my prayer. You have come!"

I said, "This is not the right time. Your store is not yet open."

The owner said, "No, God has listened to my prayers. Please, please, come inside."

I said, "I have no money."

He said, "You do not have to give me money now."

I said, "I have very limited money. I cannot buy anything."

Hostile forces always make fun of me! I chose a few saris, mostly to please him. I had only 120 rupees with me. He said, "You give me 100. Afterwards when you come back, you will give me the rest."

The man put the saris in a bundle, and packed them very, very nicely. I said, "All right. I trust you, and you trust me. You have got 100 rupees. I trust you to such an extent, I do not need a receipt from you. You are such a nice man. In the morning you are praying. God knows when I will be back, but during the day I will come. Now I am going to see my sister."

His whole forehead was besmeared with ashes and white paste. He looked like the greatest devotee. I said, "He is such a nice man."

Late afternoon came. Already I had gone to see my sister three times. I said, "Let me go back to that store." My sister was so happy that I was going shopping. She had begged me to go and get saris, but I had said, "This time I am not interested." When I told her I had bought some, she was very happy.

I went back to the store and got the package. I gave him the money. He was very happy to find such a sincere person. As I was carrying the package out of the shop, all of a sudden, some divine forces acted through me. I said to myself, "The best thing is to count again to see if all the saris are there or not." To me, the package looked exactly the same; in the morning we had counted everything. But I said to him, "Can you open it?"

The man said, "Why? Can you not see it is the same?"

I said, "Something is telling me. Just open it. I am absolutely sure all are there." He had given me the receipt and everything.

Reluctantly he opened the package and I counted the saris.

Four saris were missing! I got so furious. I said, "I am calling the police!"

The owner said, "No, no!" He ran into a corner of the store. Those four missing saris he had kept at one particular place. He grabbed them from the corner and brought them to me.

I said, "How could you do this? Police, police!" He deceived me shamelessly. The package looked exactly the same the way he had re-packed it. If you take away only four light saris, how will somebody know? He had tied the cord around the bundle in exactly the same way.

When I was about to come out of the store with the package, the owner, his son and perhaps his grandson were blocking the door with their arms. They said, "You have to drink some soda." They were afraid that I would tell the police.

I said, "I promise I will not go to the police. You have given me my saris back, so I am not going to the police."

The owner said, "I know you will not go to the police, but you have to drink some soda."

I had to wait there for five minutes because they had sent for soda for me. Otherwise, they would not allow me to leave. This is called emotional demand. It was all fear, fear.

For this kind of deception there is something called the law of karma, but the law of karma does not operate immediately. God waits for us to pray to Him for forgiveness; God gives us the scope to pray for forgiveness. Unfortunately, instead of using this time to become better, many people become worse.

34. Another missing rickshaw

When I came outside with the bundle of saris, my rickshaw was missing. The driver was supposed to be right across the street. Where had he gone? It is my eternal rickshaw fate. There I saw only twenty or thirty bicycles. I was looking this side and that side, but there was no trace of my driver. I said, "What is happening?"

He did not tell me that he would be going somewhere. I had to stay in the store for another ten minutes until the driver came back.

I asked him, "Where did you go?"

He said, "I was hungry." He had gone to eat. At last, he brought me back home safely. This is India!

35. Ganesha was not thirsty

While I was in India, magazines, newspapers and radio were telling about statues of Ganesha drinking milk. This miracle happened in many places around the world. But in one case it was not true. About forty metres away from my house there is a Ganesha *Mandir*. Always I heard the music. It was one house away from our house. Unfortunately, that Ganesha was not thirsty. At every hour of the day and night, women were sleeping in front of the temple and outside on the street, but this particular statue did not accept the milk that they offered.

36. Avoiding the Florida lady once again

In four days how many sad experiences you can get! I have forgotten to tell you about the Florida lady. She had bothered me so much on my previous trip. I was very happy that she did not come to see me when I arrived.

One day I went to my dearest boss Amrita's centenary exhibit. The 19th of September was his birthday, so they had an exhibition. It was smaller than the smallest. I was extremely happy that they observed his centenary, but I was so unhappy and sad that it was such a small exhibit. The exhibit was prepared by his youngest niece, Kumuda. If she had not insisted, there would have been nothing.

The exhibit was at the ashram school. As I came out of the building, the Florida lady screamed: "Ah, Chinmoy, when did you come?"

She greeted me at the ashram school gate. I said, "Enough, enough, enough!" Then I told the *rickshaw-wallah*, "Go away from here as fast as possible."

We drove to the nursing home, and I came home after two hours at least. The Florida lady was waiting in front of my house. I begged her, "I have come here only to see my sister, my dearest sister. Do not bother me."

This time I hoped she would listen to my prayer.

37. Plagued by the Florida lady

Every day I would walk two miles early in the morning. Then in the evening at ten o'clock or ten-thirty I would go out again and walk two miles. On my fourth day, I went walking at three-thirty in the morning. After 400 metres, all of a sudden my right foot was aching like anything. The pain was so bad. I said,

"How could it be?" Then I said, "All right, God does not want me to walk today."

I sat down. It was still quite dark; the sun had not risen. I was meditating very powerfully facing the sea. I meditated for about forty-five minutes. I was so happy. Now that I had meditated for forty-five minutes, I could go home.

I stood up. The sun was still not visible. I said, "The best thing is to imagine the sun. Let me take a few stretching exercises." I was taking stretching exercises, moving my arms and so on. At one point I turned around. Just thirty metres away, the Florida lady was doing the same exercise. I had not seen her before. I was so embarrassed. I said to myself, "Where could she come from?" O God, O God, she was there. I had not seen her when I went there to meditate. Can you imagine?

Then she followed me home. I was walking slowly because I was being cautious. My foot was still aching. I said to her, "I am begging you. Please do not bother me. This time my sister is dying. I am all the time thinking of her. Please, please, please."

But she would not listen.

38. *Flowers for the Samadhi*

On my last day in India, I went to the Samadhi. The man who was in charge of Sri Aurobindo's room was there. He said to me, "You are not planning to come to Sri Aurobindo's room this time? You must come."

I gave him a very sorrowful face. I had been coming to the Samadhi every day. But for Sri Aurobindo's room there is a fixed hour; only at eleven o'clock can you go there. That was the hour I was more interested in spending with my sister. I could not say anything. The man gave me some flowers. He said, "All right, if you cannot go, I understand."

I put the flowers on the Samadhi, and I was very, very happy.

39. Aging ashramites

When I see the ashramites who are older than I am, how pitifully they walk! They take four inch-long strides and their whole body bends in different directions. Their faces are completely changed. While walking along the street, out of fifty people I would only see perhaps only one ashramite that I knew from before. So many people who are older than I am by five or ten years have passed away. Wherever I went, there were all new faces. The old ones have all gone. When I went to the Samadhi, I could not recognise anybody. At the meditation hall, I could not recognise anybody. They are all new.

I think there are practically the same number of ashramites – two thousand or so – but most of them are new. People with whom I was brought up have all gone. Even many who were younger than I am have passed away.

My aunt is an exception. She is ninety-five years old. She is blind; she cannot see at all. She wants to live another five years, and then celebrate her centenary. There are three people who are one hundred years old in the ashram. Let us see how many years more they can cover.

In India so many people die after the age of fifty years. It is from our Indian heat. If I had stayed more than two months there, I too would have gone to the other world! I suffered so much from the heat. The fan was emitting only hot air. When you stand in front of the Bay of Bengal, it is unbearable. The hot countries that we visit at Christmas are nothing in comparison to Indian heat.

40. Greatness versus peace

Before I left, one of my friends came to see me. I said to him, "God has given me a few things and God has made me great, but God has given you something which He has not given me."

My friend asked, "What has He given me?"

I said, "Look at your eyes, look at your face, look at yourself. How peaceful you are! What am I doing? I have thousands of students here, there and everywhere, but I have only worries and anxieties. I am ready to give up all the name and fame that I have and all my disciples. Everything that I have in my possession I am ready to give up if God would give me just a fraction of the peace that you have."

Then I said to him, "Which one do you want? Name and fame like me or peace?"

He said, "Name and fame I do not want."

I said, "Do you not feel that you are leading a peaceful life?"

He said, "It is true. I know it and I feel it."

I said, "I have got name and fame, everything, but I have not got peace."

My friend looked at me so pathetically. He is of my age. He leads a very simple life. He has such peace inside him. I can see it in his face and in his eyes. I have name and fame; everything I have got. But peace I find only in my meditation. There I go beyond, beyond. In my outer, daily life, I have only worries and anxieties.

41. *No refuge from the Florida lady*

On the last day, I went to my sister's place for an hour. We were talking, talking, talking. My sister was cutting jokes with me and I was cutting jokes with her. She was saying, "Take care of your health. I can see how fat you have become."

I said, "I have lost weight."

On the last day, my sister was giving me absolutely so much joy. Alas, the Florida lady! How could she come into my sister's room at the nursing home? When I saw her, I said, "O my God!" My sister was so sad and upset. Of all people, that lady was coming with some flowers, standing ten metres behind us, near the other patients. I said, "O God, this is too much, too much!"

Then I looked at my sister and I meditated very powerfully for four or five minutes. I said, "I may come once or twice more, but today is the last day. We have cut so many jokes. Now let me meditate. I am not going to pay any attention to that lady. You also do not pay any attention to her. Let us meditate."

When I was about to leave, the Florida lady said, "Please wait, wait. These flowers are from Sri Aurobindo's room."

I was so surprised. I said, "How, how could you get flowers from Sri Aurobindo's room?"

Then she said, "Oh, they are not actually from Sri Aurobindo's room, but while I was plucking them, I thought of Sri Aurobindo's room. So I brought these flowers."

First she said they were from Sri Aurobindo's room. Then she said she thought of Sri Aurobindo's room while plucking them. The last time I went to Sri Aurobindo's room in January, she was there to bother me. This time I did not go. Perhaps she knew somehow. Perhaps she had been observing me. When I challenged her about the flowers, she said, "No, but I was thinking of Sri Aurobindo's room when I picked them."

She brought the flowers near my sister to give them to her, but I got disgusted and I started to move away. Instead of giving the flowers to my sister, that lady had to follow me! Look how sincere her compassion for my sister was!

42. *The doctor's genuine compassion*

When I was leaving, the main doctor happened to be there. I said, "I have to talk to you."

The doctor said, "Please, please come."

I went to the doctor's room, and we talked and talked. The doctor was very, very nice. With his compassion he melted my heart. I have no complaint against either of the doctors. While we were talking, I was praying to the Supreme that the Florida lady would leave. When I came out, she was not there. I was so happy.

43. *My friend becomes my bodyguard*

I was supposed to leave at five o'clock in the afternoon. By three o'clock I had been to see my sister four times. Around five o'clock I was upstairs putting everything in my suitcase. Since my sister was not there, I had to do everything myself. I had no help. Somebody knocked at the door downstairs. At that hour, the Florida lady had to come!

My brothers opened the door and she came in and sat down. Then my two brothers came to talk to me upstairs. In such a hurry I was getting ready.

My saviour was the driver, who is a very close friend of mine. He dislikes the Florida lady like anything. He opened the front door to take my suitcase from the staircase. He called out, "Chinmoy, why are you so late?"

I said, "I am late because I have no sister here."

He was shouting from downstairs; I was shouting from upstairs. In Bengali we were shouting at each other. It was all friendship. When the lady saw him, she went out of the house because she knew that he would insult her. She was standing outside. On my previous visit, when she came, I finally gave her some money. This time also she came with the expectation of getting some money.

Last time my friend saw that I was forced to give her something because she was not coming out of our house. At the door, I had given the Florida lady two hundred dollars. This time my friend was my bodyguard. He would not allow me to give any money to her. I came down with some money in my hand, but he ordered me to enter into the car, and I obeyed him. The Florida lady was across the street, so she did not get a chance to get the money.

My two brothers came out. I was very affectionately saying goodbye to them, and the lady was so miserable that I could not give her money. Perhaps she cursed me and that is why everything went wrong at Madras airport.

44. *Reconfirmation precaution*

For my trip back to New York, I had to reconfirm my flights. I do not blame Ashrita, but I blame his fate. His sincerity, his eagerness to do the right thing I appreciate, but the fate that he has is unbearable, and I suffer.

Last time when I went to India from Myanmar, instead of listing my name with a G, it became C: Chose instead of Ghose. This time Ashrita gave me the itinerary. From India I was supposed to come directly via Air India to London. From Madras to Bombay and from Bombay to London, it would be the same plane. The flight number was 101. To reconfirm my flight, I went to a travel agency in the ashram that is very reliable. The name of it is Auro Travel, and the owner is my very good friend. They are so expert. For twenty-five years they have been in that line.

My friend's assistant said that no reconfirmation was needed since I was in executive class. He said that reconfirmation is usually only needed if you stay longer than a week, but for executive class it is not needed at all. In my case, it was not necessary. But my friend, the boss, disagreed. He said, "It is necessary. This gentleman is my friend. You have to reconfirm it. If anything goes wrong, it will be our fault."

My friend, Gautam, has so many assistants. I was sitting right in front of him, and one of his assistants phoned up Madras, telling my name, this and that. Everything was reconfirmed. My flight number was 101.

45. Waiting at the airport

My friend who was going to drive me to Madras airport from Pondicherry advised me, "No matter when the flight is, you should be there five hours before."

I fully agreed with him. I said, "Otherwise, something may go wrong."

The plane was supposed to leave at 2:15 in the morning. He brought me to the airport at nine o'clock. I said, "Do not worry about me. I will read. I will buy some books."

I went to the counter and saw that the flight number was 401, instead of 101. The stupid thing is that they do not mention the destination, only the flight number. They should say it is Bombay. Then I went and bought eight or ten books: books of wisdom, books of proverbs and all kinds of things. I sat facing the counter, only fifteen or twenty metres away. People were coming and going.

Around 10:30, long before the scheduled time, I went to the counter and showed my ticket just to check. The man said, "Your ticket says 101. Can you not see this is 401?"

I said, "Yes, it is 401, and mine is 101."

The man said, "101 is a later flight."

I believed him.

46. Tearing up my books to reduce my luggage

I had ten or twelve books. I was reading them, but since they were so thick, I said, "Let me tear out the pages that I want."

Any place that was important, I ticked off, and then I tore out the pages that I had marked. The man who was sitting beside me asked, "What are you doing?"

I said, "I have to go to America, so I do not wish to carry all these books. They are so heavy."

These were Chinese proverbs, a book of wisdom, a book of friendship and others. From each book I got perhaps four or five pages.

The man sitting next to me asked, "Can I take these books that you have discarded?"

I said, "Yes, by all means take them."

So the man took the books, while I kept only a few pages from each one.

47. Acting on wrong information

Many passengers gathered for flight 401, which departed at eleven o'clock. Around 11:30 I went again to the counter. I said, "Now, tell me, when will the other plane arrive?"

The man said, "What are you saying? Flight 101 leaves from Bombay. Here it is 401."

I said, "Your colleague told me that flight 101 will be later. Now you are saying he was wrong."

The man said, "101 is from Bombay."

I said, "It said 401. Mine was reconfirmed as 101." I showed them the receipt even.

He said, "It is all over. At 11:00 the plane left for Bombay. From here it was 401. The flight number changes to 101 in Bombay."

Such wrong information was on my ticket. When my friend called British Airways from Pondicherry, they could have told him at that time. The airport officials were saying to blame British Airways because they issued the ticket.

I said, "Why should I blame British Airways? When I reconfirmed here, at this counter, why did you not check it? When I first showed you my ticket, why did you not tell me that 101 is from Bombay but from here it is 401, even though my ticket says 101?"

Who can deal with these people? They said, "You can go and speak to the duty manager." The duty manager was a fat lady. I told her everything, and she told me, "It is the fault of British Airways."

I said, "How can it be? I came to India on British Airways, but I am going back on Air India. When I showed my ticket here at the Air India counter, they told me my flight was later. They could have informed me at that time that flight 401 becomes 101."

The duty manager insisted, "No, it is not our fault."

I said, "Somebody has to take the blame. If it is not your fault, then when I came before, at that time why did the man say 101 was later, instead of saying it goes from Bombay?"

She maintained it was not their fault. I said, "What can I do now?"

She said, "Tomorrow morning there is another flight at 7:15 from Bombay to London, but you will miss it. By the time you arrive in Bombay, it will be gone. I can give you a direct flight from here to London. You have to be here tomorrow morning. It leaves at half past seven."

48. The departure tax

O God, I had to wait another eight hours at the airport! From time to time, I would go and get tea to stay awake. One I drank was very strong. By this time my books were all finished. I said, "Let me buy two or three newspapers. Since the flight is at 7:30, I should be there at 4:30." Actually, I was already there, since I was reading and moving around right near the counter. I wanted to be first in line.

At 4:30, I was standing at the counter. Somebody else came around five o'clock. He was a friend of the ticket checker, so he went first. Then I needed to pay the airport departure tax. The man who was in charge of collecting the departure tax was fast asleep. Here I lost my first place. I was knocking and knocking. Finally, he opened up. When I went to pay, I found I did not have enough Indian currency. They needed three hundred rupees. I had only American hundred-dollar bills. The man said to me, "Are you crazy? Why do you want to give me so much money?"

I said, "I do not have enough rupees."

I searched and found a fifty-dollar bill, but fifty was also too much for him. I searched again and found a twenty-dollar bill. At last he gave me change. After paying my departure tax, I said, "Now I have to keep myself awake for God knows how long. Let me go out again to buy another tea."

This time, however, the tea man was fast asleep! I did not want to torture him. I waited until they announced the flight, and then I boarded the plane.

49. My London experience

My "direct" flight from Madras to London went to Kuwait, Cairo, Italy, France and so many places! Flying from London to Bombay took only eight and a half hours. This way it took ten or eleven hours.

When the plane finally arrived in London, the equipment was not functioning properly, so we had to come down from the plane using ordinary stairs, not a covered walkway. It was really raining hard. The workers had umbrellas, but for us there were no umbrellas. They said that if we wanted umbrellas, we would have to wait for a few minutes. Who wanted to wait? After such a long flight, nobody wanted to stay on board. The workers were saying to be very careful and to hold onto the rail.

In order to make my connection to New York, I had to go to Terminal 4. There I had to get a new boarding pass. Terminal 4 was quite far from the place where we had arrived. A few other passengers were with me. The officials said that within fifteen minutes a coach would come to take us to Terminal 4. The first coach we missed. Then we waited another fifteen or twenty minutes. I said, "What can we do?" There were three of us who wanted to make this connection and we had very little time. About half an hour later the coach came, and we three entered. We went to Terminal 4, which was quite far. By walking it would have been impossible, and it was raining.

People say that the British are very, very polite, but I think politeness is found in the dictionary only. Our waiting area was empty. When I went to the man who was supposed to take care of us, he said, "Just a minute," and he left. After five or ten minutes he had not returned. His jacket was still on the seat but he was not coming back.

I did not know how much time I had. Already my plane from India had been late. I could have only half an hour left at most before the flight left. I was so sad. I said, "Everywhere I will have this kind of fate."

On the other side it said "First Class". The man who was taking care of first class said to me, "Now that there is no passenger here, you can come."

I went to him very thankfully. He said, "I can give you the boarding pass, but I am unable to give you the seat number."

I said, "It is only half an hour before the plane departs."

He said, "I am sorry, but I cannot give you a seat number. For a seat number you will have to go to gate number 10, and they will give it to you."

Gate 10 was quite far. I walked and walked and went to gate 10. Although it was clearly written "Gate 10", I saw that nobody was there. I said, "The plane will leave in half an hour, but nobody is here. How could it be? He definitely told me gate 10.

I suspected that something had gone wrong. Usually I never read the schedules on the television screen. This time I said, "Let me look for the British Airways plane that goes to New York." On the screen it said that the gate was number 4. I said, "I have been sent to gate 10. Now I have to go to gate 4, which is so far away. Here I am in trouble."

Luckily, an airport official arrived. I said to her, "I was sent to gate 10 and there is nobody here. Now the screen says it is gate 4."

The lady said, "Yes, we thought it would be 10, but it has changed."

I had to return to gate 4. I was forced to walk extremely fast. The whole way I was only cursing myself for believing these people who give me wrong directions.

At gate 4, almost everybody was on board. There were hardly three or four persons ahead of me. Both my knees were hurting. Everything was hurting: physically, vitally and mentally. I was so disgusted. I said, "Civilization is not only lacking in Indian, but in India's once-upon-a-time boss."

50. *Sitting in a cloud of smoke*

I entered into the plane. I was so happy that at long last my problems were over. I showed my boarding pass to the steward. My seat number was 14B. This steward was so careless and callous. Instead of 14B, he pointed out to me 14E. I did not say anything. Perhaps he had his own reasons. I sat there. Soon afterwards, somebody came and told me that it was his seat number. He said, "Yours must be 14B."

I explained, "The steward asked me to sit here."

Then I took my bag and moved to 14B. I said, "Even here I have to get wrong information? This is too much."

I was seated on the aisle and next to me, on my left, was a very fat man, but there was plenty of space so it was no problem. Across the aisle, on my right, there were three seats. In the first was a businessman with lots of papers, and next to him was the young man who found that I had made a mistake.

The pilot made an announcement: "We shall deeply appreciate it if you do not smoke." When I was given my seat, I had no choice as to whether I was in a smoking or non-smoking area. At that time I did not care, as long as I was finally inside the plane. Now I discovered that smoking is allowed in executive class.

The pilot himself made the announcement requesting people not to smoke, although it was not forbidden. Then the man who was on my right side started smoking. The plane had not taken off yet. Luckily, the smoke was not coming towards me. Suddenly, the young man to the right of the businessman stood up and said to him, "The hell with you." The businessman smiled at him. Then the young man left and went to the economy section. He had bought a ticket for executive class, but he went to the economy section to find a non-smoking place. He did not come back.

I counted six cigarettes. One after the other the businessman was smoking, and he did not know how to stop. Still, the plane had not yet started. There was a very nice-looking man who was sitting next to the one who had left. This second innocent man also stood up to find a place in the economy section, but nothing was there. He was so miserable. He had to come back and sit near the big business executive.

I said to myself, "God has saved me." But God does not know how to save me. At intervals of fifteen or twenty minutes, the businessman would get the inspiration to turn towards me and blow his smoke in my direction. Usually he would blow his smoke on the right side, but sometimes he was relaxed and he would get the inspiration to smoke turning in the other direction. I was so disappointed. The man who sat on my left side became furious, but what could he do? Both of us were suffering like anything.

So many people were suffering because of this man who would not stop smoking. And this particular flight lasted seven hours and forty minutes.

51. *The police and the stewardess*

At the airport in London, the stewardesses and their luggage had to be examined thoroughly, like us. The police came inside the plane to take one of the stewardesses back to airport security because she had not been examined. She said, "Yes, I will go, but I hate the person who examines us."

The police said, "Then come with us, and we will find somebody else."

So the police took this stewardess back into the terminal.

52. The final note

When I came back to New York, Aushadi was my saviour. At customs I did not have any problem. His friends or colleagues or bosses were so kind, so kind. Everything was faster than the fastest when I dealt with them. They were cutting jokes with me. I had so many unfortunate experiences during my journey back to New York, but this last experience was very good.

NOTES TO MY EXPRESS VISIT TO INDIA

1. *(p. 507)* On 20 September 1995 Sri Chinmoy made a sudden trip to India to visit his sister, Lily, who was seriously ill. He stayed in Pondicherry for four days and returned to New York on 26 September. He narrated the stories in this book upon his return.

APPENDIX

BIBLIOGRAPHICAL NOTES

Salutations *(1981-1983)*

The *editio princeps* was published in a series of twelve separate books. These books have later (1981-1983) been published in a series of three books, each including four books of the editio princeps.

Parts 1 to 4: Switzerland (part 1), Italy (part 2), Germany (part 3) and Puerto Rico (part 4). Sri Chinmoy has visited Switzerland, Italy and Germany as part of a European lecture and concert tour and he had a meeting with the Pope in the Vatican. In September 1980 Sri Chinmoy was invited to Puerto Rico to deliver the opening benediction at the Pan American Masters Games.

Parts 5 to 8: Florida, 11 March to 20 March 1981 (part 5); Canada, where Sri Chinmoy gave a series of lectures and concerts, 4 May to 10 May 1981 (part 6); England, where he offered a series of lectures at Oxford and Cambridge, 14 to 20 May (part 7); Brazil, 21 May to 1 June 1981 (part 8).

Parts 9 to 12: Florida, November 1981 (part 9); Mexico (with a group of his disciples for their Christmas holiday), during December 1981 and January 1982 (part 10); Puerto Rico, for the second annual Sri Chinmoy Marathon in San Juan, December 1981, and again in February 1982 (part 11); Bermuda, in January 1982 and at an earlier time (part 12).

I love shopping *(1985-1994)*

Some of the recollections in part 1 and part 2 are accompanied by drawings not by the author. The front cover of part 3, part 4 and part 5 show two (same) photographs of Sri Chinmoy.

The world-experience-tree-climber *(1986-2005)*

Sri Chinmoy told the stories in part 1 from 19 October 1980 to 11 June 1982, in part 2 from 21 July 1982 to 31 March 1983, in part 3 from 19 December 1982 to 28 September 1984, in part 4 from 10 October to 20 January 1986, in part 5 from 27 February 1986 to 27 June 1987, in part 6 from 18 July 1987 to 14 September 1988 and in part 7 from 8 October 1988 to 20 January 1991. Stories in part 8 were offered during his trip to the Bahamas, Guatemala and Mexico in December 1997 and January 1998. Some of the anecdotes in part 1, part 2 and part 3 are accompanied by drawings, not by the author. The front cover of part 2 to part 8 show a photograph of Sri Chinmoy. Additionally, the front cover of part 2, part 4 and part 6 also show some of Sri Chinmoy's bird drawings.

Sri Chinmoy visits India *(1995)*

Recollections about Sri Chinmoy's travel to India in early 1995: his stopover in Calcutta, Wednesday, 11 January 1995 (5 hours), his stay at the Sri Aurobindo Ashram, Pondicherry, late evening Wednesday, 11 January 1995 to early morning Monday, 16 January 1995 (four days and five nights), and his journey back, from Pondicherry to Maui with route: Monday, 16 January 1995, drive to Madras. Then by plane to Calcutta, Bombay, Tokyo (overnight), Honolulu (overnight) and arrival in Maui early on Thursday, 19 January 1995.

The front cover shows a photograph of Lily-di, Sri Chinmoy's sister. Page iii shows a photograph of Chitta and Mantu, Sri Chinmoy's brothers. The back cover shows a photograph of Chitta, Lily and Mantu.

My express visit to India *(1995)*

On 20 September 1995 Sri Chinmoy made a sudden trip to India to visit his sister, Lily, who was seriously ill. He stayed in Pondicherry for four days and returned to New York on 26 September. He narrated the stories in this book upon his return.

The front cover shows a photograph of Lily-di.

BIBLIOGRAPHY

SRI CHINMOY:

SALUTATIONS (3 VOLUMES)

   −*Salutation, numbers 1-4*, New York, Agni Press, 1981.
   −*Salutation, numbers 5-8*, New York, Agni Press, 1981.
   −*Salutation, numbers 9-12*, New York, Agni Press, 1983.

Suggested citation key: SLT.

I LOVE SHOPPING (5 VOLUMES)

   −*I love shopping, part 1*, New York, Agni Press, 1985.
   −*I love shopping, part 2*, New York, Agni Press, 1986.
   −*I love shopping, part 3*, New York, Agni Press, 1994.
   −*I love shopping, part 4*, New York, Agni Press, 1994.
   −*I love shopping, part 5*, New York, Agni Press, 1994.

Suggested citation key: LS.

THE WORLD-EXPERIENCE-TREE-CLIMBER (8 VOLUMES)

–*The world-experience-tree-climber, part 1*, New York, Agni Press, 1986.
–*The world-experience-tree-climber, part 1*, New York, Agni Press, 1993.
–*The world-experience-tree-climber, part 1*, New York, Agni Press, 1993.
–*The world-experience-tree-climber, part 1*, New York, Agni Press, 1994.
–*The world-experience-tree-climber, part 1*, New York, Agni Press, 1994.
–*The world-experience-tree-climber, part 1*, New York, Agni Press, 1994.
–*The world-experience-tree-climber, part 1*, New York, Agni Press, 1994.
–*The world-experience-tree-climber, part 1*, New York, Agni Press, 2005.

Suggested citation key: WE.

SRI CHINMOY VISITS INDIA

–*Sri Chinmoy visits India*, New York, Agni Press, 1995.

Suggested citation key: VI.

MY EXPRESS VISIT TO INDIA

–*My express visit to India*, New York, Agni Press, 1995.

Suggested citation key: EV.

POSTFACE

Publishing principles

The works of Sri Chinmoy series aims to obey the Author's wish: scrupulous fidelity to his original words, use of typographical style by him selected, specific spelling choices, end placement of any editorial content (i.e. not written by Sri Chinmoy himself), particular treatment of some personal nouns in special cases, etc.

Textual accuracy

The series has been checked to ensure faithful accuracy to the originals. Although much effort has been put in proofreading and comparing different versions of the text, this print may still present lingering errors. The Publisher would be grateful to be apprised of any mistypes via postal mail or facsimile, possibly with scan of the original page where the text is different. Please use original books only, specifying the year of publication, as no online version can be considered authoritative.

Ongoing reprints will include any revised text from these errata.

Acknowledgements

The Publisher is very grateful to the late Professor Lambert and his équipe for his invaluable advice. For many decades Prof. Lambert conducted a small publishing house specialising in hand-made prints of philological edition of the classics. The standard of this edition would not have been the same without his scholarly advice.

The Publisher is also grateful to the international team of collaborators that spent countless hours proofreading and checking the current text against the originals.

Our deepest gratitude to Sri Chinmoy. His living presence can be felt breathing throughout his writings. It is a privilege to be involved with his works, in any form.

Citation keys

Citation keys can be used throughout *The works of Sri Chinmoy* to allow accurate cross-reference of texts across titles and editions. Examples: EA 13, ST 50000, UPA 7. Suggested citation keys can be found in the bibliography at the end of each volume.

Sri Chinmoy Canon

We could not use better words than Professor Lambert's, who kindly offered the name *Sri Chinmoy Canon*:

> «By defining Sri Chinmoy's first editions as *editio princeps* we chose to follow classical scholarship criteria, not because we consider Sri Chinmoy's work antique, but because we believe it is among the few post ‹classical antiquity› works to rightly deserve to be considered a *classicus*, designating by that term *superiority, authority* and *perfection*.
> «The monumental work Sri Chinmoy is offering to mankind is awe-inspiring and supremely pre-eminent in proportions and quality. It is manifest that Sri Chinmoy's work — which we feel right to call *The Sri Chinmoy Canon* — will be of profound help and source of enlightenment to anyone seeking a higher wisdom, truth and reality supreme.»

[Translated from French by M. G.S.]

TABLE OF CONTENTS

PART I

SALUTATIONS, BOOK 1	5
I — SALUTATIONS TO SWITZERLAND	5
II — SALUTATIONS TO ITALY	19
III — SALUTATIONS TO GERMANY	25
IV — SALUTATIONS TO PUERTO RICO	28
BOOK 2	37
V — SALUTATIONS TO FLORIDA	37
VI — SALUTATIONS TO CANADA	50
VII — SALUTATIONS TO ENGLAND	59
VIII — SALUTATIONS TO BRAZIL	63
BOOK 3	71
IX — SALUTATIONS TO FLORIDA	71
X — SALUTATIONS TO MEXICO	78
XI — SALUTATIONS TO PUERTO RICO	90
XII — SALUTATIONS TO BERMUDA	102

PART II

I LOVE SHOPPING, BOOK 1	115
I LOVE SHOPPING, BOOK 2	145
I LOVE SHOPPING, BOOK 3	177
I LOVE SHOPPING, BOOK 4	205
I LOVE SHOPPING, BOOK 5	227

PART III

THE WORLD-EXPERIENCE-TREE-CLIMBER, BOOK 1	251
THE WORLD-EXPERIENCE-TREE-CLIMBER, BOOK 2	283
THE WORLD-EXPERIENCE-TREE-CLIMBER, BOOK 3	321
THE WORLD-EXPERIENCE-TREE-CLIMBER, BOOK 4	347
THE WORLD-EXPERIENCE-TREE-CLIMBER, BOOK 5	369
THE WORLD-EXPERIENCE-TREE-CLIMBER, BOOK 6	387
THE WORLD-EXPERIENCE-TREE-CLIMBER, BOOK 7	413
THE WORLD-EXPERIENCE-TREE-CLIMBER, BOOK 8	439

PART IV

SRI CHINMOY VISITS INDIA	467

I – MY STOPOVER IN CALCUTTA	467
II – AT THE SRI AUROBINDO ASHRAM (PONDICHERRY)	475
III – MY JOURNEY FROM PONDICHERRY TO MAUI	493
PART V	
MY EXPRESS VISIT TO INDIA	507
APPENDIX	
BIBLIOGRAPHICAL NOTES	
BIBLIOGRAPHY	
POSTFACE	
TABLE OF CONTENTS	

*Composition typographique par imprimerie
Ab Academia Aoidon, Paris & Lyon.*

*Un grand merci à Prof Knuth pour
l'utilisation avancée de TEX.*

A LYON, LE 13 AVRIL XII Æ.G.

www.ingramcontent.com/pod-product-compliance
Lightning Source LLC
Chambersburg PA
CBHW030110240426
43661CB00031B/1361/J